D1582075

WARTIME NOTEBOOKS
AND OTHER TEXTS

Marguerite Duras

WARTIME NOTEBOOKS
AND OTHER TEXTS

Edited by
Sophie Bogaert and Olivier Corpet

Translated from the French by
Linda Coverdale

MACLEHOSE PRESS
QUERCUS · LONDON

First published in Great Britain in 2008 by
MacLehose Press
An imprint of Quercus
21 Bloomsbury Square
London
WC1A 2NS

Initially published by Editions POL/MEC, Paris,
as *Cahiers de la guerre et autres textes* in 2006.

English Translation Copyright © 2008 by Linda Coverdale

A CIP catalogue reference for this book
is available from the British Library

ISBN (HB) 978 1 84724 251 8
ISBN (TPB) 978 1 84724 519 9

10 9 8 7 6 5 4 3 2 1

Typeset by Deltatype Ltd, Birkenhead, Merseyside
Set in Linotype Didot
Printed and bound in Great Britain by Clays Ltd, St Ives plc

CONTENTS

Preface

An oeuvre without remnants: nothing written by Marguerite Duras was left behind. Characters, places, subjects circulate among the texts and echo one another; the abandoned scraps of a manuscript are picked up again in the next one, integrated into a new composition. In short, the entire archive has been used in her oeuvre. And when the "papers" of Marguerite Duras arrived at the Institut de la Mémoire de l'Édition Contemporaine (IMEC) in 1995, they made that same impression on those who first examined and sorted them. No matter how diverse they may appear, the manuscripts for each of the works do not seem, as often happens, to be an accumulation of disjointed pieces but appear to be a coherent totality, as if composed in a single flow of writing.

Amid the riches of these archives, the *Wartime Notebooks* stand out immediately. Marguerite Duras had kept these four small exercise books, which are among her oldest papers, in an envelope she had labelled with that name. We have retained this title, and the *Wartime Notebooks*, in fact, form a homogeneous whole: behind the material unity established by Marguerite Duras lies a coherence both chronological and thematic, since the notebooks were written during and just after the war, between 1943 and 1949, and to varying degrees, they all evoke that crucial period in the author's life.

In addition to a long autobiographical account retracing her childhood and youth in Indochina, the first notebook contains rough drafts of what will become *The Sea Wall*, as well as the initial versions of narratives Marguerite Duras will publish many years later in the collection *The War*. The next two notebooks, devoted almost entirely to the original version of *The War*, were made famous by the preamble in which the author recalls, in 1985, the "blue armoires at Neauphle-le-Château" where they had lain forgotten. Finally, in the last notebook, the rough drafts of future novels – including *The Sailor from Gibraltar* and *Madame Dodin* – are interspersed with long autobiographical texts in which descriptions of daily life on the rue Saint-Benoît right after the war accompany some first attempts at fiction. The ten unpublished "other texts" that round out the volume, written at around the same period as the *Wartime Notebooks*, cast essential light on this pivotal period when Marguerite Duras came into her own.

Two biographies of Marguerite Duras bear particular witness to the considerable value of the *Wartime Notebooks* from a biographical point of view.[1] In that respect, this edition allows texts that until now have been quoted only piecemeal to be read in their entirety, and establishes in particular the fact that they do not constitute a personal diary, properly speaking, although the writing closely follows the events related in *The War*.[2]

Marguerite Duras herself considered these notebooks to be very special, and she refers to them repeatedly in her oeuvre. After publishing certain excerpts from them in a literary magazine in 1976, she mentions the notebooks in *Les yeux verts* in 1980;[3] in the preamble to *The War*, she even describes "this thing I can't yet put a name to, that terrifies me when I reread it", as "one of the most important things in my life".

Many of the narratives published here do touch on major, seemingly vital events in her life (the deaths of her first child and her brother; her activities in the Resistance; the deportation and return of her husband Robert Antelme; the birth of her son Jean), and the primordial figures of her oeuvre are already taking shape, including her mother, her brothers and her first lover. It is clear why she herself would consider these texts unique and of exceptional importance.

But even more clearly, these works are of precious literary value. For although a large part of the *Notebooks* consists of preliminary drafts later revised by the author, they are neither simple sketches nor flawed outlines, and it is striking to observe, for example, how much her final version of *The War* represents a process of refinement that leaves untouched both the linearity of the first creative impulse and the vivid, sometimes brutal spontaneity that gives the tale its strength.[4] Thus the *Notebooks* reveal a freshness and rhythm that uncannily recall those of the author's very last works, which no doubt explains the disbelief expressed by some readers when *The War* was published – and which deeply wounded Marguerite Duras – regarding the real existence of those "notebooks in the blue armoires".[5]

Besides their astonishingly modern style, the *Notebooks* display that conspicuous interweaving of fiction and autobiography so characteristic of the author's late manner. Whereas the novels she published in the 1940s and '50s remain rather classic in style and are obviously intended to be fiction, the *Wartime Notebooks* reveal a sensibility that from the outset perceives the personal through a literary lens. This entanglement of the real and the imaginary culminates in *The Lover*, and it is surely no coincidence that the novel that gave the author her greatest public success brings together, as do these *Notebooks*, memories of both her childhood and the war. The close relationship between those two periods is made explicit there: "I see the war in the same colours as my childhood." In the rough drafts for *The Lover*, this filiation is affirmed even more strongly: "The war is part of my childhood memories ... It does not belong to the rest of my life, in my memory. Childhood overflows into the war. War is an event that must be endured throughout its reign. Just as childhood endures its own state ..."[6]

To Marguerite Duras, consequently, childhood and wartime have this in common: they impose the experience of submission and foment a revolt for which writing becomes the instrument. One can thus understand that the evocation of the past, in these texts as in the rest of her oeuvre, is never guided by the complacent fascination characteristic of certain autobiographical works. On the contrary, far from all nostalgia, the past digs its roots into the most immediate present, making the author's childhood "an inexhaustible, extraordinary time [she] feel[s] [she] can never fully measure". This "boundless childhood", to use her lovely term for that atmosphere of family life, informs these *Notebooks* even in their imperfections, just as it breathes epic life into the published works.

And so the startling revelation of the power of these texts, still fresh in their appeal, inspired their publication here. Neither simple sketches nor scattered fragments, the *Wartime Notebooks* represent the birth of the oeuvre of Marguerite Duras. It is striking how completely this matrix of future works contains the primitive architecture of the entire Durassian universe. These texts, which those familiar with the author's books will encounter with feelings of both recognition and discovery, thus clearly provide an essential light by which to read her work.

Once the question of publication was settled, there remained that of how best to make available texts that were sometimes fragmentary or difficult to decipher. One initially attractive possibility was to present all the texts in facsimile, accompanied by their transcription and the appropriate body of notes; this option, however, might have deformed the writing in several ways. It would have fetishized the manuscript-object in its physical form, so that any reading of the notebooks risked focusing on their aesthetic and visual aspects rather than their contents. In addition, the necessarily imposing dimensions, and thus the cost, of such a volume would have thereby limited its audience to a select group of experts and devotees, when the writing itself is limpid and quite accessible. In the end, the editorial protocol we adopted emphasized legibility: the goal was to establish the texts but without smoothing them

out too much or forgetting their status as archival documents –
witness the two notebooks incorporating drawings.

The approach chosen in the end thus offers ease and continuity
of reading. We have provided an index of fictional characters and
persons known to Marguerite Duras who appear in the *Wartime
Notebooks*, as well as a brief further consideration of the connec-
tions between these texts and the author's life and published
works.

Since this edition has deliberately omitted all explanatory
notes, the reader will consult the available biographical works
for all details regarding the names of people, places and events
mentioned in these texts. The collection of original documents
may be consulted at the Institut de la Mémoire de l'Édition
Contemporaine, moreover, where experts will be able to examine
closely, if necessary, the editorial process behind this volume.[7]

We have tried, above all else, to respect the intermediate status
of the *Wartime Notebooks*, halfway between archival documents
and the acknowledged works; it is here, at this fragile point of
equilibrium, that the oeuvre of Marguerite Duras was born.

Sophie Bogaert and Olivier Corpet

NOTES

1. Laure Adler, *Marguerite Duras* (Chicago: The University of Chicago Press,
2000); Jean Vallier, *C'était Marguerite Duras* (Paris: Fayard, 2006).
2. Although Marguerite Duras herself refers to these texts in her preamble
as a "diary", she adds that it "is inconceivable [to her] that she wrote it while
waiting for Robert A. to return". She also confides to Marianne Alphant in
Libération, 17 April, 1985: "In my opinion, I must have begun writing *The War*
when we were visiting convalescent homes for deportees," in other words,
several months after Robert Antelme's return.

3. "I'd like you to read what I'm doing, I'd like to give you – to you – some fresh, new writings, fresh despairs, those of my life now. The rest, the things lying around in the blue armoires of my bedroom, they'll be published one day in any case, either after my death or before, if I ever again run out of money." *Les yeux verts*, "La Lettre", Paris, Petite bibliothèque des Cahiers du cinéma, 1996, p. 10.

4. Marguerite Duras mentions this work of rewriting in particular in her interview with Marianne Alphant: "The text of the book was not laboured over, it was tossed down on paper to be written out later. And then, you see, I didn't write it out. Most of my work for its publication was removing, for example, what had to do with religion, with God." *Libération*, 17 April, 1985.

5. As she confides in particular to Luce Perrot in the interview "Au-delà des pages" produced for the French television station TF1 in 1988.

6. Manuscripts of *The Lover*, in Fonds Marguerite Duras/IMEC.

7. IMEC, Abbaye d'Ardenne, 14280 Saint-Germain-la-Blanche-Herbe. See www.imecarchives.com for further information.

Note on the Transcription

Since fidelity to the text was the paramount concern, the transcription of the *Wartime Notebooks* required making choices and adopting certain conventions.

The texts have been transcribed in the order in which they appear in their notebooks, with the exception of those in the fourth notebook, the scattered pages of which have been grouped thematically. The texts are also presented in their totality, aside from the very rare exception of a few fragments that were too brief or illegible and were therefore dropped. Incomplete sentences (which usually followed or preceded a missing page) were also removed.

Square brackets – [ ] – identify all significant interventions on our part, meaning when a word was either illegible, or uncertain, or syntactically necessary and obviously overlooked by the author.

Through a concern for legibility, we finally decided to remove all crossed-out words and, where necessary, to choose what appeared to be the author's last correction. (The only crossed-out words we retained are those that Marguerite Duras did not replace and which remained indispensable to the meaning of the text.) The punctuation was occasionally very lightly modified: principally, commas were added to the longest sentences, and quotation marks were inserted where obviously required. Certain particularly dense passages were opened up with new paragraphs. Numbers were written out; lastly, spelling mistakes were corrected, along with errors in agreement and the sequence of tenses.

Note on the Translation

The *Wartime Notebooks* are precisely that: notebooks, not novels. Although Marguerite Duras certainly knew that anything she wrote might someday be published (what writer does not?), not one piece was published by her as it appears in the *Cahiers de la guerre*. In that sense, these are *private* papers, and they present a translator with a particularly prickly problem.

The writing in these exercise books is by its very nature "imperfect": exploratory, impassioned, sometimes rushed or overworked, often brutally frank, incomplete, even incomprehensible at moments, because the author has not licked these bear cubs into their final shape and sent them out into the world with her blessing. A translator always micro-edits while melting a work down in one language and recasting it in another, doing small things here and there to smooth out the rough spots and irregularities that inevitably appear. The author, after all, has taken care to present the original language *just so*: this way, and no other. Mixing and matching, the translator works to present the original text in a new language but with the same degree of linguistic craft and finesse that distinguished the author's creation.

What happens, however, when the work is, as all these texts are, works-in-progress? There is a great temptation to help out, to make things more coherent, less abrupt, more musical, to tweak the writing subtly into a form perhaps more friendly to the reader – and less likely ever to set that reader wondering whether something strange might be going on in the translation.

Yet the whole point of this book is, in a way, its "imperfections": the sudden shifts in tone, in point of view, the verbs veering between past and present, the same subject showing up in yet another guise, the chop-logic when the author wheels the narrative off in a different direction, just to see ... Different styles are tested, like lenses in an ophthalmologist's office. Is it better this way, or that way? With, or without? The writing here is protean, fluid, like water seeking its own level any way it can, as Duras exercises her voice, learning as she goes, and there's something for everyone here. Fairly conventional prose sits next to work that flows like what she later called "*écriture courante*"; we see her fiddling with compressive phrasing, techniques of repetition, the gaze as the *primum mobile* of writing; there are texts as brusque as a no-nonsense film or theatre script, others where she's imagining out how to hide things in plain sight, and always, always, those moments of mathematical elegance when the writing hits its full stride and captivates us with the ruthless power of a voice like no other. Readers familiar with her published works will find their earliest expression here, and those who read her for the first time will see the startling and dramatic events of her tumultuous life just coming into focus as she begins creating and recreating her identity as a writer. The very rawness of this writing matches the raw material of a life whose themes appear here in their first and, perhaps, most honest avatars.

And so, these texts must be translated with even *less* linguistic leeway than usual, because their irregularities and idiosyncrasies are so revealing. I have tried to pay attention to the rhythm of the language on the page rather than follow by-the-book punctuation and phrasing. If Duras indulges in an orgy of comma splices, so be it. If her pages thicken with staccato exchanges of he said/she said, become overripe or strangely mannered, or turn maddeningly telegraphic, well, that's her choice. Here Duras is already, clearly, some kind of a writer, and this book is her workshop, gymnasium, kitchen, treasure chest, the magic mirror in which she longs to see herself and which shows her to us, in a seductively elusive *mise en abîme*, as she would come to be.

A few practical considerations.

The French editors' additions are in square brackets: [ ]. (The brackets around small inserts like "on" or "to" have been dropped.) My additions are in curly brackets: { }. They represent useful clarifications too slight for endnotes. Some of these clarifications come from the published works for which these texts were rough drafts.

The French editors supplied endnotes only for their preface and the introductions to the *20th Century Press Notebook* and Part II: Other Texts. All endnotes to the material in the notebooks themselves are the translator's, and when notes have been added, they appear at the end of the individual sections in each notebook: "Ter of the Militia", "Rue Saint-Benoît" and so on.

Linda Coverdale

I
THE WARTIME
NOTEBOOKS

Pink Marbled Notebook

Introduction

The first of the *Wartime Notebooks*, called the *Pink Marbled Note-book*, is the longest of the four. This exercise book with a thick cardboard cover contains 123 pages, some fifteen of which are filled with a child's drawings (probably added later by Marguerite Duras' son, Jean Mascolo, born on 30 June, 1947).

The chronological references in the text indicate that Marguerite Duras began writing this notebook sometime in 1943. The first seventy pages contain a long autobiographical narrative focused on events from the author's childhood and adolescence in Indo-china, including in particular the first known version of her relationship with the man who will become "the Lover". Written in an even hand with few deletions, this entire section appears to have been composed in a rather continuous fashion. Although the text occasionally alludes to the reactions of a potential reader, implicit in the impersonal pronoun "one", the only explicit moti-vations for the writing are personal: "No other reason impels me to write of these memories, except that instinct to unearth. It's very simple. If I do not write them down, I will gradually forget them" (p. 38). Certain episodes will reappear, however, sometimes in an almost identical form, in published works (the novella *The Boa* and, especially, *The Sea Wall*).

The rest of the notebook is more disconnected, with more crossings-out. It contains various fragments of *The Sea Wall* (in which the first person gradually gives way to fictitious characters,

Suzanne and Joseph), followed by texts later rewritten and published in the collection *The War*, there entitled "Ter of the Militia" and "Albert of the Capitals". In *The War*, the names of the characters in particular are different: {in both stories} the main character, Théodora (or Nano), becomes Thérèse {and Albert, one of the leaders of the interrogation centre, becomes D.; the other leader, Jean, becomes Beaupain in "Ter of the Militia" and Roger in "Albert of the Capitals"}.

Childhood and Adolescence in Indochina[1]

It was on the ferry that plies between Sadec and Saï that I first met Léo. I was returning to boarding school in Saigon, and someone, I no longer remember who, had given me a lift in his car along with Léo. Léo was a native, but he dressed like a Frenchman, he spoke perfect French, and he was just back from Paris. Me, I wasn't even fifteen yet and had been to France only when I was very young. I thought Léo was quite elegant. He was wearing a big diamond ring and a suit of tussore, a lightweight raw silk. I'd never seen a diamond like that except on people who until that moment had never noticed me, and as for my brothers, they wore white cotton.[2] Given our resources, I found it almost inconceivable that they could ever afford to wear tussore suits.

Léo told me that I was pretty.

"You know Paris?"

Blushing, I said no. He knew Paris. He lived in Sadec. Someone living in Sadec knew Paris and this was the first I'd heard about it. Léo flirted with me, to my profound amazement. The doctor dropped me off at the boarding school in Saï, and Léo managed to tell me that we'd "see each other again". I'd realized that he was extraordinarily rich and I was dazzled. I was so impressed and unsure of myself that I couldn't answer Léo. I returned to the home of Mademoiselle C., where I boarded with three other people: two teachers and a girl two years younger than I named Colette. Mademoiselle C. relieved my mother of about a quarter of her schoolteacher's salary, in return for which she guaranteed a thorough education. Only Mademoiselle C. knew my mother was a teacher, which we tried hard to hide from the other boarders, who would have taken offence. Teaching positions in native schools were considered demeaning because they were so poorly paid. I took great pains to conceal this secret as best I could. Returning that evening to Mademoiselle C.'s house, I sank into despair – I told myself that Léo, who lived in Sadec, would surely discover my mother's occupation and inevitably turn away from me. I couldn't tell this to anyone, certainly not Colette, who was the daughter of an important government administrator, or Mademoiselle C., who would have sent me packing – which, I had no doubt, would have promptly killed my mother. But I consoled myself. Even though Léo knew Paris and was quite wealthy, he was a native and I was white; perhaps he would be satisfied with a teacher's daughter.

Being a teacher's daughter had worked to my disadvantage in school, where I only kept company with the daughters of customs officials and post-office employees, the sole positions on a par with teaching in a native school. Because she was broad-minded and because my mother still had a great reputation for integrity, Mademoiselle C. had been willing to accept me, but she was both more strict and more intimate with me than she was with Colette. For instance, Mademoiselle C. had a cancer below her left breast and showed it to no-one else in the house except me. She usually showed it to me on Sunday afternoon, when everyone had gone out, after we'd had our snack. The first time she showed it to me, I understood why Mademoiselle C. gave off such a stench – but showing it to no other boarder except me conferred on us a kind of complicity, which I attributed to my status as a teacher's daughter. I was not offended and told my mother, who took some pride in this mark of confidence. It would all take place in Mademoiselle C.'s bedroom. She would uncover her breast, go over to the window and show me the cancer. Tactfully, I even contemplated the cancer for a good two or three minutes. "You see?" Mademoiselle C. would say. "Ah! Yes, I do see, that's what it is." Mademoiselle C. would tuck her breast away, I'd begin to breathe again, she would do up her black lace dress and sigh; I would then tell her she was old and it wasn't important anymore. She would agree with me, be comforted, and we'd go for a walk in the botanic garden.

My mother had been teaching in Indochina since 1903, and as a civil servant and the widow of a civil servant, she had obtained from the colonial administration a concession of rice fields in Upper Cambodia. At the time these grants were paid for in very modest annual instalments and passed to the beneficiary only if the land had been put under cultivation by the end of x years. After endless efforts, my mother obtained a vast grant of 2,100 acres of lowlands and forests at the back of beyond in Cambodia, between the Elephant Mountains and the sea. This plantation was 37 miles along a dirt track from the nearest French outpost, but that should not have posed any real problem. My mother hired fifty or so servants who had to be transplanted from Cochin China and installed in a "village" we had to build entirely on marshland, a little over a mile from the sea. That time was one of intense joy for us all. My mother had waited her whole life for that moment. In addition to the village, we built a bungalow on stilts beside the track that ran along the edge of our plantation. That house cost us 5,000 piastres, a vast sum in 1925. Set on stilts because of the floods, it was built entirely of wood that had to be felled, squared and cut into boards on-site. None of these enormous potential disadvantages stopped my mother. We lived for six straight months at Banteaï-Prey (the name of the plantation), my mother having obtained a leave of absence from the Department of Education in Saigon. During the construction of our house, we lived – my mother, young brother and I – in a straw hut next to the one for the household staff (the servants' village lay four hours by boat from the track, and thus from our house). We lived completely as our servants did, except that my mother and I slept on a mattress. I was eleven at the time, and my brother thirteen. We would have been perfectly happy if our mother's health had not failed. Nervous irritation and the joy of seeing us so close to leaving all our troubles behind coincided with her change of life, which was particularly difficult. Then my mother had two or three epileptic fits that left her in a kind of lethargic coma that could last all day. Not only was it impossible to find a doctor, since telephones simply did not exist in that part of Cambodia in those days, but my mother's illness dismayed and frightened the native servants, who would threaten to leave each time she had an attack. They were afraid of not being paid. For as long as those fits lasted, the servants sat silently on the adjacent embankments all around the hut in which my mother lay unconscious and groaning softly. My brother or I would come out occasionally to reassure the servants and tell them that my mother wasn't dead. They had a hard time believing us. My brother would promise them that even if our mother died, he would pay them and send them back to Cochin China no matter what the cost. My brother, as I said, was thirteen at the time; he was already the bravest person I've ever known. He found the strength to both comfort me and persuade me not to cry in front of the servants, since there was no need for that: our mother was going to live. And indeed, when the sun would leave the valley to set behind the Elephant Mountains, our mother would regain consciousness. Those attacks were unusual in that they had no lasting effects, and my mother was able to resume her customary activities the very next day.

The cultivation of 500 acres of the plantation that first year, added to the construction of both our house and the village, plus the transportation and installation of the servants, completely consumed the savings my mother had accumulated over twenty-four years of civil service. But that was of minor importance to us, confident as we were that the first harvest would recoup more or less all our setting-up expenses. This calculation worked out by my mother, and carefully checked by her night after sleepless night, would of course prove infallible. We believed in it all the more because my mother "knew" that we ought to be millionaires in four years. In those days, she was still communicating with my father, dead for many long years; she did nothing without seeking his advice, and it was he who "dictated" to her all the plans for our future. These "pronouncements", according to her, only oc-curred at around one o'clock in the morning, which justified my mother's wakeful nights and endowed her in our eyes with fabu-lous prestige. The first harvest came to a few bags of paddy rice. The 2,100 acres granted by the colonial administration were salt land, flooded by the sea for part of the year. The entire standing crop "burned" in one night of high water, except for the few acres around the house that were far enough away from the sea. As soon as the water dropped and the river running along the edge of our plantation was navigable again, we went to see our 500 acres of salt-burned rice – thus making an eight-hour round trip by boat to confirm our complete ruin. But that very evening, my mother decided to borrow 300,000 francs to build dykes that would place our rice fields definitively beyond the reach of tidal flooding. We could not mortgage our plantation, given that it did not yet belong to us and that, even if it had, considering that it lay on alluvial salt lands regularly invaded by the sea, it was worthless. All the credit banks to which my mother turned formally refused to lend her that considerable sum, which we could guarantee with nothing. In the end, my mother went to a *chetti*, a Hindu moneylender, who agreed to advance her that amount in return for a bond on her teacher's salary. All three of us were deeply ashamed when the arrangement could not be made without the knowledge of the Department of Education. My mother was therefore obliged to return to work. On Friday evenings she used to leave Sadec, where she taught, covering 500 miles by car and setting out on her return trip Sunday night. The *chetti* demanded so much interest that he personally consumed about a third of my mother's salary. For as long as those dealings lasted, my mother never lost heart. The construction of the dykes, which were to be gigantic, propelled her into boundless excitement. My brother and I were quite close to her and shared her exaltation. My mother consulted no expert to determine if those barriers would be effective. She believed in them. She always acted by virtue of a superior and unverifiable logic. We brought in several hundred workers, and the barriers were constructed during the dry season under our supervision. Most of the money loaned by the *chetti* was spent on them. Unfortunately the dykes were chewed up by swarms of crabs that burrowed into the mud in high tides – and when the sea rose the next year, those barriers of loose earth, undermined by the crabs, melted almost completely away.

The whole crop was lost a second time. It was obvious that we could not build dykes without shoring them up with stones. My mother understood this; unable to find any stones, she considered criss-crossing the trunks of mangrove trees at the base of the embankments. Once again she'd found the answer. The evenings when she made such discoveries and told us of them are among the most beautiful of my life. Her own ingenuity filled her with an ecstasy so infectious that the few remaining household servants came to share it as well. The agricultural workers, who lived isolated from us, stayed only because my mother treated them with extravagant generosity. They had come to settle in as farmers, but since the rice fields produced almost nothing, my mother found herself obliged to treat them as workers – which didn't help our finances. The last of the money loaned by the *chetti* went into the mangrove scheme. It wasn't that bad an idea: one section of the embankment held up, the other collapsed. The hundred acres of rice fields Mama christened "the conclusive test" were her pride and joy. The crop flourished and we went to see it every Saturday. Alas, we were disappointed again when harvest time arrived: working together, the village servants gathered the crop in secret and returned to Cochin China by sea – with the only paddy rice we'd ever managed to produce in three years. Once more, my mother made the best of it. The construction of the dykes had absorbed all her attention for three years. To her, the fact that one section had held fast represented a signal success. My mother's purity of soul was equalled only by her high-minded detachment. Tiring of the barriers, she tried to ignore the fact that the following year, those that had survived intact now crumbled in turn. Nevertheless, she continued afterwards to sow a few acres every year on a trial basis. She claimed that the sea would soon withdraw from her rice fields and that she would reap the reward for her efforts. The acquisition of our millions was further off, she felt, but no less certain. Sometimes we doubted that alluvial land could silt up in just a few years, but my mother reassured us. She had emotional convictions like that, which we still shared.

We were utterly ruined. My mother more or less abandoned the plantation and tried to figure out how to reimburse the *chettis*. Turning her attention to me, she decided to see to my education and was as relentless in this project as she had been in constructing our house and the dykes. She didn't bother with my brother, whom she found unintelligent, and took me in hand. She considered me more promising educational material than he was, but her judgement was tinged with contempt. My brother didn't either {*sic*}. My brother used to say to me, "I'm not very smart, myself – I'll stay on the plantation," or "Me, I haven't got your intelligence, I don't deserve the sacrifices that Mama makes for you." He was sincere. And he would tell me, "Of course I have to stay in Sadec so you can study." He stayed in Sadec. My brother's humility caused me constant sorrow. My mother had decided that he was obtuse, and he adjusted to that "demotion" in all simplicity. In the same way, my mother had decided that I was naturally suited for study. My grades at the lycée were disastrous: I was at the very bottom of the class in every subject until the eleventh grade, but an acceptable mark would occasionally come my way in French – and then my mother would weep with joy and say her sacrifices had been worth it. At the beginning she often came to see me at Mademoiselle C.'s home with my brother, in our ancient Citroën, but since they were then making ends meet thanks only to my mother's incredible ingenuity, their visits quickly tailed off. That's when I began going to Sadec on my own sometimes, taking the Saturday bus the French never used because it required eight hours for a trip that usually took four. That's how I came to accept the occasional ride home and how, during one of them, I met Léo.

The day after that encounter, back at Mademoiselle C.'s house, I heard a car honk loudly. It was Léo. Colette was with me, I was afraid to go out onto the balcony. Léo drove by thirty-five times in a row. He would slow down in front of the house without daring to stop. I did not appear on the balcony. No-one else thought to look outside; I must have been waiting for Léo and particularly attentive to the sounds in the street. I felt rather embarrassed, I might add, when I thought of the trouble Léo was taking to please me. Still, I dressed as nicely as I could and at two o'clock went downstairs to go to the lycée. Wearing another tussore suit, Léo was waiting for me along the way, leaning against his car door. He came towards me and said, "It's not easy to meet you." He invited me into his car. Léo's car truly fascinated me. The moment I got in I asked what make it was and how much it cost. Léo told me it was a Morris Léon-Bollée and cost 7,000 piastres. I thought of our Citroën that had cost 400 piastres, which my mother had paid in three installments. Léo also told me that it wasn't his only car, that he had another as lovely as this one but a touring car, also a Morris Léon-Bollée, which was his favourite make of automobile. Léo seemed quite pleased that we were having such a relaxed conversation. He asked me where I would like him to drive me. "To the lycée," I said. "I'm late." In gracious and carefully considered

terms, Léo asked me if I wouldn't like to go for a drive; I said no.
He drove me to the main gate of the school and asked my permission to come and pick me up that same evening. He came that
evening and returned the next day and all the days that followed.
I was so proud of his car that I depended on people seeing it, and
I lingered in it on purpose to be sure my classmates would notice
me. I was certain at the time that my using such a car would cause
a definite stir, thus making me suitable company for the daughters of important Indochinese officials. None of those girls had a
limousine like that at her disposal: a green and black limousine
specially ordered from Paris, of impressive dimensions, of such
royal elegance, with a liveried chauffeur. Unfortunately, in spite
of his wonderful car, Léo was Annamese. I was so dazzled by the
car that I forgot this drawback. My lycée classmates dropped me
permanently from their society. My only previous companions no
longer dared compromise themselves in my company. I had no
girlfriends and wasn't unduly upset by that. For several weeks I
continued to see Léo. I always contrived to make him talk about
his fortune. An only son, he owned a huge number of buildings
scattered throughout Cochin China and had access to considerable
wealth. The figures comprising Léo's estimated fortune staggered
me: I dreamt of them at night and thought about them all day long.
They had nothing in common with any I'd ever heard at home.
For as far back as I could remember, I'd known that my mother
didn't have enough money. Her one preoccupation was to earn
some, although her adventurous streak often led her a merry chase
towards her goal. It didn't matter – our mother had inculcated
in us an almost sacred reverence for money. Without it, one was
unhappy. Without it, virtue would not "pass" and innocence was
open to reproach. My mother was convinced that if she succeeded
in earning money, a series of happy consequences would follow.

"There are teachers in native schools who married their daughters to bankers. They exist, believe me, I know some. But they're
the ones who found ways to give their girls dowries."

When I met Léo, we were managing to live and to pay off the *chettis* each month only by selling what remained of our furniture and jewellery. We did this in secret, selling our jewellery to native jewellers as quietly as possible. "If anyone finds out, we'll be disgraced," my mother said. She had kept on our old housekeeper and the cook, however, because if people in Sadec had learned that my mother did her own cooking, they would have cut us dead. And Mama did have to make and receive a few official visits. My mother did not sit in judgement, by the way; she had neither the time nor the inclination for that. I never heard her complain that money trumped all the other values of the Indochinese colonial world. At that time, fortunes were springing up like mushrooms in Indochina. Rubber planters were swarming through the colony, earning millions. Saigon was one of the richest and most corrupt cities in the Far East. There reigned the strictest of hierarchies, based on wealth and all its outward signs. The planters came first, and then the body of high-ranking Indochinese civil servants. Bribery was accepted, organized and facilitated our access to high society: a customs official who had managed to smuggle in three million in contraband opium would thus soon find himself hobnobbing with the local administrator. The corps of top Annamese public officials paid exorbitant (fixed) prices for honours and decorations. It was common knowledge that the Legion of Honour cost 18,000 piastres.

Although such considerations exceed the scope of my narrative, they have a bearing here precisely because we never gained any foothold in that society, and because my mother's natural humility fuelled her constant desire to achieve entry there at all costs and by any means. I've forgotten to mention that among the French in the colony, "Annamitophobia" was the rule. A very few Annamese moved among French circles. In principle, any "native-lover" in the civil service was doomed never to rise in the ranks, and we were, given our mother's position, at the bottom of the civil-service ladder. People said my mother had some merit, but no-one received her. Our only friends were either post-office employees or customs officials, or worked as she did in primary-school education. The very fact that my mother had never left the colony and that she had many Annamese friends there discredited her for good among the French. On that point, my mother was particularly uneasy and uncertain.

I don't wish to paint a portrait of Indochina in 1930; I want to speak above all about what my youth was like. My mother was often of two minds not so much because of external conditions and conventions but by nature. And so, when the question later arose of my marrying Léo, my mother hesitated because he was native – which would have reinforced the disrepute from which she suffered so unaffectedly. The important thing is that she hesitated, although she knew, deep down, that anybody would have considered the whole thing absolutely unacceptable.

We suffered a lot from our poverty, and hiding it added insult to injury. It wasn't so obvious on the plantation, where we lived in perfect isolation. In Sadec, we stopped at nothing to prevent the sixty French people on the post from learning anything about our plight. So on the last evening of every month, when my mother would take the *chetti* a third of her salary to pay off the interest, she went in secret and after nightfall. Several times she wasn't able to do so, I no longer remember why. Then the *chettis* would come to our house. They'd settle into the sitting room and wait. Several times Mama wept in front of them, begging them to go because the servants could see them. The *chettis* did not leave. Silently, they stayed. They knew they had only to appear, that for a white woman, borrowing from *chettis* was the very depth of shame. Finally Mama would throw the money in their faces. They would gather it up and go off smiling.

In such situations I'd shut myself into a room in the house, forcing Mama to come looking for me, which generally resulted in a proper beating. Mama often beat me, usually when "her nerves gave way" and she couldn't help herself. Since I was the smallest of her children and the easiest to control, I was the one Mama beat the most. She used to hit me with a stick, and easily sent me spinning. Anger would send such a rush of blood to her head that she'd speak of dying of a stroke. The fear of losing her would thus defeat my rebellion every time. I always agreed with Mama's reasons for beating me but not with her methods. The use of the stick I found radically shocking and unaesthetic; the blows on the head, dangerous. But the slaps that marked my cheeks were my despair – especially while I knew Léo, to whom I couldn't possibly admit "what was going on at home". I knew he would not understand, that he would never approve of Mama's attitude towards me, while I agreed with her completely and could not have tolerated anyone criticizing her, not even Léo.

I'll have occasion to return to these blows. I really did get a lot of them. Shortly before I met Léo, when I was fourteen, my eldest brother, who was studying in France, returned to Indochina. Through some strange rivalry, he picked up the habit of beating me as well. The only question became who would hit me first. When he didn't like the way Mama was beating me, he'd tell her, "Wait," and take over. But soon she'd be sorry, because each time she thought I'd be killed on the spot. She'd emit ghastly shrieks, but my brother had trouble stopping himself. One day he changed tactics and sent me tumbling; my temple struck a corner of the piano, and I could barely get up again. My mother was so frightened that from then on she lived in obsessive fear of those battles. My brother's massive biceps compounded my misfortune, and his Herculean strength overawed my mother, which probably spurred him on. I was quite small and thin, without any of my two brothers' superbly athletic appearance. In her good moments, my mother would tell me, "You, you're my little waif." Such marks of affection, which revealed that my mother loved me for the very reasons that so often turned her against me, were beyond price,

especially since they were so rare. My brother's return home introduced insults and vulgarity to our household. Until then we had
been polite through ignorance. My eldest brother came back from
France with an education (the only one, since four years of tutor-
ing with a priest had failed to earn him his baccalaureate diploma
at the age of eighteen) in new insults, which arrived in the nick of
time at a house where jangled nerves were reaching a flashpoint.
My naïveté may seem exaggerated, but it was nonetheless real.
When my brother beat me and called me a little crab louse, I had
no idea what that meant and no chance to find out until years
later, actually. Which doesn't mean that I didn't resent the insult
"crab louse" – on the contrary, I resented it all the more violently
in that I was more or less confusing "crab louse" and "crap house"
to get "stinking little thing", so I became even angrier at being
beaten for my tininess, which was hardly my fault. My brother
insulted as he beat me. His usual terms of abuse, aside from "crab
louse", were "piece of shit", "you're not even worth spitting on,"
"you pile of garbage", and "dirty slut", which last also remained
a mystery to me but stabbed me anyway – I don't know why,
perhaps because of the obscene sound of that word *slut* – right in
the heart. "Bitch" seemed to me particularly unacceptable, much
more so than "sonofabitch", which I thought was the diminutive
version. The word *degenerate* troubled my conscience and upset
me, especially while I knew Léo, because my brother used it a
lot during that relationship, along with "snake in the grass" and
"venomous serpent", which, although more intellectual, seemed to
me more treacherous. "Stinker", "shit-ass", "ass-wipe" or "whore"
did not require backing up by blows, they were already everyday
expressions. There were others and I'm greatly saddened not to
remember them. I cannot hear them without feeling in my very
soul the true taste of my youth; they have the aura of summers
gone forever, of the raw, vivid angers of my fifteenth year. I received them with a seriousness that may be laughable but that I
will never feel again no matter what anyone says to me. I believed

in them. I no longer do. They put me through the sorrows of hell. Even Léo, in whom I confided regarding my brother, could not manage to grasp how they could make me suffer so.

The difference between my mother's and my brother's blows is that his hurt much more and that I refused to accept them in any way. Every time, a moment would come when I believed my brother was going to kill me, and my anger would give way to fear that my head would come off my body and roll along the ground, or that I would be beaten senseless. When my brother took up opium, his violence even increased, so that I could not speak to him without provoking an attack. When he had smoked too much, he beat with skill and cunning, slowly, pausing after each blow to enjoy fully its effect.

He also beat my brother {sic} at first, but as the opium took its toll, he no longer came out on top as often, and backed off.

One may wonder why my brother treated me like that. I wonder as well. I no sooner glimpse reasons than they slip away from me. He beat me because he couldn't bear me. My mother couldn't bear me either, even though she loved me deeply. I note that I did not have any friends in my lycée either, and that the girls and even most of the boys in my year found me unlikable. When my mother removed me from Mademoiselle C.'s care later on and placed me in a state boarding school, I was the bête noire of the prefects and most of the students. (True, I did have one friend there, Hélène, as well as three other girls who worshipped me with a kind of adoration that was rather ambiguous but quite far from true friendship.) In those days I didn't try to understand; I endured the situation with fatalism. I didn't feel sad about it. I was detestable the way the others were amiable; I was as uninteresting to most of the girls my age as they were fascinating to me, because before I came to the lycée, before I was fifteen, I'd had precisely no contact whatsoever with French girls. There were specific reasons for their antipathy and indifference. First of all a kind of perfectly understandable unsociability that I tried to conceal with arrogance, if not total viciousness. I was never pleasant with anyone. Amiability, terra incognita. When I encountered white society in Saigon, I discovered amiability. I thought it was the prerogative of wealth and happiness. It never occurred to me to smile. I'd never felt pleasure except with my mother and brothers, and at home we knew only wild, uncontrollable laughter, since smiles had been banished from our relations. We were modest and hard with one another, using speech to hurl insults or inform ourselves about various strictly material things. Chatting was unknown at home, except on certain evenings of general gaiety that occur in any family but which in mine took on a frenzied note, probably because they occurred after months of silence. And that chatter, in fact, was not the real thing. The main idea was to have some fun, because we could no longer stand going without it. Then we could laugh at anything – we even went so far as to turn the story of our plantation into an irresistible farce. And all on behalf of the cause. "It's falling-down funny, the story of our dykes," my eldest brother would say. "I don't know anything more hysterical. Everything turned against us, even the crabs that chomped them right out from under us – trust Mama to come up with an idea like that." On those evenings I'm sure we all attained the highest state of bliss. We'd lost everything but would laugh ourselves silly (there's no other word) over losing everything.

Well, when I arrived in Saigon, I had no intention of changing. I remember what a painful chore it was to shake hands with my classmates. During the three years I remained at the lycée, I never got used to that, it provoked an involuntary coldness in my manner, just as I could never answer my teachers' questions without arrogance. I had one English teacher who took such a dislike to me that he actually felt ill at the sight of me, he *could not stand* to look at me any more, and, flouting the custom observed in co-educational schools, he seated me at the very back of the classroom, claiming that I was hopeless at English. At the boarding school, I made a prefect "sick" through my mere presence in the study hall and dormitory. She could not speak to me without choking. And yet I wasn't unruly, and given how indifferent or hostile most of the other students were to me, I could hardly have induced them to misbehave.

If I stress this aspect of my relations with others (with both my family and my classmates), it's because this is important – and left its mark on me for years. I lived in a more or less constant state of guilt, which only increased my arrogance and spitefulness, because I took pride in never feeling sad about this. A single person, before Léo, took an interest in me. He was one of the class dunces, a half-caste. I wouldn't let him touch me because he had rotten teeth. Everyone looked down on him. His father ran a store in the Chinese quarter. He was over twenty and still in the ninth grade, he'd been left back so many times. We both sat in the last row in English class and he regularly asked me for a ring I wore. I would pass it to him. Saying that it was still warm from my heat, he'd hold it tightly in his hand, bring it to his mouth, kiss it and close his eyes, breathing deeply, and each time I'd be afraid he might swallow the ring. I'd look at him, curious; I didn't know what he was talking about when he'd tell me that the ring was making him excited. That creature was a calamity. I couldn't bear seeing him because he embodied the species to which I belonged – and from which I wanted to escape: the poor and despised. For more than a year he pursued me like an evil spell. At that time in the school in Saigon there were some planters' or governors' sons who had their own cars, and who crossed the girls' courtyard with tennis rackets tucked under their arms, arriving with "their" girls. And some of them were handsome. I used to hide and watch them go by. Seeing them hurt me, because I already knew that they would never take me away in their cars. I gazed at them as if they were displays in a shop window; sometimes I would dream that one of them noticed me, and I'd wake up in tears.

I think that I lacked the slightest bit of charm to an unbelievable degree – especially since my mother rigged me out after her own

taste, which must have lagged ten years behind the current fashion. Unlike the other girls, who wore straw hats, I was outfitted
with a colonial helmet with a large, round brim that probably
protected my shoulders as well as the back of my neck. It was a
model of an impressive size that my mother had ordered specially
for plantation life, and which I dragged around for years. When
I managed to lose it at last (it fell into the river during a ferry
crossing), my mother bought me a man's fedora that was origi-
nally the {brownish-pink} colour of rosewood and later turned a
yellow mottled with green. Everyone wore white sandals in those
days. My mother, well, she saddled me with black patent-leather
court shoes I wore on bare feet. My frocks were consistently made
to my mother's specifications by our Annamese housekeeper.
They were the very same ones I wore at eleven or twelve years
old; the hems were let down as I grew up, and that was that.
Those frocks were so huge ("Above all, let's be practical," Mama
used to say) that at fifteen I was still wearing them. They were
usually of Japanese or native fabric, and my mother, for reasons
of hygiene, had them laundered, which meant that their colours
soon washed out of them. I remember a vivid blue cotton frock
(seams on the shoulders and at the sides: the pattern followed
for sixteen years of my life) with a design showing a flowering
cherry branch reaching from my right shoulder to my left knee;
on this branch, at my waist, an enormous bright-pink bird was
poised to take flight – a design repeated in reverse on the back.
If I remember that frock, it's because I suspected that it wasn't in
good taste and felt that the fabric was better suited to a folding
screen. My mother assured me peremptorily that the frock was
wonderful and I believed her. It's true that she herself dressed in
a more or less similar fashion and was famous throughout Cochin
China (I only learned this much later) for her almost unique way of
dressing. I believed in my mother as much as in God. If she liked
a frock, I do believe I would have worn it proudly before the jeers
of the whole world. I forgot to mention that when I met Léo, I was

wearing the brownish-pink fedora that Mama particularly liked and that she placed on my head herself in a rather unusual way, tilted to the side, like those cowboy hats in American silent films. Léo spent a whole month trying to make me understand through increasingly direct allusions (and with good reason) that this hat was unsuitable for a girl. But I had such faith in my mother's taste that, even though I had never seen anyone wear a hat like it, and even though Léo finally told me emphatically that it upset him, I wore it anyway, behind Léo's back and before the eyes and under the nose of the entire lycée.

Besides lacking charm and dressing in a manner so absurd that it almost defied description, I was not conspicuous for my beauty. I was small and ungainly, thin, covered with freckles, burdened with two carrot-red plaits that hung to the middle of my thighs – I say plaits, but *cables* would be the better word, my mother pulled and twisted my hair so tight. I was sunburnt from being almost always outdoors on the plantation and at the time, white skin was the fashion in Saigon. My features were reasonably even and might have passed for beautiful but were so distorted by my stubborn, disagreeable, tight-lipped expression that no-one could notice them. I had an evil look my mother described as "venomous". I'll simply say that when I come across any photos from those days, I look in vain for a hint of softness, of sweetness in my face. My mother's few friends would tell her that I would turn out pretty, that I had beautiful eyes but needed to wear spectacles because there was certainly something wrong there, my gaze didn't look right. In the outpost of Vinh Long, where my mother taught when I was just a little thing, that look had already provoked comment from the administrator's wife. I had turned around towards her at Mass and the look in my eyes, it seems, had "frightened" her. A kind soul, she told my mother to have my eyes checked. My mother never did – she knew there was nothing wrong with my eyes, and she claimed that if I had a venomous gaze it was also intelligent. She would tell me as well that I was very pretty;

she told me so in private: "Don't worry, you're awfully pretty." I didn't worry. I think my mother was trying to convince herself that she had a pretty daughter. My eldest brother, on the contrary, positively insisted that, "Aside from me, your kids are all duds." It's true that he was astonishingly beautiful. I'm not saying that lightly: within a month of his arrival in Cochin China, he was known as the handsomest man in the colony. My brother had this quirk: he could not mention any woman he found pretty without adding a remark aimed at me ("So much for you!") or my mother ("So much for your daughter!"). Sometimes he looked at himself in the mirror and called me over. "You ever seen a mouth like this?" he'd ask me, pointing to his. I'd reply prudently that with a thorough search, one might perhaps be found. "Stinker," my brother would answer, "so much for you ..."

Nothing distressed my mother more than to have my brother question my beauty. True, I had no dowry, and my mother agonized over the thought that one day she'd have to marry me off. When I turned fifteen, this became a topic of discussion at home. "To get her hitched," my eldest brother would say, "you can just whistle for it: you'll still have that one on your hands when she's thirty." This was a sore point with my mother and she'd get angry: "I'll marry her off tomorrow if I feel like it, and to whomever I please besides." I found the idea of winding up a spinster chilling – even death paled in comparison. I kept my ears open. I knew my mother was lying when she said she could marry me to anyone at all, but I still hoped that I might find "a match". My mother preferred to confide in my younger brother, and would sigh, "How will we marry her off?" My younger brother was an idealist, and he was fond of me. "You never know," he'd say, "but we should get her out and about." He was the one who insisted that I go to boarding school. "If she's well brought up and has a profession in hand, even without a dowry, she just might find a husband." I think all mothers with children worry about these things. In my house, though, they thought it wise to let me know how matters stood. "She has to understand what life is like," my mother said. The professions they wanted to "place" me in varied from year to year. They considered in turn that I would be nothing less than a teacher, lawyer, doctor, newspaper editor and explorer. I had my own ideas; until I was fifteen I wanted to be a trapeze artist or a film star. "You'll do as you're told," my mother would say. The most surprising thing was that my brothers never gave a thought to their future. "They'll have the plantation," my mother said, which wasn't a solution; long after experience had shown that we couldn't count on that, she continued to say that my brothers would "have the plantation", which reassured her all the same. My brothers never went to the lycée or any kind of school. There wasn't ever any question of that. They lived in Sadec, and the complete idleness of those young men of seventeen and eighteen seemed scandalous to everyone, except of course to us. We made no effort to excuse it. When people told my mother that the situation was "a great misfortune", she would regularly reply, "You're telling me!" – but without any real conviction. My younger brother had decided to become a hunter, the greatest hunter in Indochina, and pass up the plantation. By the age of fourteen he was hunting in the Elephant Mountains, and at twenty-one he had bagged twelve tigers and a black panther. "It's a goddamn lousy profession," my older brother kept telling him, only to be told that it was the sole career suitable for a man who had "courage but no talent for studying".

Léo's intrusion into the family changed all our plans. As soon as we learned the extent of his fortune, it was unanimously decided that besides providing everyone in the family with his or her own car, Léo would pay off the *chettis* and finance various undertakings: a sawmill for my younger brother and a studio-workshop for my elder one, the blueprints for which my mother studied carefully. I was delegated to inform Léo of these projects and "sound him out" on them, without promising anything in return. "If you could manage not to marry him," my mother said, "that would be better:

he's native, after all, no matter what you say to me." I rebelled and said I would marry Léo, to which my mother's answer was always "If you're clever and know how to manage it, you can definitely avoid that." If I persisted, I got a beating. My mother would make me swear "on her head" that I would never give myself to Léo. "You can do absolutely whatever you like, but don't sleep with him: get everything you can out of him, you have the right – think of your poor mother – but don't sleep with him, or no-one else will want you." My mother had complete faith in the virginity of girls: "A girl's greatest treasure is her purity." If I slept with Léo, nobody would ever want me, not even Léo. Later, a year after I'd met Léo, he announced that to his great sorrow he could only marry me completely disinherited by his father, who would not accept such a marriage at any price. My mother then spoke of "taking him to court" for having compromised me. My mother had so counted on Léo that she considered this refusal a disaster not only for me but for my brothers, who had been naïve enough to bank on him. But my mother was kind and allowed Léo to keep seeing me anyway. She saw him rather often herself; perhaps she hadn't given up all hope that he would marry me, and meanwhile she and my brothers took considerable advantage of the situation, and I'll return to that.

Why did Léo notice me? He found me to his liking. The only explanation I can think of is that Léo himself was ugly. Left badly scarred by smallpox, he was distinctly uglier than the average native but was always dressed with perfect taste, meticulously groomed and unfailingly polite, even at my house where rudeness was the rule, even towards him. Léo was, moreover, truly generous but sharp enough so that one couldn't ask "just anything" of him. So when he met my family he was shrewd enough to realize how dangerous they would be if he didn't watch his back. Despite this natural caution Léo was more or less unintelligent. He was the worst kind of "European" snob, yet he seriously impressed me because he knew how to dance the Charleston, he ordered his ties from Paris, and he'd seen Joséphine Baker in the flesh at the Folies-Bergère. He missed Paris, trailing an aura of nostalgia that was not without charm. For almost two years he dragged my family and me through every nightclub in Saigon. He would come fetch me in his Léon-Bollée, in which he carted my mother and two brothers around. My mother would request "special permission" from the directress of the Pension Barbet, my boarding school, and I would go out with them. That's what Léo called "doing the town" or "going on a razzle". My family annoyed him and he would have gladly dispensed with them, but I'd told him in no uncertain terms that if he didn't "hit the high spots" with them, I wouldn't go out with him. My mother was unshakeable on this point: a girl must not go out alone with a young man, or she'll be compromised for ever and won't find a husband. But my refusal to go out alone with Léo reflected above all – aside from the trust I placed in my mother's words – the most sincere and steadfast desire to see my mother and brothers profit as well from my good fortune. I felt as if I were "taking them out" in turn, because without Léo that would never have happened, since at the time my mother could not buy even a few gallons of petrol to come get me in Saigon.

How often did Léo haul us around like that? No doubt many, many times. They all blend into one. We were known in every bar, tearoom and nightclub in the city. We used to go above all to La Cascade, which was about 12 miles outside the city and featured a "night" swimming pool cut right into the bed of a mountain stream. This pool was lighted from within by electricity, and the swimmers' bodies, fluid and supple, were silhouetted in the diverted waters of the torrent. My brothers and I would swim there before the ritual cold supper and dancing. Those were strange evenings; they were not cheerful occasions. My brothers, who despised Léo, wore set expressions of silent dignity; my mother displayed a fixed sad and gentle smile as she proudly watched her children dancing. As usual, her frocks looked like peignoirs, with side and shoulder seams, no belt, and she wore cotton stockings with her down-at-the-heel shoes. She sat a little to one side of the table, holding on her knees the large handbag she "never let out of her sight", in which she always carried the land-office map of the plantation and her receipts from the *chettis*. At that time people were calling her a martyr to her sons, especially the eldest for whom she went daily deeper into debt without any idea of how she could ever get out. She would say to herself that she was a martyr and we believed her; she said it every day, each time she beat me, and whenever she was resting, taking time to think. To us she had by slow degrees reached the condition of martyrdom the way one advances towards a diploma in disaster. She was a "martyr" the way one would be anything else. She used to say, "I'm chained to my troubles"; "I'm worn out, it would be best if I died"; "I'll have to shoulder my burden until the end"; "Sometimes I wonder what I did to Heaven to deserve such tribulation". She talked like that too often, we never listened any more. People criticized her in those days for being too indulgent, especially because of that business with Léo, which did her serious harm. They would say, "Madame D. lets her daughter go out with Annamese – that girl is completely ruined, it's a shame." They always saw us with Léo and his friends, and said that I "slept with natives". I was fifteen. Léo hadn't yet touched me when all Saigon considered me "the dregs of the city". We suspected as much, but we would interpret that gossip in a reassuring way. Finally, when no-one would have anything to do with us any more, Mama said, "They're jealous, who cares?" I think my mother found real relaxation in those nights spent in the clubs. She did not touch the champagne. Her big hands resting on her purse, she was entirely at our service, never saying a word about going home. From time to time she would say something nice to Léo, as a token of gratitude and because she felt my brothers were too frosty with him. (I can see my mother's hands now, clutching her purse as if clinging to her fate. God's hands do not seem more beautiful to me. When I was very little and noticed something disturbing or had a frightening thought, for example the possibility of my mother's death, when I learned at the age of five that she was mortal, I would go to her and tell her. Then she would pass her hand over my face, gently, and tell me, "Forget." I would forget and go away comforted. With those same hands, later on, she beat me. And she earned my daily bread by correcting exercise books or doing accounts all night long. She devoted that same full effort to it. She beat hard, she slaved hard, she was profoundly good, she was made for tempestuous destinies, for hacking her way in exploration through the world of emotions. She was deeply unhappy, but she found her share of happiness in that very misfortune because she loved work and sacrifice, and what she preferred above all else was to forget herself, to lose herself in endless illusions. My mother dreamt the way I have never seen anyone dream. She dreamt her very unhappiness, she spoke of it with pride; she never knew real sadness but only pain, because she possessed a soul of royal fierceness that would have disdained to wallow in the acceptance all sadness entails.)

If she seemed sad while we were dancing, it was without realizing it; she wasn't sad in fact, she was simply pleased. Her manner could be misleading. Léo would not have allowed me to dance with anyone but him, aside from my brothers. In the cabarets my brothers spent their time watching girls they found attractive. When there was one they both fancied too much, things almost always ended badly, so Mama, who kept an eye out, would announce she was tired and suggest that we leave. I didn't like dancing, except with my younger brother, with whom I waltzed. Léo, who danced consistently off the beat, considered himself a fine dancer. At first the other customers laughed at us, but in the end everyone knew us and no-one paid any attention. Léo was short and wore suits with sloping shoulders, which did not look good on him. There was a tango he considered irresistible because he had danced it in Paris: "Not That I'm Curious, But I'd Like to Know Why Blondes Always Have Black Muffs".

Léo was perfectly laughable and that pained me deeply. He looked ridiculous because he was so short and thin and had droopy shoulders. Plus he thought so much of himself. In a car he was presentable because one couldn't see his height, only his head, which, albeit ugly, did possess a certain distinction. Not once did I agree to walk a hundred yards with him in a street. If a person's capacity for shame could be exhausted, I would have exhausted mine with Léo. It was just simply awful. I would dance only tangos with him because the bright lights were then replaced by a very subdued, reddish glow, which allowed the two of us to escape much notice. I'd come to an agreement with him about dancing only the tango; since that dance was quite popular at the time, I danced enough with Léo for him to feel it was still worthwhile to take us out. I claimed that I loved no other dance but the tango (which, by the way, I haven't much cared for ever since). I'd already had an instinctive dislike for that dance, which I soon hated. Since it was for months Léo's only chance to get close to me, he danced it in a rather lewd fashion, glued to me, his belly thrust forward, with an expression of painful concentration. As for the Charleston, it was all the rage in Paris, but in Saigon it was only beginning to catch on. Léo knew the Charleston and loved it madly. For months he begged me to learn it so that we could dance it together. The prospect of dancing with him on a half-empty floor always repelled me. I never learned the Charleston. Given the way I felt, the very idea drove me to despair whenever Léo unfortunately insisted that we try. A few rare times, crazed by his exasperated longing for the Charleston, he danced it with some other girls in the room; since he was native, and to avoid being rebuffed, he could only try inviting the girls who seemed decidedly middle-class and displayed a certain coarseness. He believed that these desperate decisions (because one never knew, he might be rejected anyway) would impress me. They did not leave me indifferent, true, but what tormented me the most was seeing the man who passed for my lover and with whom I was supposed to spend my life making such a fool of himself.

When Léo talked to me it was exclusively about love. In general he complained about me, and claimed I was making him suffer terribly. His jealousy poisoned our relationship. But looking back after fifteen years, I do realize that without that jealousy I could never have continued seeing him. He squabbled with me and imposed conditions on our "outings", which he had realized I enjoyed. He'd tell me, "Now that I've pulled you out of the soup, you're going to betray me." He was obsessed with that and must have been innately predisposed towards jealousy, because from the beginning I took our relationship quite seriously and never gave him any reason to be jealous. After the Charleston, it was films Léo loved, American films. So he would tell me, "It's real simple: if you betray me I'll bump you off." How could I have betrayed him, and with whom? I only slept with him once and after two years of pleading. What he called "betrayal" would have been kissing someone else, for example, or dancing with a European. I gave him a detailed schedule of my activities, I yielded to all his arbitrary demands. I obeyed them rigorously. I thus spent a certain part of my life creating imaginary obligations for myself and observing them with uncommon strictness. I truly believed I was at fault where Léo was concerned, and I felt wretched for not being able to "do more". I spent a good part of my time with him swearing on the heads of my mother and brothers that I was faithful to him. But Léo never entirely believed me. My elder brother would tell him, "My sister's a tart," and Léo would [press] me to give him explanations I could not provide. To the best of my recollection, the rare moments I spent alone with Léo were formal interrogations. Or else, when the surroundings were convenient, serious struggles during which Léo tried to kiss me on the mouth. Yet I was in love with him in my fashion, and when he would go a week without seeing me, to punish me, I was very unhappy. I was in love with Léo-in-his-Léon-Bollée. Sitting in his magnificent limousine, he made a considerable impression on me, and I never became accustomed to it. I was also in love with Léo when he paid for the cold suppers and champagne in the nightclubs. He did it casually, with an offhandedness that went straight to my heart. Never, precisely never, would my mother or my brothers have offered to pay for anything at all; never (although yes, perhaps once in two years, and I'm not even sure about that) was he invited to lunch in our home. Often, before going to the nightclubs, he took us to dinner at a Chinese restaurant in Cholen. That would happen when I had been "nice"; then he'd cough up a hundred piastres (a thousand francs in 1931) and that was just for a start. My mother and brothers felt he never shelled out enough and often groused about it, but they didn't dare say so to his face.

It was to me they said or argued that. "He should already be quite happy to go out with a white girl," my mother would say. My elder brother, when he did mention him, never referred to him as anything but "the foetus" or "your lousy foetus" or "your syphilitic jerk". I was willing not to argue, indeed that's all I was, not being very enterprising. Timidly, I began to complain to Léo about needing money. I still wonder how I wound up taking such a drastic step. Search as I may, I can't find a clear motive for that decision any more. Obviously, above all, I was trying to make sense of myself. I had brought Léo to the house and with him the considerable comfort of his cars, as well as the distraction and luxury of our nights on the town. But that was not enough. Léo would get the hump: he did a lot but not *everything* that was asked of him. For example, he had indeed placed one of his cars at our disposal – to be driven only by his chauffeur: my brothers were not permitted to touch it. This condition struck them as a grave affront, and my elder brother considered it a provocation. He could not climb into the car without remembering it. "If this isn't pathetic, to have to put up with stuff like this ... If I weren't

holding back, I'd bash in the ribs of that lousy foetus of yours."
And my mother would add, "Let it go, things won't always be this
way." To understand such naïveté, which might seem far-fetched,
one must realise that we were sunk in a boundless childhood
from which, all in all, we were trying in vain to escape. We were
even spending our whole lives trying to get out of it any way we
could.

When I say that I was trying to make sense of myself, I mean
something quite specific. I was seeking this meaning within my
family, where my insignificance was such that every time I tried to
assert myself, if only by offering my opinion, I was energetically
put back in my place. When I first brought Léo to the house, I
hoped to become an interesting and perhaps even an indispensable person. My family soon became accustomed to the comforts
and opportunities Léo provided. They got used to everything with
disconcerting ease. When an advantage went missing, they became
indignant with the utmost sincerity. Whenever Léo happened to
"go down" to Saigon without taking them along, they felt this was
a dirty trick that spoke volumes about what Léo really was. "I saw
through him long ago, that little runt," my elder brother would
say, adding, "One day I'll get him back for all this." I must note
that we also became accustomed to the worst inconveniences as
well as the pleasant changes. In the same way that we had grown
used to running out of money, to selling our remaining jewellery
and, later, the furniture, so that we could eat until the end of the
month, we got used to nasty gossip ("slander", my mother called
it, saying, "Let them foam at the mouth, my conscience is cleaner
than theirs"). Likewise, we grew accustomed to Léo but with this
difference: the acquired advantages immediately joined our most
basic needs. All acquisitions were permanent, and our eyes then
turned towards possible future gains. And so, I had no right at all
to rest on the laurels of any advantages Léo offered through me,
which meant I was always on the alert, constantly looking for what
Léo might do next for my family. Léo needed a lot of coaxing, he

was stingy, and he told me that my family disgusted him deeply, which neither bothered nor angered me in the least.

When he was willing to give me some money, I led him to believe that it was for me to buy certain things I needed. These sums were not large, but still, they were something. I would waltz home in triumph, planning my performance, and announce, "Léo gave me fifty piastres." My mother would come over to me and say, "Give." Basically, I wasn't very nice: "Why should I?" I'd say, wanting to be begged. My elder brother would show up in turn; when there was talk of money, when he heard it mentioned in conversation, he arrived all aquiver, like the hunter who hears the tiger roar. "How much?" he'd ask. My younger brother would declare, "I think this is revolting." Me, I still had the money, and while I had it, I knew what happiness was. It didn't last long. "Give me that money," my mother would insist, adding remarks such as "You cannot keep that on you, it's not proper, hand it over, I'll give it back to you." She never did give me back anything whatsoever, poor woman, it would have been completely impossible for her – the little bit of money I gave her was immediately swallowed up by the family's needs. I made them plead with me, it was a kind of revenge. For a moment I experienced the illusion of power. I'm not saying that my mother didn't feel a twinge of shame at such moments, but money had an extraordinary power over her. When she knew that I had some, she went into a kind of trance. She would dog my footsteps all through the house: "Give." My brother prowled around us, bare-chested in his silk trousers. I'd announce my news in a loud voice, on purpose, because my mother had told me one day, "Don't tell your brothers anything, it's not worth it." I wanted to know how far, to what extremes, my mother would go; I felt a terrible joy in watching the limits to her injustice expand with each passing day. My mother knew this, but she never had the strength to do otherwise. Afterward I was punished, but I deserved it, I knew that as well. Things weren't to be pushed too far; even in that case, there were boundaries to be observed. The moment when I had to hand over the money always arrived: "You're going to give it to me this instant." The hand was suspended above my face, ready to fall. I gave. The money vanished into the purse and we thought no more about it – that's a manner of speaking, by the way, because once Léo began giving me some money, my brother's insults acquired a fresh nuance. From "crab louse" I passed to the status of "tart", "bit on the side" and "bitch who sleeps with natives". My mother, speaking of that aspect of my relations with Léo, would say, "It's a dreadful misfortune." Still, fifty piastres – why let them go to waste?

Such reflections do prove that they more or less realized that the situation was somewhat scandalous, but they always managed to make that all my fault. Especially since my mother was not unaware that such behaviour (I was sixteen) might present a few drawbacks for the future. The particular nature of her attitude sprang precisely from the contradiction between her conduct and her observations. Regarding the conduct of young women my mother's opinion never changed, and although her ideal was doubtless a touch naïve, she believed in it passionately, an ideal that never, ever, became more flexible or nuanced, even when she accepted my behaviour with Léo and his money. "There is nothing more beautiful than a pure young woman," my mother would tell me, and she described her so well and with such grace that she tortured me, because I recognized none of my traits in those portraits. Even when my reputation was such that it was now nearly useless to try passing me off as "marriageable", I could not arrive anywhere without my mother whispering to me, "Smile, a girl should smile," and she herself would present a kind of pathetic grimace she probably considered the happy-smile-of-the-happy-mother-of-the-smiling-young-woman.

I add that her chief character trait was a complete incapacity for despair. Until the last day of my time in Indochina, she hoped to marry me off. This idealistic aspect of her character was balanced by a kind of unshakeable good sense: "Demand whatever you like from him," she'd tell me when speaking of Léo, "you can accept everything, but don't sleep with him." And when I managed to extract some money from Léo, she felt a certain pride in that. She would say of me, "I'm not worried about her, she'll manage." I began to hand over the money Léo gave me to my mother, but my elder brother quickly asked me to help him out. On such occasions he was charming and irresistible – and I could not resist him. "Dear little N., couldn't you let me have ten piastres?" I'd give it to him in secret; there wasn't a single time when I didn't believe we would be friends again for ever. My gullibility was equalled only by my stupidity. When my brother and I later lived in France and I began playing my little game with the boys at the lycée, he got into the habit of turning out my pockets every evening. Then he'd beat me, claiming that I was being "kept" and that he'd "teach me how to live", that he was "doing this for my own good". I refrain from passing judgement just as I refrained from doing so at the time. I would like to keep intact the radiance of the unique Event that my elder brother was for me. He was unfair and cowardly, like fate itself and every destiny. There was something thorough and fundamentally pure in his ferocity towards me. His life unfolded with the implacability of the inevitable, and he filled us with respect. The weave of blows and insults he gave me is the very fabric of which his soul was made, there was no extra margin. He was always of the *greatest* injustice, what no-one could surpass, which best evokes the unjustness of Destiny and falls upon you with the unpredictability of fate. Not for anything would I want that, in the name of some morality, no matter how all-inclusive, he be found reprehensible and judgement be passed on him. My brother was cruel, of course, but with a cruelty such that I never found any human measure for it, and that is the important thing, that is why I ask not for indulgence, but for a reprieve from all morality. If he is found blameworthy, along with my mother, I consider that these recollections are not those I would have liked them to be. No-one is entitled to offer explanations for the conduct of others, or even to try, everyone certainly agrees on that. Even when I was tiny, I believed that my mother and elder brother were answerable directly to God: they beat and passed judgement by virtue of superior reasons, imbued with infinite mystery. When, older, I rebelled, it was always a bit reluctantly, and the joy I felt thereby was not unrelated to a blasphemous delight. I always felt a twinge of guilty conscience when accusing them in turn, and forcing them to a lucidity that diverged, however slightly, from the quasi-divine irresponsibility in which they moved with incomparable ease.

One may well wonder why I write down these recollections, why I present behaviour I announce it would displease me to see judged. Doubtless, simply, to bring such behaviour to light. I feel, since I began recording these memories, that I am unearthing them from a thousand years of drifting sands. It was barely thirteen years ago that these things happened and that our family broke up, except for my younger brother, who never left my mother and who died last year in Indochina. Barely thirteen years. No other reason impels me to write of these memories, except that instinct to unearth. It's very simple. If I do not write them down, I will gradually forget them. That thought terrifies me. If I am not faithful to myself, to whom will I be? I no longer really know what I used to say to Léo. It's so frightening, and at the same time it isn't very important. Believing in the insignificance of one's childhood is, I think, the sign of a deep-seated unbelief: definitive, complete. What can I do about it? Everybody agrees about childhood. All the women in the world would weep over the story of any old childhood, be it even that of murderers, tyrants. Not long ago I saw a photo of Hitler as a child in embroidered petticoats, standing on a chair. From childhood on, every destiny is infinitely piteous. I am doubtless led to believe only in the childhood of others, for in mine I see nothing but a precocity more likely to horrify me on the whole. My childhood photographs nauseate me. Whenever I happen to read accounts of someone's childhood or youth, I am astonished at the world of unreality they contain. Even in the stories of children referred to as "unhappy" (as if there were happy children), one finds artificial hells, desperate recourse to dreams, escape into enchantment, the supernatural. That always staggers me, and I tend to believe that it's a question more of involuntary betrayal – or, more simply, a poetic transposition with which people feel childhood must be endowed, else it would be dishonoured. For as far back as I remember, my childhood unfolded in a stark and barren light, nothing like the world of dreams, which was barred from my earliest years. It's always awkward to assert such things. I can therefore say that I do not recall having dreamt about anything whatsoever, be it even a better life. If I was dreaming about marrying Léo, my "hell" was following me into the dream, and the dream – that was the confrontation between this reality and what one might call happiness.

I state immediately that this lack of dreaming does not imply that I was lucid. No. I remember (and perfectly) that at school, I was worse at studying than most of the pupils. Not that I was particularly unintelligent, but I didn't know how to work, I didn't find it at all interesting or useful. I think that despite my apparent attention, I was almost completely distracted. For example, I would listen to the teacher talk about some subject. What would intrigue me was how he went about it, his way of explaining, more than what he was explaining. I make an exception nevertheless for mathematics, which fascinated me, even though I was basically hopeless in that subject as well as everything else until the eleventh grade. Sometimes I would receive an "outstanding" mark in French, it depended on the teachers. For six months I had a French teacher who considered me far and away his best student, and he never gave me less than 90 per cent. He left; his successor banished me to the bottom of the class, and never gave me even an average mark. I felt truly repelled by certain subjects or classic authors. Madame de Sévigné filled me with a discouraging disgust against which I struggled in vain. A paper on her {close} relationship with her daughter earned me a failing mark and I was singled out for criticism. I no longer remember very clearly what I did to deserve that mark. On the other hand, Molière and Shakespeare entranced me, whereas Corneille and even Racine bored me to bits. There were some classes I decided to "skip" because I felt they were useless. For a few weeks, I dropped out of English; they were reading *A Christmas Carol* at the rate of ten lines per class hour, and every class almost gave me a nervous breakdown. I did the same thing later with biology when it went too slowly for my taste, and then with history, and geography. This meant saving many hours, which I devoted to Léo. The principal of the lycée noticed, of course; I was threatened with expulsion and summoned to the vice-principal's office. I went to see him in an indescribable panic, but he invited me in and let me know right away that if I was nice, he would not expel me. Then he tried to kiss me on the mouth, and the session wound up in a boxing match [since] I didn't want to kiss him because of his huge black beard, and because I'd promised to remain faithful to Léo, whom I told about all this. Léo didn't believe me, he took it very badly, and would have liked me to leave the lycée immediately, which I found a bit excessive. As for my mother, she was delighted, even though she affected a sincere indignation: "That's what it's like – when you have pretty daughters you must keep a sharp eye out."

I stayed in school where I did exactly nothing at all. My reports were catastrophic. At the end of the year, the overall evaluation was: "Does not use her great gifts." My mother, who remained more or less indifferent to my marks, took only the general evaluation seriously, and she was jubilant: "When I say she's intelligent, I know what I'm talking about." At such moments she looked after me more, had new frocks made for me, and she'd say, "Eat, sleep, start building up your strength to be at your best when you go to college." She thought the marks I received were unfair and managed to make me believe that the professors had it in for me personally in the same way everyone had a grudge against us. "Don't let it bother you," she'd say; "they'd never give such grades to the daughter of some administrator." End of discussion. Besides, there was some truth to that. The sons and daughters of planters and important officials were seated in the front rows of the classroom; behind them came the minor civil servants, then the natives. And among the natives, those with well-to-do fathers were placed immediately behind the French students.

It is not for me to criticize that state of affairs, but it deeply amazed me. I'm not saying that some students' marks were related to their higher social standing, but it is true that those students received more attention. When they entered tenth grade, any native students considered anti-French were singled out for stricter supervision. I knew one, the son of a native doctor, who became a close friend; he was exceptionally intelligent and in ninth grade began winning all the first prizes. I admired him greatly, because he regularly refused to have anything to do with the French, and he never abandoned his pride. He refused to sit near the front of the class, for example, and stayed resolutely with his compatriots. He was said to be "dangerous". And so, even though he was by far the best student, he was never congratulated by the teachers' committee, which "passed over" his marks. How many times did I hear French people say, "With that race, you have to be careful, you mustn't flatter them, they'd immediately start thinking they're our equals." We saw one another in secret, since he didn't want to be seen with a French girl. He was a boarder at the lycée because his father couldn't afford to pay for a room in town. I believe we came very close to being in love. The day before school ended for the summer, just before my departure for France, we met in an empty room after our last class. Saying goodbye to one another affected us deeply. "You're French," he told me, "I'm Annamese, I can't allow myself to love you. I'll be going to Hanoi to study law because I don't have enough money to go to France, and besides I don't want to, I don't like the French." Having no faith in the possibility of a Franco-Annamese rapprochement, he was in despair. I haven't seen him since, and don't really know what happened to him. He was afraid he had tuberculosis; I have no idea if his fears were justified. If he is alive, I suppose he's a leader in the Indochinese Nationalist Movement and I think of him and all his brothers with emotion, and I wish to tell him here of my admiration and complete sympathy.

(A remark, which is perhaps out of place here, but which I do wish to make: the school in Saigon admitted only the Annamese sons of French citizens, exclusively. Moreover, European dress was strictly required. In 1931, when I left Indochina for ever, a few Annamese girls were attending the lycée. They were forced to disguise themselves as Europeans, which did not suit them at all, for the most part, and that bothered them. European dress was likewise obligatory in the state boarding school where I lived. On Sundays the Annamese boarders could be seen out walking in the streets of Saigon, all dressed in the French style and making fools of themselves in public. What is the point of unforgivably stupid measures like that? I think such requirements, which may at first seem insignificant, come close to being criminal. In addition, the children of non-citizen natives were not allowed to go beyond primary school. Granted, tuberculosis and leprosy have been considerably contained in Indochina, thanks to us, but the physical world provides no possible moral compensation. To save children from death only to restrict them later to a sanctioned, limited development, the very limits of which are codified, seems to me much more reprehensible than it was commendable to save them from death.)

Léo had no interest in politics. The management of his wealth and its astounding dimensions were a constant shelter from such preoccupations. Let's remove him from the Annamese setting and consider him as what he was. I mean that I'm returning to my adolescence. The more I think about it, the more I believe that Léo displayed a very characteristic stupidity that was not, however, without charm, at least for me. He had spent two years in Paris on one long spree during which, as he said, he had "learned how to live". He claimed to have known many women there, and as proof he showed me some photographs: in one of them he was sitting on the floor, his head in the lap of a laughing, heavily made-up brunette of about forty. Other women, each one supplied with an Annamese, lounged about either on divans or on the floor, in equally erotic poses. The setting must have been a hotel room, at night. The women were all stamped with a sinister vulgarity. It's not for nothing that I remember so well that photo in which Léo, his head clamped between the woman's knees, had his eyes half-closed and resembled a corpse. It was a revelation for me: I told myself that I was following these other women in Léo's life and, I don't know why, the anguish this thought gave me was like that I later felt at the idea of death. It then dawned on me that Léo was a truly pathetic fellow, and that I would spend my life in his company, that it was my lot to have Léo after having had my family and that I would never escape. I didn't leave Léo because of that, however; I never even mentioned anything to him. But after seeing that photo, I spent an entire month trying to familiarize myself with the idea of an absolute abandonment. I said nothing about this to my mother. I could not have done that. It was through the photo that I thought I understood that she had abandoned me, as had my brothers: she was letting me sink imperceptibly into that liaison with Léo, when she should have realized that he would not bring me happiness. I [thought] she was abandoning me not willingly but because of a weakness I sensed was without limit or remedy, and which meant that from that moment on I loved her differently.

Léo showed me that evidence of a past life to try to make me fall in love. The things he said to me were not so different from those scattered through American films and cheap romance novels. He told me he would love me "till death", that I had "a heart of stone" and that I was "breaking" his own heart; I loved him "for my money", he said, and "not for myself". He said that he was "born to be unhappy", that "money can't buy happiness", that he was too sentimental and that the world was cruel. He would also say, "What I want is quite simple – a humble home, a loving heart, and I ask for nothing else on this earth." He said that I was "made to make men suffer" and to back this up, in his moments of despair, he would sing, "Women love to drive men mad, live to make their poor hearts sad …" in such a mournful voice that I begged him every time never to sing that song, which I told him was passé. That's the language my first lover used with me for two whole years – a singular contrast with the way my family talked. I was aware of how shabby and outdated Léo's words could be, but that nonsense touched me, I usually found it flattering. I gave up trying to change Léo. He said things that ought to have proved to me a thousand times over his profound stupidity. An example of Léo's finesse: "Parisiennes are adorable. Whenever I arrived at my mistress' place later than the appointed time, I'd find my photograph upside down. It was a charming way to let me know that she was hurt because I was late. When we're married, will you often turn my photograph upside down?"

I gave up trying to change him because it was too much work. I accepted Léo's trite remarks. I accepted everything. My mother, my elder brother, the showers of blows. Everything. I thought the only way to extricate myself was still to marry Léo, because he had money, because with that money we'd go to France with my entire family and there life would be good. I did not plan to leave my family in Indochina, because I thought life alone with Léo would be beyond my strength. Therefore I accepted everything with a certain simplicity: I was not without hope, but I did not separate that hope from a present that was rather fearsome. I thought that one day I would no longer be beaten or insulted, that people would listen to me, that I would be beautiful and brilliant, rich, that I would ride around only in limousines, that perhaps someone other than Léo would love me. Someone other than Léo ... But for that Léo's millions were needed so I could have my nose straightened (advice from my elder brother, who was aware of the new profession of plastic surgery), and patronize the great fashion designers (more advice from my elder brother), and know "how to talk to men" (advice from my mother). It was as clear as day. I believed it all. Without that, no chance of a future. When I claim that I come from the most colossal stupidity, that in losing my youth I lost an empire of stupidity, I certainly know what I'm talking about. Whenever I'd managed to make Léo angry and he was sulky with me, I was despondent because in losing Léo I would lose everything, I'd fall back into my family, and grow old in their shadow. It was horrible to contemplate. To escape all that, I needed Léo.

How did I manage to overcome the kind of physical loathing I felt for Léo? The first time he kissed me on the mouth, it was one evening in his Léon-Bollée. He had come to get me after school and was taking me back to Sadec for the weekend. I rarely saw him alone and at that hour; perhaps it was even the first time that had happened. Along the way, Léo put his arms around me and I felt desire for him. I think it was desire. It was a peacefulness that fully contented me. I was comfortable, there, in Léo's arms. I believe it could have been anybody, I would have felt the same. Léo was anybody: anybody could have told me what Léo told me, anybody could have had Léo's arms and kindness in the darkness of the car, in the black night that was my youth. When his cheek touched my cheek, it was pleasant. I did not see his face. It was a cheek that wanted my cheek – Léo's cheek, and nothing else. I sensed that he desired me because his hands were shaking and because they sometimes encountered my breasts; I preferred to have them around my waist, where I put them back, so that was fine. Quite moved, Léo said, "You have lovely breasts." I said nothing. Léo's desire slipped gently into me and induced mine. I did not desire Léo directly, I desired Léo because he desired me. His desire aroused mine without him having anything to do with it. I found that desire was good to experience, I felt it as a kind of solution to all sorts of things. While Léo held me in his arms, when I thought of my family, I suddenly pitied them for not being as happy as I was, and I thought it was good to think that. I was reconciling myself with the world: I hadn't felt that plenitude except when coming home from hunting with my younger brother, when there had been a storm, and we were returning barefoot in the soft mud of the rice paddies. "Give me your breasts," Léo was saying. I did not want to give him my breasts to touch, I didn't think that was worth it, that would not have added anything more. What I wanted was to feel his desire, that was all. "I love you," Léo said quietly. He did not rush me, he knew I was a virgin, he had principles concerning "the first time"; he left my breasts alone and settled for my waist and my hair, my cheek. When he told me he loved me, I felt penetrated by a kind of fierce generosity and was forced to close my eyes. Anyone else could have said it to me. Under the same conditions, it would have had the same effect.

I had read a {popular sentimental} novel, *Magali* by Delly; this book played a major role in my youth. It was the most beautiful/the only one {*sic*} I'd read, and in it the words "I love you" were pronounced a single time, during a conversation between the two lovers that lasted barely a few minutes but justified months of waiting, of pain, of devastating separation. I'd heard that declaration at the cinema, and each time it overwhelmed me. I thought one said that only once in a lifetime, the way it was in *Magali* and {romantic} films about Casanova: only once to only one person, and never afterwards to anyone else, like the way it was with death. I was convinced of that. And that evening, when Léo told me he loved me, I felt giddy. Not only was he saying it, but he would never say it again – and he was saying it to me. I was so young and so naïve that I imagined that once those words had been spoken, you couldn't say them again without being ashamed and dishonoured to such an extent that suicide was the sole remedy for such despair. Later, Léo said them to me many times, and although I was not as deeply stirred as I had been the first time, I was moved all the same. Those words had a magical effect on me. Later on, I often asked Léo to say those words: "Say them to me" – and I received them the way one receives the wind, eyes closed, paying attention with all of one's being. Later on, long after Léo, other men happened to say them to me, when their meaning seemed more than doubtful to me. Nevertheless, the words have always obliged me to listen to them seriously, even when they were said only in the distraction of desire. I used to say to Léo, "Even if it isn't true, say it." They were key words: even in moments when I felt the most foreign, the most closed to Léo, those words opened me up and I became kind to him.

It was on that evening that Léo kissed me on the mouth. He did it by surprise. All of a sudden, I felt a cool and moist contact with my lips. The revulsion I felt truly cannot be described. I shoved Léo, I spat, I wanted to jump out of the car. Léo was at a complete loss. In a single second, I felt myself stretched tight as a bow, ruined forever. I kept saying, "It's over, it's over." Léo was saying, "What do you mean?" He did not understand. At one point, he laughed, and explained to me that it wasn't letting herself be kissed on the mouth that cost a girl her virginity. "I know that," I cried, "but it's still over." He tried to calm me and put his arms around me again but I shouted, I begged him to stop the car and let me out. It was mid-evening in the middle of nowhere, but I wasn't thinking of that any more. I'm retracing the scene the way it happened; I cannot explain it. I was disgust itself. But as for explaining what I meant by "over", I cannot do it, I don't know any more. I did calm down, however, and slid over to the end of the seat, as far from Léo as possible. And there I spat into my handkerchief, I kept spitting, I spat all night long and the next day; whenever I thought about it again, I spat some more. Obviously quite miserable, Léo no longer tried to touch me; he could see that I was spitting and asked, "Do I disgust you?" I could not reply. I was remembering his face, which was at that moment in darkness: his pockmarked face, his large, soft mouth; I recalled the photograph in which he was so pathetic and I was thinking that the mouth, the saliva, the tongue of that contemptible creature had touched my lips. Truly, I felt a kind of aftermath of rape. Nothing could make it so that he had not touched my mouth with his mouth that had touched so many others, that opened only to tell me despicable or ridiculous things, that seemed to me degraded, vain and stupid, lost, as Léo was lost. "I see that I disgust you, you don't need to hide." I did not reply. I thought about the words my brothers used to describe Léo. "Foetus": I had been kissed by a foetus. Ugliness had entered my mouth, I had communed with horror. I was violated to my very soul.

If I wanted to jump out of the car, it was to put an end to the horror: I was discovering my existence in a horrifying light, naked and bleak. For once, I was not deluding myself, and I *knew* what I would find in Sadec. My elder brother befuddled with opium, my mother in a frenzy of exasperation, and the blows, the blows, endless, the inadmissible blows, the shameful blows. It was as if a machine to manufacture lucidity had suddenly started up inside me. I saw things clearly. I was setting out in life with the mis-shapen creature that was Léo and there was no escape for me. I couldn't escape from anything – perhaps that was what it was to be "over": I had nothing left. Whereas I hadn't known a moment before that I still had my mouth, now it no longer belonged to me, I didn't recognize it anymore. I was suffering its violation, its pollution, just as I was suffering what I thought was life: my life. I rinsed my mouth with my own saliva which I spat out into my handkerchief, and with my handkerchief I rubbed my lips. But that wasn't enough – never enough: I still believed that some portion of Léo's saliva yet remained in my mouth and I spat again

and again without stopping. Of course I knew that Léo must have
been terribly hurt by all this but I put that off until later, there was
nothing else I could do. I was busy cleansing my mouth. I opened
it and dried it in the onrushing air. But when I closed it and my
saliva began flowing, the tragedy would begin again, I would imagine that my saliva was forever mixed with Léo's. At some point
I cried, and then I drew closer to Léo and said, "I'm being silly,
it's because it's the first time." He put his arms around my waist
and said, "You're making me suffer dreadfully." I clung to him,
my head against his chest, hidden, and I tried to start swallowing
my saliva again in tiny amounts, to get used to it. When I couldn't
manage it, I would spit discreetly into my handkerchief. "Above
all, you mustn't be angry with me," I told Léo. I wanted him to
console me; he could not. But his enveloping arm consoled me. I
could count only on Léo's arm and I used it that evening as much
as I could. I found that arm inoffensive and kind, it wished me no
harm, it was willing to have me, and I managed to make do with
that for consolation.

My elder brother had a monkey, a marmoset, which he loved
to distraction. He could shed tears over this monkey. When he
was forced to leave it at the plantation – after the adventures I
am about to relate – he sometimes worried seriously about it:
"I wonder what those bastards are doing with my monkey." At
the time I'm speaking of, my brother had gradually reached the
point of smoking {opium} for much of the night and was coming
home at around six in the morning. He would go to bed right
away and get up for lunch, then go back to sleep, after which
he would play with his monkey until our five-o'clock snack,
then play with his monkey again, have dinner, and go off to
smoke. We kept this monkey in a cage, in a small courtyard. It
was an exceptionally intelligent and amusing animal. He wound
up playing a major role in my brother's life. When my brother

wasn't sleeping, he would let the monkey out and put him on his shoulder; he would play the piano to him and would give him so many sapeks (a bronze coin of the native currency) to put in his mouth that his jowls were stuffed full and so heavy that he could only move about with his head hanging. The monkey would then take the coins out and give them back to my brother one by one. My brother found this howlingly funny – I've never seen anyone laugh like he did. He would call my younger brother and me to come and see the performance. We had to be there or risk making him dangerously angry. We had to watch. Sometimes it took an hour.

Whenever I didn't laugh, my brother was furious. Sometimes my mother would appear and tell him, "I beg you, do something, anything at all but do something, don't waste all your days ..." My brother would put her in her place more or less roughly, it depended, but he'd keep playing with the monkey. We were also raising a rooster, which my brother sometimes put into the monkey's cage, where the monkey would pluck out its feathers with shrieks of joy. The rooster would squawk and the scene would amuse everyone, even my mother, so there were some things that brought us together. Perhaps it was cruel, but we didn't think about that. One day the monkey escaped and spread panic through the native girls' school where my mother was the principal. Within a minute the entire school fled outdoors, the girls all screaming. My brothers and I were in heaven although my mother took it quite badly, spoke of being dismissed and persuaded my brother to send the monkey back to the plantation. That was when he began taking an interest in the place, going out there to see his monkey, which was pining away from boredom. One day the animal began to lose his teeth because he wasn't being given enough to drink; my brother couldn't resist bringing him back to Sadec, where the monkey, having picked up a few vices, would spend his entire day masturbating, to the huge disgust of everyone but my elder brother. My brother would show

CHILDHOOD AND ADOLESCENCE IN INDOCHINA 51

the same infatuation with certain people for a while, then drop them as completely as if they'd never existed.

Why remember the cinema all of a sudden? Urgent to write it down. It happened when she was fourteen, that girl I once was. I did not want to go walking with the young ladies of the Pension Barbet every Sunday, in a crocodile, through the streets of the city. I was ashamed of going out all lined up. It was just impossible to consider – impossible. I had said so to my mother. My mother understood that this was impossible. She knew that certain things I felt were impossible should simply be abandoned. Or was it that I managed to win her over? I don't think so. Just as my mother had given up hope of making me say sorry, she gave up hope of seeing me go out walking in a crocodile with the Pension Barbet. I had told her, "That's impossible," without explaining myself. I had added, "It's ridiculous."

I would have been unable to explain myself, I was not in the habit of doing that. I had never explained what I meant about anything whatsoever.

Everyone in my family was like that. Never, anywhere, in any milieu, have I encountered such an acute sense of the immodesty of language. Never was it used for anything except describing actions to be taken or situations requiring definition. Insults could not have been more gratuitous: we could have refrained from insulting one another, so if we insulted one another, it was thanks to a spirit of poetry. Never in my home did words serve to describe a mood, to express a complaint. My elder brother's "You make me fucking sick" meant, to us, that *everything* made him fucking sick, and that he found himself in a state of what in another milieu is conventionally known as despair. And so it was not without solemnity and respect that we avoided speaking to him at such moments. Insults – they were our poetry, sharing its truest, most undeniable characteristics. First, gratuity, which was not rash but said exactly the right thing, lit us up with anger, and flooded us with revelations of all kinds. "Your house is a shithole," my brother would tell my mother, "a real shithole and boring as shit." Those words found in us that "always hollow" space evoked by Saint John of the Cross, and they filled us with something evident, with a revelation. In such cases, I could tell that the house really was a shithole, that I was up to my neck in shit, and I suspected that everything was a shithole and that no-one ever got out of it. There were the words, and the look that went with them, and the tone – clipped, unaffected, utterly suitable and sincere – that drove all doubt from those golden words.

I have not experienced revelations that powerful in my life, as powerful and as supremely convincing as certain of my elder brother's insults, save in my reading of Rimbaud, of Dostoyevsky. My brother was perhaps the first to inculcate in me that tendency I still possess to prefer the work of inspiration to absolutely any other, and to hold human intelligence in disfavour. In the matter of intelligence, I am tolerably responsive only to that of certain animals, precisely those that possess so little of it that the rare traces they do display seem to spring from sudden inspiration. For example I prefer stupid cats to intelligent ones. I can't help it. I prefer cats that don't recognize me to those that do. When my brother caught syphilis, he said, "Rotten fucking life, I'm fucked rotten." From then on, I felt infinitely compassionate and fraternal. I felt inconsolable, just inconsolable to learn that such things happen in life, but I did indeed learn this, and no-one, afterwards, had to teach me that lesson better than he had.

When I insisted to my mother that it was impossible for me to go walking with the girls of the Pension Barbet, my mother must have felt that I couldn't help it. She was so accustomed to "things one can't help" that she gave in. She went to see the principal of the Pension Barbet. I waited for her outside the office door. It was an awkward request. The discussion lasted a long time. My mother emerged flushed and still unsettled, and she told me that I'd been excused. I don't know what argument my mother used, but she was not a little proud of having carried the day. The principal felt strongly about those Sunday walks, she wanted to put the perfect behaviour of her students on public display. I still wonder what made her give in, especially since my mother had asked her to allow me to go out alone, which should have seemed inadmissible to her. At that time, I did not know Léo, and my mother surely never thought I might misbehave on my walks; to tell the truth she wasn't thinking of anything, and she didn't wonder what I could do on my own in the city, at fourteen years old, every Sunday afternoon.

Indeed, the following Sunday, when I faced this prospect, I had no idea what to do with myself. I got dressed at four o'clock, however, and I went out. I had a bright-green straw hat my mother had bought me in a sale (of course) to be worn on outings. I was wearing a dress of raw silk with blue flowers. It was only when I got outside that I found myself helpless to deal with the utter absurdity of my outfit, which seemed somehow inevitable. It never even occurred to me to change any part of it. Just as I had the mug of a "crab louse", of someone to whom one would say, "So much for you," so also that outfit prescribed by my mother was part of my public image, and I dragged it around as sadly as I did my face. Through the city, off I went. Believing the human race spent Sunday afternoon the same way in every city in the world, I did so as well. I had always been taught the significance of social conventions, whose meaning had been deeply instilled into me. And I can affirm absolutely that throughout a great part of my youth, I strove to be "like others", to "pass", which brought me a considerable amount of pain and a latent despair that stayed with me for a strangely long time. After leaving the Pension Barbet, I set out to walk along the street with the air of a girl who knows where she's going, someone behaving normally. Well, once outside, I stiffened up and walked so bizarrely that people were looking at me. I think I must have been walking with an expression of extraordinary concentration – especially since I didn't know where I was going. I was mulling over what had led up to this outing: my refusal to walk in the Pension Barbet crocodile; my wish to go off on my own. At that time, colonials all had their own cars. One hardly ever saw a French pedestrian. Because of the throngs of natives in the streets, girls went out with their parents – one certainly did not encounter a girl on her own, it just wasn't done. One kept girls "on a tight rein". As for me, in the shade of the tall tamarind trees, I walked along and as I walked, it became ever clearer that where I belonged was not where I was. People noticed me, looked back at me, smiled, surprised, sorry for me. No, it's difficult to imagine. I was fourteen, with breasts, an apple-green hat, a blue-flowered dress with a hem below my knees, patent-leather shoes, a small handbag, and I was walking with downcast eyes, looking at no-one, just my feet, in a state of horrible embarrassment I've never experienced since. I felt disguised; I was. I encountered bands of girls going to play tennis, bareheaded, all in white, athletic, tripping lightly along. Me, I could have been taken for either a little girl or a little whore. I was a walking ambiguity. I didn't know, others didn't either, looking at me and wondering what this was that no-one had ever seen before: she might have been young, except for that drawn expression, that age-old look of shame and misery shrivelling her made-up face. I did not dream of going back. It was not possible. Not possible to retreat; furthermore, that never occurred to me. It was Sunday afternoon, and I was out for a walk. No-one to visit; I knew no-one in the city. I walked, I walked, I left the wide avenues, I took the little streets. I couldn't go back until seven o'clock. I was waiting for evening, for darkness, to hide, and meanwhile I tried to conceal myself as best I could in narrow suburban streets edged with houses, where I knew there would be no French people, where only natives would be astonished, which seemed less serious to me, more bearable, because there were many more of them than there were French people, it was less important, less painful, everything was relative: a native would be less astounded, unprepared to take the full measure of my absurdity. I was bathed in perspiration: sweat poured from my hair down my face. Even so, I did not return to the Pension Barbet. I became stubborn. I decided to go to a film matinee. That abrupt resolution came to me at the moment when my strength deserted me. I turned back and headed for the centre of town. I kept running into French people. On my apple-green hat there was a red rose. "Moss rose", my mother called it. And my little handbag for that older look, "all dressed up", the finishing touch that gave me a serious air. I was suffering like a soul in hell. I walked very fast to go to ground in [the Éden Cinema].

I arrived there and went to the ticket window. I hadn't thought about this. I had barely enough money for a seat "down in front". The front seats were taken only by the "scum" of the city. Half-castes, Annamese, all piled into rattan chairs, three rows separated from the orchestra seats by a great gap: difference.

I found enough money for my ticket by counting out some small change, without fainting. When I went inside to the theatre, the lights were still on. I was too early, the show hadn't started yet. At the back of the orchestra, there were already three rows of French patrons. Down in front, a gang of rowdies laughed and whistled. I had to walk the length of the theatre watched by everyone in the orchestra. Alone. Because no-one escorted the patrons down in front to their seats. Not one white in the front rows. I did not flinch. I walked down the aisle. The crossing of that theatre by my public persona took place in the profound silence my public entrance had provoked. I remember that I no longer remembered how to walk. The whole of humanity was watching me. I was white, no doubt about that. Nobody had ever seen a white girl in the front seats before. Everything, I knew everything people were thinking, and I was thinking the same thing at the same moment. Everything danced before my eyes, and I found myself in a truly advanced state of unreality. I had bonded deeply with shame. I was a walking shame. I was simply ridiculous. I had no business being in that cinema and my outfit was not normal but laughable to say the least, if not pitiable. Everything was giving way. I found myself giving way, on a rattan chair, my handbag on my lap, streaming with sweat. I could not say anymore whether ten minutes or an hour went by before the lights went out. But suddenly it was dark, and someone began playing the piano. I roused myself from my torpor. They were showing *Casanova*. I found this film to be decisively beautiful. I left consoled. I had seen Casanova confess his love to a woman and kiss her on the mouth.

In the evening, there was a faint, dry clatter on the Ramé road. "It's Paul coming home," my mother said, and soon afterwards he appeared in his small open carriage on the flat road to Ramé. We were in such need of money that he had come up with the idea of providing public transportation. So he'd bought an old horse and a cabriolet and all afternoon long he shuttled between Bantai and Ramé, which brought him at most enough to buy himself some cigarettes. My mother had gone along with the project.

From a distance we watched three natives alight from the carriage, pay Paul their fare, and Paul then turn into our road and arrive at the house.

"Filthy job," said Paul.

My mother was having palm trees and flowers planted along the side of the house. She had been supervising a servant hard at work all afternoon. For a long time now we had known there was no hope of earning any income from the plantation. The mother {sic} could not bear idleness; she had flowers planted and kept her servants busy that way. The scorching dryness, moreover, had defeated her efforts several times. But the mother still kept trying.

That day I had spent part of the afternoon in the shed under the eaves where we kept the game my brother bagged. Four does and a stag were hanging there from iron hooks. I often shut myself up inside, without my mother knowing. It was cool in that shed, and no-one disturbed me there. The does were losing their blood drop by drop, and the soft sound – ploc – of the blood dripping on the floor must have lulled I don't know what faraway melancholy in me. My brother's hunts poisoned my existence; they were my mother's pride. As soon as evening came, my brother would go out onto the veranda and sniff the air: "Tonight, I'm off," he'd say. I had made it a sort of personal duty to visit the dead does in the shed. I too was proud of my brother's exploits, but above all I found them wrenching. The animals decomposed quickly in the heat and were then unhooked and thrown into the river, where they drifted downstream to the sea. We ate so many that we grew sick of them, and in the end preferred something else, for example the black-fleshed wading birds my brother killed in the mangrove swamps along the seashore and which we ate almost raw, barely roasted over a wood fire. At one time, we would feast on the pickled flesh of young crocodiles, but in the end we tired of everything. The region offered little in the way of meat; the only pigs there were [*illegible*] and fed on sewage from the village. We were reluctant to eat them. The region was very poor. The natives made up for that with dogs; one of our servants would chase them with axes and decapitate them in mid-gallop: they would keep on running, covering 10 yards or so without their heads, which literally threw me into a panic. We could not bring ourselves to eat dog, which my mother had always opposed because she loved dogs. We could not keep a single one, unfortunately, without seeing it end up in that pitiable fashion.

When I'd heard the rumbling of the carriage, I had come out of the shed. I went over to my brother. He was pouring with sweat, rapidly unharnessing the horse, which had grown even thinner.

"I don't know what's wrong with him," my brother was saying. "He's going to give up the ghost. He must be tubercular."

He released him into the meadow. The animal was no longer eating. We looked at him for a moment.

"He won't last much longer," my brother said. "Come swimming."

I went quickly back up to the bungalow and put on my suit. In his room, my brother did the same. Going back down we passed my mother.

"You're going there again," my mother said.

Without answering we made our way through the rice field towards the little wooden bridge where the river ran deep. My brother, a wonderful swimmer, jumped in first. The cove itself was wide and rather shallow; he went round in there like a goldfish in a bowl. I always hesitated, because of the things one encountered in that water. The river flowed out of the forest a few hundred yards from there, and often dead birds, squirrels, even tigers – in the rainy season – would go down that river. We almost always emerged from it with leeches. My brother would insist, and I always gave in at last. He was teaching me to swim. We'd stay in the water until nightfall, when we heard my mother yelling, threatening us with punishment. We'd go back up and rinse away the muddy river with jars of rainwater.

We used to tear leeches out from between our toes. My mother always noticed.

"You'll wind up bled completely dry," she'd say.

NOTES

1. The Union of Indochina was created in 1887, comprising Laos, Cambodia, Cochin China (the southern part of present-day Vietnam), Annam (central Vietnam) and Tonkin (northern Vietnam).
2. Born in 1914, Marguerite Donnadieu was the youngest of three children. Her brother Paul was born in 1911, and the oldest child, Pierre, in 1910.

Ter of the Militia
(Rough Draft)

It all started three days ago. Maxime had come back reporting that he'd put {the prisoners} in a barn in Levallois with some clean straw and they'd been joking around, saying "*Kaputt.*" Maxime was laughing. This was in the canteen. The others laughed, listening to Maxime. Théodora had insulted them, then burst into tears. She'd been unapproachable ever since. "She's awful, she's a savage," the other women at the centre were saying about her. Maxime and Théodora had shouted at each other. Almost everyone was on Maxime's side. For three days now, he'd avoided speaking to Théodora. Obviously disgusted with her, the women were keeping their distance. Albert was the only holdout. "Just leave her the fuck alone, alright?" he told the other women. He agreed with Maxime about how to handle {the prisoners} but made sure that everyone knew not to give Théodora any shit about it.

"I'm off," said the girl. "Tell Albert I came by."

"Everything's a goddamned mess," said Théodora.

It was quite hot. Still machine-gun fire. The women took care of the canteen or the mutual-aid centre. Théodora wasn't doing anything. As a rule, she stayed in the bar[1] because of the phone numbers. Still machine-gun fire in the distance. It seems to be getting closer. It's hot. The militiamen[2] – eleven in a room on the fourth floor – must really be hot; maybe they need some water. It has already been over now for three days. In a small room across from the bar, six collaborators are playing cards; they've banded together because they found those out in the corridor too lower-class. "I've had it with prisoners," thinks Théodora. She knows one prisoner who is perhaps being shot at that very moment. Shot by the Germans. He was at Fresnes[3] three weeks ago; now she hasn't any idea any more. Yesterday, in another centre linked to the Richelieu centre, there was also some shooting: a Gestapo agent. That was on the rue de la Chaussée-d'Antin, in a courtyard. She, Nano, had gone there with Albert and Ter, the militiaman. Ter had to be interrogated.

Entering the big empty room that was headquarters at the rue d'Antin centre, they'd passed a stretcher going out: flabby, still soft. "Two minutes ago," Jean had said, "you just missed it." The Hernandez group had done it, he explained. Three revolver shots in the back of the neck, out in the courtyard. Albert and Théodora had gone to see the courtyard. On one stone, a puddle of blood was already congealing. In the corridor, it was hard to talk over the loud voices of the Spaniards; in the courtyard, there was only some blood. The fellow had wept and pleaded while the Spaniards argued about who would get to kill him. Jean and Albert were talking about it; Jean was pale, like someone who's seasick. "I don't like it," he told Albert.

The militiaman, leaning back against the fireplace, had seen the Gestapo agent's corpse go by, and, looking through the doorway, he'd seen the blood. He was quite pale. Of all the prisoners in the centre, he was by far the one Albert and Théodora liked the best. "If you've brought me here to shoot me," he'd said very quietly to Albert, "I'd like to know it: I'd like to write a note to my parents." Suddenly, while they were talking to Jean, they'd realized that the militiaman had seen the corpse of the Gestapo agent. Ter's pallor was the kind that should happen only once in this life. "No, we didn't bring you here to shoot you," Albert had replied with a smile. "Oh, good," the militiaman said, "because I would have liked to know." Then he'd said nothing more. For a moment, Albert had remained thoughtful.

In the two neighbouring rooms, men were carefully oiling their guns. Sweating heavily, Jean was giving orders about where various groups would be staying that evening. The Spaniards were yelling in the empty rooms. Smiling, Albert had offered a ciga- rette to the militiaman. Albert was friendly with the militiaman and Théodora. He'd also offered Théodora a cigarette. He liked Théodora, he took her just about everywhere; he found women a nuisance but not Théodora. The militiaman had smiled back at Albert when he'd offered him the cigarette. Théodora had smiled too, of course. It was a nice moment. The militiaman was smok- ing his cigarette as hard as he could, taking deep drags. He was twenty-three. You could see his trim waist, and the muscles in his long young forearms. He would have blended right in with the other men moving around and oiling their guns if he hadn't been so pale, and smoking like that. But he had a dirty past; if men's pasts could be forgotten, there would never be any war. Smoking his cigarette, he might have managed to believe he was starting to live again and that this past had vanished, but no. Off in every corner men were oiling their guns and preparing to go out again. Albert might have offered that smile and that cigarette to just anyone, once this man had passed, alive, from the utter certitude of death to life. But just anyone would not have smiled at just anyone like that. Albert was intelligent. He was even the triumph of intelligence, that Albert, thought Théodora, in the sense that this smile was one of understanding with the militiaman. He was not kind but was so understanding that you could say nothing escaped him, while he understood everything. Standing by the fireplace, Albert waited for Jean. "When you have a second, can I ...?" "Now is good," said Jean. The militiaman didn't wonder what he was doing there. He smoked his cigarette. Since he hadn't been shot, he was now at a loose end. He must have suspected he'd be a topic of interest but only vaguely. That was no ordinary smile they'd exchanged, he and Albert: a smile of complicity. A priest wouldn't have done that, because religion has disfigured death, and that's the least of its crimes. Neither Albert nor the militiaman believed in God. No other way.

Jean has a second. He and Albert talk. Théodora stays by the fireplace with the militiaman. It was yesterday they'd interrogated him. She knows him as well as she knows her own brother. He was a friend of Bony and La-font. He went off on the razzle with them. He rode around in Lafont's armoured car. "Why did you join the militia?" "Because I wanted to have a gun." "Why a gun?" "Because guns are swell." For an hour they'd been after him relentlessly to find out what he'd done with it, if he'd killed anyone in the Resistance with that gun. "I was the lowest of the low," he'd said. "They wouldn't have let me kill any Resistance fighters." He hadn't said that he wouldn't have tried if they had let him. Albert's group had arrested him in another FFI group,[4] one that didn't take prisoners, so they'd unloaded him back on Albert's men. "What the fuck were you doing in the FFI?" "I wanted to fight." "With what weapon?" "With my gun." "Was it to hide out?" "No, because I knew that sooner or later … It was to fight." "Why weren't you wearing an armband?" Then Ter had smiled. "Come on, you must be kidding …" That answer was what had made Albert and Théodora take a liking to the militiaman. In one year he had made six million in a German purchasing office, and he'd spent it all. "How much did it bring you?" "Six million in 1943." He'd come right out with it. Théodora thought he looked like a guy who liked sex and good times. He was convinced that he was going to be shot. During his interrogation, he'd looked at Théodora in a certain way. Now she knew he must have been a lady's man. A fucking idiot, too, but that wasn't the moment to think about it.

Albert had rejoined Ter and Théodora. "We're leaving." They'd made straight for the door. On the way out, Albert had given a friendly wave to Hernandez, and so had Théodora.

Hernandez was a Spanish giant in the FAI[5] who said he was in training to return to Spain. It was his group that had executed the

{Gestapo} agent, and all the French considered those seventeen men to be their battle-hardened superiors. The agent's execution made Albert feel his friendship was well founded; the friendly wave he'd given him confirmed this. Hernandez would have died in an instant for the Spanish Republic: he had the right to kill. The honour of executing the agent had fallen to his group, and rightly so. Even though the agent was French, the French hadn't protested. They'd been less than certain that the man deserved to be executed; Hernandez, no. Now Hernandez was laughing, as usual. He was a barber by trade, and a Spanish Republican by conviction: he would just as willingly have blown his own brains out to advance the civil war. When they weren't fighting, the Spaniards oiled the guns they'd gotten their hands on. The insurrection in Paris made them homesick, and they thought of Spain. They felt they'd be able to leave the following month. "It's Franco's turn," Hernandez kept saying. They were sure about that, and anxious to regroup, but the Socialists were setting conditions unacceptable to those in the FAI. The FAI and the Communists wanted to leave for the border immediately; the Socialists wanted to wait, and talked about an organized expeditionary force. They had all left their jobs to go back.

Going past Hernandez, Théodora thought he might be the one who would execute the militiaman in a few days. She preferred Hernandez. She smiled at him. Only Hernandez knew how necessary it was to kill him. No question of meddling in that: preventing Hernandez from killing would have been a crime against the people. The Gestapo agent's death had been a true execution, Hernandez didn't doubt that. Théodora had even less doubt on that score – a few days earlier she'd wanted to kill the German prisoners. Théodora didn't know what Jean and Albert had said to each other. Why had the militiaman been brought from Richelieu to the d'Antin centre? Théodora couldn't figure out what Albert had in mind. But that wasn't important.

When they got into the car, Terrail had politely opened the

door for Théodora. He was naturally pleased to be leaving the d'Antin centre, but it was also because Théodora was driving, and women who drove must have impressed him. The militiaman had sat beside Théodora; Albert, in back, with a small – very small – revolver. It didn't work, this revolver; it was all that he had left, since his comrades had stolen the rest of his guns. The militiaman didn't know this revolver didn't work; he sat quietly, sticking out his arm at every turn, paying attention to the driving. At one point, Albert and Théodora had exchanged gleeful looks over the revolver: if he only knew … The militiaman, though, was serious, quite serious, signalling the turns with his arm. This militiaman was the kind of person who can enjoy a car ride even if he knows it's his last – after all, at least it's something – and for whom the handling of a car in Paris is fascinating in itself. He had kept his gun with him for the same reason.

In the streets, no police. Swarms of FFI vehicles went in all directions. In particular, cars went in the wrong direction along one-way thoroughfares, especially Haussmann, which Théodora had taken to return from the Chaussée-d'Antin centre. Still no police. Lots of accidents. From almost every car {bristled} the barrels of rifles and machine guns held by guys with the mugs of proles. Now and then, the warbling of machine guns: the shooters on the roofs. Every evening, people come to the centre to report seeing shadows passing across neighbouring rooftops. That's how Théodora almost got some American soldiers killed when they were setting up an anti-aircraft defence post on a bank roof. There are women in all the jeeps, and little tarts as well, as in the FFI cars. The biggest whingers are the AS.[6] A whole bunch of them had turned up – in uniform – at the Richelieu centre the day after Leclerc's entrance into Paris.[7] They had complained indignantly about the disrespectful treatment they'd received. They had come "to take possession of the premises". When she'd gotten back there yesterday, Théodora had run into them in the corridor as the general was saying, "I thought we'd be able to keep them, but they're too much in the way, it's impossible." He was talking about the FFI.

Théodora was sorry that the insurrection was over and they hadn't been allowed to wipe out the mothball brigade.[8] Many things saddened her, and not the least of them was those mothballs. It was one of the most depressing things she'd ever seen. They had come "to put an end to irregularities". Addressing men who hadn't washed or slept properly in two weeks, they'd said, "Boys, these mattresses must go, enough of that." The mothball general never went anywhere without six other mothballs, even to order the corridor swept, whereas petrol-bottle "missions" were carried out by two men.

Albert was ashamed for the mothballs. The men at Levallois were moaning like crazy. Those at Porte Champerret, while they were at it, wanted to burn the whole place down. Only the prisoners were reassured, because they'd wind up in the hands of the military police. The mothballs had spent the last two weeks taking inventory of everything the FFI had stolen from collaborators. In the end the list became so long that they'd given up trying to get it all back and had started minding their own business. They impressed no-one but the prisoners; the Levallois men didn't even step aside when they passed them in the building. The FFI men had been hard up for food for several weeks, but the mothballs were eating like kings, on tablecloths and at noon. The FFI ate the leftovers at half past one.

The same day the Gestapo agent was executed, Théodora had gone that evening to the Prisoners' Bureau to get some bread-requisition coupons. There she'd encountered a number of people conscripted for public service who'd come to get paid. In the office of the minister's secretary, a man was saying, "I've got a stiff and no idea where to put it. It was dropped off at the station three hours ago, the morgues don't want it, I'm fed up!" The secretary had told him that she had other things to do. "It's from the rue de la Chaussée-d'Antin – I've phoned all the hospitals, he's downstairs in the vehicle, and what am I supposed to do with him?" Théodora hadn't said a thing. It was the agent. The secretary was growing impatient and so was the guy, who finally went away, leaving on the secretary's table a small gold medal on a chain: "They found that on him; it's got nothing to do with me." And he'd left. Théodora, who knew the secretary, had ventured to look at the chain. A first-Communion medal. She'd wondered why the guy had taken it off him, that complicated things. "And me, what do you want me to do with him?" the secretary had said with a shrug. The guy had slipped away. While Théodora was signing the requisition coupons, the chain had been lying on the table like any old thing. She had felt like touching the chain to see if it was still warm. That was silly. The guy had said that the stiff hadn't a single paper on him, he hadn't a clue who it could be. Théodora didn't know either, but she could have found out by phoning Jean. The thought had never even crossed her mind. She'd laughed. And then she had left. Although she'd laughed, the chain had also made her feel sick. That was enough of that.

NOTES

1. "That's what we called a kind of checkroom with a counter where we'd distributed provisions during the insurrection." *La Douleur* (*The War*).

2. In January 1943, a collaborationist militia run by Joseph Darnand became the Milice Française (French Militia), a volunteer force with political and paramilitary powers charged with supporting German operations against the French Resistance. Pierre Laval was its first head, but the Milice was led by Darnand and underlings such as Paul Touvier. The Milice also worked with the likes of Klaus Barbie to round up the men, women and children sent to French detention centres for shipment to German concentration camps.

3. Built at the end of the nineteenth century just outside Paris, Fresnes

prison was used by the Germans to house political prisoners, some of whom were executed there, while others were sent on to Germany for execution or internment in concentration camps.

4. The Forces Françaises de l'Intérieur (French Forces of the Interior) refers to the Resistance fighters of various organizations in France placed under the command of General Koenig by Charles de Gaulle in June 1944 to unify domestic armed opposition to the Germans. About two hundred thousand strong, the FFI wore civilian clothing with an FFI armband and mostly used their own weapons. General Patton, among others, paid tribute to their invaluable support in the liberation of France.

5. The Federación Anarquista Ibérica (Federation of Spanish Anarchists) was a militant Spanish trade-union organization that fought against Franco in the Spanish Civil War, and was one of several such Spanish groups that fought later as independent but integral forces within the French Resistance.

6. By the end of 1942, some independent Resistance organizations had combined into the Mouvements Unis de la Résistance; the armed wing of the MUR was the Armée Secrète. The armed wing of the Communist-led Front National, formed in May 1941, was the Francs-Tireurs et Partisans Français. The more right-wing MUR recognized De Gaulle as their leader and thus benefited from his – and Allied – support, whereas the Communists, more suspicious of the general's growing authority, retained their independence but were often left to scrounge for their supplies and weapons.

7. As the Germans lost control of Paris during the last stages of the Allied advance, brutal fighting broke out in the capital among the German occupiers, collaborationists and the French Resistance, whose strongest element in Paris was the Communist movement led by Colonel Henri Tanguy (Colonel Rol-Tanguy). General Philippe Leclerc entered the capital at the head of the first detachment of the second armoured division on 24 August, 1944. General Dietrich von Choltitz surrendered the next day.

8. *Les naphtalinés* – members of the French armed forces who decided not to fight the German occupation – put their uniforms away in mothballs to be safely donned years later at the Liberation, when they smelled richly of naphthalene.

Wife to Marcel

I'm the lowest thing there is in society, I'm wife to Marcel. Marcel works nearby, at the factory. Before the war he made aeroplane engines, now he makes churns. He's a skilled worker, makes good money. Yes. He makes enough, I've no complaints. He's a working man. We had three children: two died, the third's a working man as well, married. He's got a four-year-old son. Me, I'm wife to Marcel. No special skills. I keep a good house. Marcel's pals, when they stop by of an evening, it's "Where's Marcel?" "He's at the working men's club," I say. So then they say, "I'll come back tomorrow … How's it going?" "Fine." They leave. Why would they stay? I got nothing to say to them. I'm wife to Marcel – other than that I don't see what. Our son comes by on Sundays: "Hello M'ma." Then he talks with his father. I fix the food. My daughter-in-law, she talks with them, and sure she helps me but we haven't much to say to each other. I've never had much to say.

Albert of the Capitals
(Rough Draft)

After a while, they'd all had enough of interrogating the prisoners. At first everyone was interrogating, then only a few, then Albert and Jean. Then even Albert and Jean had got fed up. Théodora had questioned the first prisoner, brought in at five one afternoon. An owner of the bistro he frequented had come by: "There's a traitor in my place, an informer – you should come get him." Three men had gone to collect him. He was the first one they'd had at the centre, a guy of about fifty. Everyone had come to see him, so they'd put him in the bar. They'd left him in the centre of the room for an hour. They just couldn't believe it: a snitch – they'd gotten their hands on one. The men surrounded him, went up to him, stared at him, sniffed him. Traitor. Bastard. Pig. A little fifty-year-old fellow. He had a squint, wore specs, a wing collar, a tie. The men went right up to his face and yelled, "Traitor!" The informer warded off blows, he was scared, sweating, saying no monsieur, yes monsieur, no madame. He had a refined voice; you might have taken him for a retired municipal employee, for example. "I assure you, monsieur, you are making a mistake." Théodora was furious, eager to deal with him straight away, but Albert had said they should wait for dinner, that they'd "take care of him" afterwards. Everyone agreed that Théodora would be the one to deal with him. Théodora's husband had been arrested by the Gestapo; she didn't know whether he was still alive, she was heartsick over it – she was the one who should deal with the Gestapo agent. The men were disappointed, but it was only fair. They had gone off to eat. Théodora hadn't eaten much. Then, after dinner, she had asked for two men. They were all busy eating in the dining hall up on the seventh floor. "Who's coming with me?" Twenty had stood up, their mouths full, and gathered around Théodora. They all had good reasons, but Théodora had picked two who'd been through Montluc, that was only fair, been through Montluc {Prison, near Lyon,} and been savagely beaten. No objections. The two young men had gone to fetch a couple of hurricane lamps; Théodora, a pencil and some paper to take notes on the interrogation. She'd heard that records were kept during questioning. There wasn't any electricity. Théodora had gone down the main stairs of the newspaper building with the two men. Outside, you could hear machine guns over by the Louvre. It was still going on. In the distance, the rumbling of tanks. Now and then, artillery. Paris was free – almost. Théodora wasn't particularly vicious, she was heartsick.

One of the young men had gone to get the informer, then the four of them had gone into a room, empty except for a table and two chairs, and closed the door. "Well?" "Go ahead, get his clothes off," {she said.} "Get undressed!" the young guys had told him. "And hurry it up." They'd been through the same thing in Montluc: first their clothes had come off and in the end they'd lost three toenails, gritting their teeth. One of them was a redhead, thirty, a garage mechanic; the other an unskilled worker, twenty-five – good guys, courageous. While the chap was undressing, Théodora wondered what she was doing; she wouldn't have known how to put it, but it was necessary. For four years, she'd been hearing, "When we catch hold of one, will he ever catch hell!" This was one of them. The informer had first removed his jacket. He was taking off his trousers. Suspecting what was coming, he was undressing slowly. He'd placed his jacket on a chair. "Speed it up," said one of the men. Maybe they were going to kill him. His tie; he was taking it off. She reminded herself: 150,000 shot. His collar; the shirt was dirty.

On the rue des Saussaies there were a hundred women waiting to give their husbands or sons packages, which had been stopped since the {Allied} landing. Théodora had waited two days running, twenty-two hours in line so he could have a package weighing a little over two pounds. The man's shirt was dirty, beneath his white collar; he was a snitch. *He* didn't have to line up on the rue des Saussaies. "You going to hurry it up or not?" said Théodora. She had stood up suddenly. The men looked at her; then, "You were told to get a move on, you bastard!" They hustled him out of his underpants. He didn't wait anywhere, he didn't line up on the rue des Saussaies: he would show a card, then go inside, then knock, then say he had the description, the address, the hours. They'd give him an envelope. Now he was removing his shoes. All his clothes were on the chair; he was trembling. In the line, there was a young pregnant woman in mourning: he'd been executed, and she was standing in line because she had received a notice – she'd been in line for twenty-two hours to get his bundle of things and the baby was due in two weeks. Now it's the socks. She wanted his things, she wanted to see them again, she'd read his last letter out loud, she read and reread that letter: "Tell our child I was brave," and she wept aloud – she must have been twenty years old and she kept saying, "It's not possible, it's not possible." All the women were crying. Someone had offered her a folding stool but she didn't want anything, she couldn't bear it except standing up. Now he's completely naked: he has taken off his spectacles and placed them on top of his clothes. The young men await Théodora's orders. He's completely naked: he has an old penis, shrunken testicles, no waist, he's fat, he's dirty. He's fat.

"Hey, you sure haven't gone hungry for four years, have you?"

"How much a head did they pay you?" says Théodora.

He whimpers.

"I'm just a poor innocent guy, I keep telling you."

"What we want is for you to tell us the truth. You're denying everything?"

"But I told you …"

Now the room is full. The women up front. The men in back. It bothers Théodora, it's as if she were doing something erotic.

And yet she can't ask them to go away, there'd be no reason. She simply stays behind the hurricane lamp, where you can see only her short, dark hair – but not her face.

"Go to it," says Théodora.

The first blow. It sounds strangely loud. The second blow. The old man tries to deflect it. "Ow! Ow!" he wails. You can see him clearly in the lamp-light. The young guys are hitting hard. The others, in back, say nothing. The men are punching him in the chest, slowly but hard. Then they stop: "D'you get it now?" He rubs his chest; without his specs, he can't see where the blows are coming from.

"How'd you get into Gestapo headquarters?"

"Uh … like everyone else …"

He's rubbing his chest with both palms. He cries as he speaks. He has the voice of someone crying.

He said "like everyone else". Rue des Saussaies, handcuffed prisoners and Gestapo agents went inside. Other people never, ever, got inside. Théodora had applied for permission to send a package; three weeks later they'd told her she had to come get a number, which she'd been given at the concierge's lodge at the entrance to the Gestapo building. Then she'd waited twenty-two hours and had shown a special paper they'd torn up at the exit. He said "like everyone else" because he's lying, plus he hopes that Théodora thinks that people could easily get inside there. He's lying. Big purple bruises are coming out on his chest. He's lying.

"You said 'like everyone else'? Everyone went inside the Gestapo building?"

There's muttering from those in the back: "Traitor, traitor, traitor, he's scared."

"Uh, yes, you had to show your identity card."

"You're sure that was enough?"

"Well, yes."

A thin trickle of blood appears on his chest. He's still lying.

They had heard about informers. And the Germans. The tortures too. Everything. Enemies. They'd shot her husband because he was a Communist, he was twenty-five years old. {This guy} turned in Communists, because he earned 5oo francs a head for them. He's a liar. His tie, his shoes, he bought them with those 5oo francs they paid him for each Communist head. "Thank you, monsieur." In the background: "Traitor, pig, sonofabitch, bastard, scum." Yes. Yes. Them, they didn't squeal: they weren't perfect, but they weren't snitches. The two young men – they never talked in Montluc.

"Go to it, guys!"

Strange, thinks Théodora: they don't hit unless I tell them to, even though I have no more authority than they do. Maybe it's because they think I know how to interrogate while they don't, but they've got fists, they clenched them in Montluc but they didn't talk, and a few days ago – factory workers, in normal life – they were throwing bottles of petrol into German tanks.

"Go to it!"

They take pleasure in it. It pleases me to give them pleasure. They're thinking of their comrades. Up against a wall: there's a man standing against a wall and in front of the man, Germans. Gunfire. The man clutches at his heart, shouts Long live France, Long live the Communist Party, falls face down in the mud. That earned him 5oo francs he spent on cigarettes and new shoes. To think that they might well not have found him, that he would have got away... The young men stop and look at Théodora.

"So what colour was your identity card?"

The two guys laugh. They know. Théodora's clever, and they like that. They've been hitting hard. His eye may have burst: blood's running down his face. He's weeping, there's bloody mucus coming from his nose and he's moaning, "Oh, oh, oh, oh, ow, ow, ow ..." He runs his palms over his chest, the many places where the skin has split open, bleeding. His hands are white. To do what he did, he never had to lift a finger. Now, whether he lives or wriggles out of it doesn't matter. There's blood on the floor.

"We asked you the colour of your identity card, you hear me? – you old bastard!"

They're ruthless, and they push their faces right up to his. Behind them a woman says, "Maybe that's enough now ..." The other women back her up. The two guys stop and try to see the women who spoke up from behind the hurricane lamp. Théodora has turned around. "Enough?" says one of the young men. "What?" says the other. "For us, was it enough?" "That's no reason," says a woman.

"For the last time, what colour was the identity card you would show?"

"Answer!"

"Answer! You're going to answer!"

In the background, another woman, her voice indignant: "It's starting up again ... Me, I'm leaving ..." Théodora turns around.

"Any women who can't stomach this don't have to stay, we don't need them – if they fuck off that suits us fine. Go to it, guys!"

"Ow!"

But the women stay, and whisper things, all against Théodora. Only Théodora's hair is visible and – when she's asking questions – her white forehead and her eyes, half closed, as if blind. The men say nothing, except for one: "Shut up!" But the women stay.

"So, quick, what colour?"

The two guys laugh. They know. They start punching again, on places they've hit before. The informer tries to fend them off. He's covered in blood. He moans.

"Well, like all the other identity cards ..."

"Go to it, guys."

They're hitting very hard. They're tireless. A man up against a wall falls clutching at his heart: he dies because he believes in something that is true for all men. The 500 francs went to buy

little treats for himself. Those shooting at the man believe in their
duty. Him, with his 5oo francs, he bought himself petty solitary
luxuries. He wasn't anti-Communist, he was earning himself some
pin money. He's still lying. A man can lie like nobody's business.
With the 5oo francs he picked himself out a tie.

Théodora stretches her legs. There's no doubt, none at all:
there's no choice.

"Go for it, guys, let him have it, and hard!"

And they let him have it, and then some. In the background:
"Traitor, scum, pig." The women leave. He groans loudly, he
pleads: "I'm begging you, please – I'm not a traitor!" But he's still
afraid of dying, because he's not yet telling the truth.

Still not enough. Théodora stands up. There is a man, a man
up against a wall, against a wall – a man she knows, who hasn't
talked, for ever, against that wall, God damn it all to hell, that
man against that wall. God damn it. "Don't make us laugh, you
and your Resistance ..." Those who say that – if they were here,
if they were to laugh, on top of everything else ... A man alone
against a brick wall; beyond that wall, nothing. She can't see
any more, Théodora. She hears the "Marseillaise" of those con-
demned to death, the "Internationale" yelled out in police vans;
the bourgeoisie peer from behind their closed shutters: "They're
terrorists ..."

"Get on with it, guys, get a move on!"

In the gleam of the hurricane lamp, he struggles. Every punch
sounds clearly in the quiet room. With each blow he cries,
"Ohhhhh!" in long wails. The women have left. Silent behind the
hurricane lamp, the men say nothing when the blows land. It's
when they hear his voice that the insults well up in the background,
through clenched teeth, with clenched fists, single words, solemn
words. It's when he speaks that the insults come because he's still
lying, he still has the strength, he hasn't yet reached the point
where the lies stop. Théodora watches the fists land, she hears
the thudding blows and thinks that in a man's body there are

protective layers that are hard to split open. When the insults rise behind her, it does her good, encourages her, she really appreciates those insults. In the silence, only once did she ask herself why the women left; impossible to understand. As for her, she can't feel her heart. When they punch his belly, he shrieks and grabs it with both hands and one of the guys takes advantage of the opening to kick him in the balls. He's bleeding a lot, especially his face. He's not like other men. You can kill him. For other men he was a lost man, informing on men. He betrayed men for 500 francs each, without bothering to find out why their enemies were paying him. A pig, now that's more valuable, you can eat it. And him, if they kill him, he'll just be something in the way.

"Enough!" says Théodora.

Her voice seems shrill after the muffled booming of the punches. She stands up and approaches the informer. The men in the back are letting her see it through, they trust her; no-one's giving her any advice, but she's not making any "mistakes", and each time she feels warmed by the fraternal litany of insults. It's quiet in the back; the two young men are watching Théodora closely. Everyone's waiting.

"One last time: we want to know what colour your card was," says Théodora. "One last time …"

The man looks at her. She's quite close to him; he's not tall, she's about his size. She's slender, she's young and cruel. And she has said: "One last time."

"What is it you want me to say …?"

He's snivelling. Not so long ago, she snivelled too. But that's because she's a woman. The men standing against walls don't snivel. The informer is giving off a peculiar odour, nauseating and sweetish: the smell of blood.

"We want you to tell us what colour identity card got you inside the Gestapo building."

"I don't know … Don't know … I keep telling you I'm innocent …"

That does it: the insults flare up. Traitor. Scum. Bastard. Pig. Sonofabitch. Théodora sits down again. She says nothing more. A brief pause. The insults keep coming, one by one.

For the first time, a guy in the back says, "Just finish him off ..." The informer has looked up. Silence. A pause. The informer is afraid. He speaks in a high, whimpering voice, one you feel he wishes could melt stones.

"If I knew what you wanted of me ..."

The two young men are sweating; they wipe their brows with bloody fists, look at Théodora and wait. Théodora seems tired and distracted.

"It's not enough yet," she says suddenly.

The two guys turn towards the informer, fists cocked.

"No," says Théodora.

She leaps up and shouts.

"Let's do it, guys, together with me."

An avalanche of fists. A final avalanche. Silence once more in the background.

"Was your card red you bastard?"

"Ohhh! Oh – you're hurting me!"

"Good," [yell] the men. "Just what we want: imagine that!"

Blood is dripping.

"Ohhh ..."

"Red? Speak up! Red?"

He opens an eye. He's going to understand.

"Red?"

Théodora is screaming. The two guys *know in advance*. The informer tries to think about his answer.

"Red?"

Still no answer.

"Harder, harder, don't hold back."

"Red? Red? Red?"

"No ..." moans the informer.

Laughter. The young men are laughing.

"Me – I waited twenty-two hours with a yellow identity card. Twenty-two hours, you bastard! Twenty-two hours. How do you explain that? It was yellow. And yet, you said you had the same one. Identity cards are normally yellow!"

Théodora is shouting. In the background voices swell, warm and full.

"Twenty-two hours! We waited twenty-two hours with a yellow card. Maybe yours was yellow?"

The informer is moaning constantly, constantly trying, now, to huddle in a corner. The two guys pull him out.

"Yellow?"

They pull him from the corner and then throw him back there. The chair with his clothes tips over, spilling them onto the floor.

"Yellow?"

He opens and closes his mouth. He'd like to answer. He's terrified. He groans. He'd like to say something. For the first time, he's beside himself.

"Yellow?"

Théodora is still on her feet. They know she won't sit down again until he has confessed.

"Noooo ... not yellow!" cries the informer.

The men keep at it. He's choking. Now he understands. They won't let up any more. Théodora keeps at it.

"Well? What colour?"

She's still shouting. Now the blows and the questions are coming with the same dizzying rhythm.

"What colour?"

Maybe he has chosen to die, she thinks. But, no: he's incapable of choosing to die – in the name of what? He'll say it.

"What colour?"

He's silent. He pretends not to hear. He's acting like a guy overwhelmed by pain. Théodora knows this as surely as if she were inside him.

"Quick, what colour?"

What will be the end of this? wonders Théodora. If he doesn't say it, we won't even be able to kill him. We'll have failed completely.

"Still harder!" says Théodora.

They're hurling him back and forth like a ball, now punching, now kicking. They're streaming with sweat.

Théodora advances on the informer.

"Enough!"

She keeps coming, compact, unfathomable. The informer recoils. He has seen her. Again, silence.

"If you say it, we leave you the fuck alone. If you don't say it, we polish you off. Go, guys. Go for it."

The informer doesn't know which way to turn. He's going to talk. He attempts to raise his head, like a drowning man tries to breathe. He's going to talk. This is it. He'd like to say something. The blows are what's keeping him from speaking. But if the blows stop, he won't talk. Everyone waits in suspense for this birth, this deliverance. But he still doesn't talk.

"I'm going to tell you," says Théodora. "*I'm* going to tell you the colour of the card you showed to get inside."

The informer starts yelling. He's still completely conscious. The blows are leaving him completely conscious.

"Green!" yells the informer.

The guys stop. The informer looks at Théodora. He isn't moaning anymore. He's consumed by curiosity. He wonders how he talked.

"Yes," says Théodora.

Silence. Théodora takes a cigarette and lights it. Then, in a tired voice: "Get dressed."

She stands up. Before leaving, she says simply, evenly, "The cards carried by the SD agents, the German Secret Police, were green. There's no longer any doubt."

While he gets dressed, both young men insult him some more.

"We'll take it up again tomorrow?" says one.

"Have to know whom he betrayed," says the other.

"We'll see," says Théodora.

She leaves. All the men leave with her. They go to the bar.

All the women have taken refuge there. They're sitting in arm-chairs, some on {wooden} chairs.

"He confessed," says Théodora.

No-one replies. Théodora understands. They don't give a damn that he confessed. There's a man with them, and he doesn't give a damn about the confession either. They're simply against Théodora, that's all. Théodora sits down and looks at them with curiosity. She herself has no idea yet what she has just done. Perhaps she has done something evil. She suspects as much: she had a man tortured. That's what it's called. The Germans tortured. She did too. While she was in that room, what were they doing in here? What? Théodora smiles, with immense disdain: they were ripping her to shreds, they must have been saying vile things about her and enjoying every second, thinking more about her than about the informer. These women know better than Théodora what has just happened to her.

"You disgust me," says Théodora.

A woman blanches with rage and shouts, "Oh! And just what about you, you've no idea ..."

She stops, choking with indignation. Albert goes over to the woman.

"Are you going to fucking leave off or what?"

Jean looks at her and shrugs. The woman says nothing. Albert comes over to Théodora and Jean. He seems quite upset by what has just happened.

"Let's have a drink," says Albert. "You'll have some wine with us, my dear Théodora."

Théodora smiles. Jean and Albert put their arms around her. The three of them are at the bar. Jean and Albert, they're the head men at the centre. Behind her back, the women remain quiet. The livid silence of hatred.

"Then you're going to go to sleep like a good little girl," says Jean.

"Yes," says Théodora. It's late.

It's an effort for her to speak. She feels like crying. Albert hands her a glass of wine.

"What a bastard he was ..." says Théodora uncertainly, looking up at Jean and Albert.

"Yes," says Albert, "a real bastard – here, drink up."

"Drink, Théodora my dear," says Jean.

Théodora drinks. She doesn't know what's happening to her. Why this sense of relief ... She has trouble swallowing. She feels like crying. The men, they drink. They talk about the informer and say he must be liquidated.

Once again, the women walk away, leaving the bar without saying good night.

"I disgust them," says Théodora.

Albert looks at her and smiles.

"It's nothing, they're just a little jealous – come on, time for bed ..."

"Jealous?" says Théodora. "Of what?"

"Yes," says Jean. "It doesn't matter if you don't understand."

He laughs. Albert laughs. They leave, with their arms around Théodora. Then Théodora remembers that neither of them had shouted abuse at the informer, not even once.

There was a big blonde called Marie, who was loyal and good-hearted. The other women were nice too, even the one called Colette, who'd never thought much about the war. And the young man who was twenty and who'd thought too much about the war – well, he was kind and courageous too. They all hated Théodora at this moment.

*

One time, Théodora asked herself how she could stand the sight and smell of that blood. I'm evil, I always suspected that. Finally, she was releasing all her cruelty. As a little girl she'd been hit many times without ever being able to hit back; she would dream that she was hitting her elder brother.

Triteness – the guys getting carried away at the last minute – one of them is vicious (Tessier); differentiate more between the two young men – light, hurricane lamp – interrogative point of departure: I would buy things from the Germans – not objective enough [about] Théodora.

They'd been put in a room on the sixth floor, in what had been the cashier's office, overlooking a courtyard. The door was sheathed in metal. The window, barred. Only a small wicket communicated with the outside. Depending on the seriousness of each case, as people were brought in they were put in either the corridor or the safe-room. In the end there were eleven, including four militiamen, an elderly Russian couple and three other couples no-one knew much about, except that they were collaborators.

The Rue de la Gaieté

The rue de la Gaieté on Sunday afternoon. People are coming along the street with the sunshine at their backs. All shops open: direct communication between the crowd and what's in the shops. The girls' heavy legs. Boys' jackets nipped in at the waist. And the crowd keeps coming. In the bus I took, there was a ticket collector who was inaugurating the new route: "Get in messieurs, get in madame, seats for everyone. Colombier! Rennes! Montparnasse, everyone gets out." He was very happy. Of course, he'd just finished four years in the metro and he doesn't work for the metro, this guy, he's with the TCRP. Because of that blasted war – no more petrol, bus routes cancelled. They'd assigned him to the metro; it wasn't his profession. Fed up with the metro, he was – got to have a feel for it to last long there. Everyone on the bus was really happy for him. Except for two Americans who hadn't a clue.

The Sea Wall (Rough Draft)

"Shit!" said Paul. "He won't go any more."

Paul and Marie looked at the horse. It was an old, grey, tubercular horse he'd bought for a hundred francs. The animal lowered its head; its flanks were so thin you'd have thought it had swallowed a wicker cage that made it look like a horse.

They'd been invited to this dance on account of her. Because the son of the flour-mill owner was in love with her. Ordinarily, given their social standing, they would not have attended. It was a huge society ball. All the important figures in the city – public, administrative and commercial – were present. The mayor was there. The man giving the ball, Monsieur Sales, owned all the flour mills in the area, and he had become impressively rich.

{The animal} lowered its head sadly and half closed its eyes. Its breathing was shallow and wheezy. This was really the end.

"Shit," said the boy.

The mother came to see the horse and looked at it thoughtfully. She was barefoot in the sand, wearing a large hat that covered her ears and came down to her eyebrows. Her dress was of garnet-red cotton, worn thin at the bust; she still had large breasts, she'd had lots of children. She began to scold her son.

"I told you not to buy him: a hundred francs for a half-dead horse – you always do the same stupid things, you're useless, you good-for-nothing."

"Shit," said the boy. "Shit and shit, there's still the carriage, I don't give a damn, I've had it, it's just not worth it. First I'm getting the hell out of here – you do what you want."

The girl arrived next and contemplated the horse. She was seventeen. She had reddish-blond plaits hanging down to her waist and was barefoot as well on the burning sand. She wore black trousers reaching below her knees, and a blue blouse. She too had a large hat that completely framed her face. Her blue eyes made two very pale, bright spots among her freckles.

"You'd be right to get the hell out," said the girl.

It was in the evening, after dinner. It had been a hot day. The man was resting on a chaise longue.

Expecting

It's between the hip and the ribs, in the place called the flank, that's where it turned up. In that hidden, quite tender place, that covers neither bones nor muscles but delicate organs. A flower has sprung up there. Which is killing me.

The Sea Wall (Rough Draft)

One day, coming back from Ramé, the mother had said to Suzanne, "I met a beggar woman who tried to give me her little daughter. If you want her, tell Joseph to go fetch her."

1) The bath. 2) The plain. 3) Encounter with Monsieur Jo. 4) Scene with Monsieur Jo. 5) Joseph.

"The reason you don't go swimming is because you're poorly assembled," said Suzanne. "Joseph is right when he says ..."

Monsieur Jo stopped knocking. Now Suzanne was rinsing herself off.

Suzanne continued: "When Joseph says that ..."

Suzanne fell silent. She knew that Monsieur Jo was behind the door. She was waiting for him to ask her what Joseph had said. When he didn't ask, Suzanne began softly to sing. A minute later, Monsieur Jo started knocking on the door again.

"One second, I beg you, Suzanne – one second."

"What Joseph said about you doesn't interest you?"

"I don't give a damn," said Monsieur Jo. "I don't care a damn about Joseph, open up ..."

Suzanne stiffened. She went up close to the door.

"Joseph says you look like a foetus," said Suzanne.

The knocking stopped. Suzanne went back to rinsing herself off. She was sure that at that moment Monsieur Jo was feeling the insult and this brought her violent satisfaction, a kind of exultant revenge.

"I believe I have never known anyone as wicked as you," says Monsieur Jo.

Suzanne laughs. Bright laughter mingling with the sound of water comes from the bathroom.

"I can't even hear you laughing," says Monsieur Jo. "You've put me in such a state ... Let me, for one second ... It's not bad to show oneself naked, I won't touch you."

"Go see if they're still over on the other side," says Suzanne.

"Right away," says Monsieur Jo.

Monsieur Jo crosses the dining room and lights a cigarette. Then he plants himself in the doorway with a relaxed air. The mother and Joseph are watching two workmen repair the bridge. The scorching white sun is going down; it's five in the afternoon. The shadows are lengthening. Many peasants in colorful *pagnes* are crossing the plain, heading for the *rac.*¹ Monsieur Jo returns.

"They're still out there – quick, Suzanne, quick."

Suzanne cracks open the door to show Monsieur Jo her white body. Monsieur Jo looks at this body and moves towards it, staring. Suzanne closes the door. Monsieur Jo remains behind it. Suzanne towels herself off and gets dressed.

"Now go into the sitting room."

"Yes," says Monsieur Jo.

Suzanne opens the door and puts on make-up. Then she does her hair and pins her plaits up around her head.

She goes to find Monsieur Jo, who is smoking and looking at the floor.

"How am I, naked?" asks Suzanne.

"You're beautiful," says Monsieur Jo. His voice is low and sad.

Suzanne sits down, looks off into the distance. They're still working on the bridge. The sun is already slipping down and part of the mountain is in shadow. They hear children shouting in the *rac*.

"You're beautiful and desirable," says Monsieur Jo.

"I'm only fifteen years old," says Suzanne. "I'm going to become even more beautiful."

"Yes," says Monsieur Jo.

Suzanne smiles. She has forgotten Monsieur Jo.

The mother and Joseph arrive, come up the stairs. Joseph wipes his forehead with a handkerchief. The mother takes off her straw hat. She has a red line across her forehead, left by the hat.

"This heat …" says Joseph. "You're a sight," he says to Suzanne. "You don't know how to use make-up, you look like a tart."

"She looks like what she is," says the mother.

With a disgusted expression, Joseph goes into his room.

"Just what have you been up to, the two of you?" says the mother. "If I ever see anything I shouldn't, I'll make you marry her within the week."

"Madame, I respect your daughter too much," says Monsieur Jo.

He stands up, adopting an offended air.

"Of course," says the mother. "The old story: dogs, that's what you are – wasn't always an old woman, you know."

"We didn't do anything," says Suzanne. "Mama, I swear we didn't do a thing, we didn't even touch each other," she says.

"Shut up, good-for-nothing, dirty good-for-nothing."

The mother collapses into an armchair.

"What a life!" says the mother, "and there's never any rest …"

"No-one's forcing you," says Suzanne.

The mother puts her feet up on an easy chair.

In the straw hut, the corporal's wife was grilling fish, and her daughter was singing.² And when night had fallen, in one of the villages bordering the plain the sound of the tam-tam was heard, rising from the plain. Indeed almost every evening, the tiger came down to the farmyards and the villages were wreathed in the smoke of great fires of green wood, and when a tiger was announced, the tam-tam called out and from all the neighbouring villages men came towards the one under threat, armed with clubs.

Joseph, still lying on his couch, heard the call of the tam-tam. He tossed away his cigarette and sat up, listening to where it might be coming from. The mother, too, had stopped moving around, and looked out the open window at the black screen of the forest. Joseph would hold out when that tam-tam was silent, but when it called he could never resist.

"I'm going there tonight," declared Joseph.

The mother went over to Joseph. It would start all over again.

"You're not going," she said. "I'm the one who's telling you: you're not going."

"Shit," said Joseph. "We'll see about that. I'm going."

"Take me along," said Suzanne.

The mother let out her usual cries.

"If I have a seizure it will be your fault – three times this week … If I die you can say you killed me."

"Take me along," said Suzanne.

"Shit," said Joseph. "I don't take women along. During the day – all right; at night – no, and you, if you yell, I'm leaving immediately."

He stood up, went over to the corporal, and asked him to go get the trackers, then shut himself up in his room to get his Mauser ready. The mother was still grumbling, but she'd begun preparing her dinner. The battle was already lost; she was carrying on for the sake of appearances. Suzanne stayed out on the veranda. The evenings when Joseph went hunting were unlike all others, because everyone went to bed late.

The mother did not sleep on those nights. She would follow all the sounds of the forest and get up to track the gleam of the acetylene lamp in the darkness. Every evening Suzanne hoped that Joseph would go hunting, and at the same time she hoped he wouldn't kill anything.

"Dinner's ready!" shouted the mother.

They were having wading birds again. The corporal's wife brought up a few fish and some rice.

"You'll have to go down to the sea," said the mother. "They're nourishing, waders."

She seemed flushed and tired in the lamplight. Her pills were starting to take effect. The mother yawned and groaned.

"Another sleepless night, with me so tired."

"It's the change of life, come on, Mama, don't worry, I'll be back early," said Joseph kindly.

"It's not because of me," said the mother. "It's you I'm always afraid for."

She rose to fetch a tin of salted butter and one of Nestlé milk. Suzanne poured a great glassful of Nestlé milk over her rice. The mother made herself some bread and butter and dunked the slice in coffee. Joseph ate the fowl, its fine flesh dark and rare.

"It stinks of fish," said Joseph, "but it is nourishing."

"That's what's important," said the mother. "You'll be careful, Joseph, you promise me?"

"Don't you worry, Mama, I'll be careful."

"So once again we won't be going to Ramé this evening," said Suzanne.

"We'll go tomorrow," said Joseph, "and, well, shit, you won't be finding any husband in Ramé, they're all married over there, except for young Agosti."

"I'll never give her to the Agosti boy, that lout," said the mother.

"In the meantime," said Suzanne, "there's no point in looking here."

"It won't be easy," said Joseph. "We'd need money. Some do get married without money but they have to be awfully pretty, and even then it's a long shot."

"Meanwhile," said Suzanne, "what I was saying about Ramé wasn't just for that – there are things going on in Ramé, there's electricity in the canteen and a fantastic phonograph."

"You're a whore who's missed her calling," said Joseph. "Stop your goddamn nagging about Ramé."

"Especially since it's not a place for young ladies," said the mother.

The mother set food down before her children: the bread the bus brought every day and her inexhaustible reserves of Swiss and American tinned goods.

The next day, as promised, Joseph announced that they were going to Ramé. The mother began by shouting, as usual, but she couldn't resist what her children wanted. On days when they went to Ramé, the mother put her hair up and wore shoes. Suzanne would wear a frock, she wound her plaits around her head, and she put on lipstick. Joseph dressed up too. It was post day. Going to Ramé meant going for a beer at the outpost canteen. Joseph asked the corporal to wash the car. It was an old {Citroën} B-12 and its battery was shot, so Joseph drove it with his acetylene lamp on his forehead; when there was a full moon, he drove without any light. The B-12's exhaust awakened all the village dogs along the way and set them barking. It took a good hour and a half to cover the 37 miles from the bungalow to Ramé.

Joseph pulled up in front of the canteen. A magnificent limousine was parked there. "Shit," said Joseph. And they went into the bungalow. It was post day; the packet boat was lighting up the sea in front of the canteen. Inside the bungalow serving as a canteen were naval officers and a few passengers. Off in a corner, sitting next to the proprietor of the canteen, young Agosti was drinking a Pernod. He was a Corsican, short and thin, with an unhealthy air; he spent all his evenings in Ramé smoking opium and drinking Pernod. He nodded at them and kept talking. The proprietor saw them and came over. He had arrived in Ramé twenty years before and never left. He was a huge apoplectic man who had taken a native wife and adopted a child from the plain who served the aperitifs and the contraband Pernod, and who fanned him when he took his siesta. The man was always sweating. He came and shook hands with the mother.

"How's business?" he asked the mother. "And the children?"

"Not bad," said the mother, "not bad. Thank God for good health."

"You have some posh customers," said Joseph. "Shit, that limousine."

"He's a big landowner from the North," said the proprietor. "They're a hell of a lot richer than we are."

"You've no reason to complain, with the Pernod," said the mother.

"That's what people think," said the proprietor. "It's a risky business. Now they're coming down every week, so it's a free-for-all. That's not a life."

"Point out this rubber planter to us," said the mother.

"The guy in the corner, next to Agosti."

He was a half-caste. He had set his fedora down on the table. He was wearing a tussore suit and on his finger, a magnificent diamond.

"Shit, that diamond," said Joseph, "but otherwise he's a monkey."

They considered the diamond, the silk suit. The face had been marked by smallpox; the rest of him was stunted and sickly. He was on his own, and he was looking at Suzanne with a complacent eye. The mother had noticed that he was looking at Suzanne.

"Smile," said the mother. "You always look as if you were at a funeral."

Suzanne smiled at the planter from the North. The mother looked at her daughter and found her pretty in spite of her freckles. When the phonograph started up, the planter from the North came over to Suzanne and asked her to dance. Standing, he cut a distinctly poor figure. Everyone was looking at his diamond, especially the people from the plain – the mother and Joseph, the proprietor and young Agosti. That diamond was worth more, by itself, than all the salt lands of the plain put together.

"With your permission, madame?" he said to the mother.

The mother gave her permission. A post-office official was already dancing with the young wife of the Ramé customs officer.

"May I be introduced to your charming mother?" said the planter. "Are you from this area?"

"Of course," said Suzanne. "Yes, we're from around here, we have some rice fields on the plain. Is that your car outside?"

"It's one of my cars. After our dance, you will introduce me to her as 'Monsieur Jo'."

"It's a really lovely car," said Suzanne.

"You like cars?" said Monsieur Jo.

"Very much," said Suzanne. "It's a limousine. There aren't any of those around here."

"Doesn't a pretty girl like you get bored out on the plain?" said Monsieur Jo.

Suzanne did not reply. She was thinking about the car. She was thinking that she, Suzanne, was dancing with the owner of a car like that. In her right hand, she was holding the hand wearing the diamond.

"What make is it?" said Suzanne.

"It's a Morris Léon-Bollée," said Monsieur Jo. "That's my favourite make. If you like, we could take a drive. Don't forget to introduce me to your charming mother."

"Fine," said Suzanne. "How much does it cost, a Morris Léon-Bollée?"

"It's a special model," said Monsieur Jo, "custom-built in Paris. I paid 50,000 francs for it."

Suzanne thought about the B-12, which had cost 4,000 francs. The mother was still paying it off. Suzanne would never have believed that a car could cost so much money.

"If we had a car like that, we'd come to Ramé every evening," said Suzanne. "That would make a nice change for us."

"Money can't buy happiness," said Monsieur Jo dreamily.

Suzanne told herself she'd heard that somewhere before. The mother said it sometimes. She also said the opposite, it depended on her mood. Suzanne definitely thought that money ... was happiness. So did Joseph.

"I would have liked to keep on dancing," said Monsieur Jo.

He followed Suzanne over to the table where the mother and Joseph were sitting.

"Allow me introduce Monsieur Jo," said Suzanne.

The mother rose to say hello to Monsieur Jo. She smiled at him. Joseph stood up too but without the smile.

"Sit here at our table," said the mother. "Have a drink with us."

"Let me invite you," said Monsieur Jo. He turned towards the proprietor. "Some champagne, well chilled," he called out. "I haven't managed to taste decent champagne since I got back from Paris."

He grinned broadly. Joseph gave him a shifty look.

"You've just returned from Paris?" said the mother.

"Yes, fresh off the boat," said Monsieur Jo. He was clearly enjoying the effect this had on them.

"It's a Morris Léon-Bollée," said Suzanne to Joseph.

Joseph seemed to wake up.

"What horsepower?"

"Twenty-four," said Monsieur Jo casually.

"Shit," said Joseph, "twenty-four horsepower. Four gears, of course?"

"Yes, four," said Monsieur Jo, "and you can start it up in second. What kind of car do you have?"

"Shit," said Joseph. He laughed. "Ours, it's not worth talking about."

"It's a good car," said the mother. "A good old car that has served us well, you shouldn't disparage it. For these roads it's just fine."

Joseph put on his mean look.

"Shit," he said. "It's easy to tell you're not the one driving. What mileage does yours get?"

"Fifteen, sixteen miles to the gallon on the highway," said Monsieur Jo, who was beginning to lose interest in this conversation. "I believe Citroëns use less."

Suzanne's eyes were shining. She was thrilled by the effect Monsieur Jo's replies were having on Joseph and the mother. Especially since the champagne was beginning to have an effect on the mother, Joseph and Suzanne. Joseph laughed heartily.

"Ours, ours gets almost ten miles to the gallon. But there's a hole in the petrol tank, so that explains it."

Joseph's merriment was contagious. The mother turned red and shouted with laughter.

"Ha-ha! It's not just the petrol tank," said the mother. "If it were just the petrol tank."

Suzanne began laughing helplessly. Joseph and the mother were shaking with laughter.

"The carburetor too," said Suzanne.

"If it were just the carburetor and the petrol tank," said Joseph.

Monsieur Jo tried to laugh. He felt as if they'd forgotten him. The mother had a full-throated laugh that jiggled her breasts.

"If it were just that," said Joseph, "but here's the thing: us, we've got tyres we stuff with, with – we drive on tyres with holes in them."

Each time, a fresh burst of laughter would shake all three of them. Monsieur Jo seemed delighted and embarrassed.

"Guess what we drive on in the tyres," said Suzanne.

"Guess," said the mother. "Oh! It's so good to laugh."

The proprietor had brought over another bottle of champagne. Young Agosti, who could hear the conversation, was laughing uncontrollably, along with the proprietor. The mother, Joseph and Suzanne were choking. Everyone was looking at them. It was hard to understand what they were saying.

"On bicycle tyres," said Monsieur Jo, pouring some champagne.

"Ha-ha!" said the mother. "That's not it, not at all ..."

"On banana leaves," said Suzanne.

"We stuff the tyres with banana leaves ..."

"And leave it to us ..." said the mother. "Leave it to – leave it to Joseph to come up with that."

Monsieur Jo really began to laugh. Joseph had reached such a paroxysm of laughter that he was strangling. The three of them hardly ever got going, but when that happened, they could hardly ever stop themselves. Monsieur Jo had obviously given up on inviting Suzanne to dance. He was waiting for things to calm down.

"That's original," said Monsieur Jo. "That's the very limit, as they say in Paris."

But no-one was listening to him.

"Us, when we go off on a trip," said Joseph, "we tie the corporal to the mudguard and hand him a watering can."

"Shut up, shut up," said the mother. "Ha-ha-ha! Oh, it's so good ..."

"Then we wire the doors shut," said Suzanne, "because, because ..."

"Because the door handles are gone."

"We don't even remember them," said the mother.

"Us? Don't need any door handles," said Joseph. "Completely useless."

"Shut up, Joseph," said the mother. "Stop it, I can't breathe ..."

"It's a pleasure to run into people as cheerful as you are," said Monsieur Jo.

They fell about laughing again.

"As cheerful as we are," said the mother, pretending to be dumbfounded.

"He said we were cheerful," said Suzanne. "It's clear he has no idea, no idea."

"If only he did," said Joseph.

Joseph was away now.

"If it were just the carburetor, the petrol tank, the tyres," said Joseph. "If it were just that ..."

The mother and Suzanne looked at Joseph. They didn't know what he would come up with. Even before he said it, laughter began welling up inside him.

"If it were just that, it would be nothing."

"What? Joseph, say it, quick!"

"We had some dykes," said Joseph, "and the crabs poked holes in them for us."

Suzanne and the mother screamed with laughter again.

"It's true," said the mother. "Even the crabs ..."

"Even the crabs are against us," said Suzanne.

"The story of our dykes," said Joseph, "it's priceless, definitely priceless. We were confident, then when the sea rose – they leaked like sieves."

"Oh, it's true," said the mother, "even the crabs. Oh yes, even the crabs."

Joseph wriggled his hand like a crab. They were still convulsed with laughter. With two fingers, Joseph imitated a crab walking towards Monsieur Jo.

"The crabs gobbled up our entire fortune," said Suzanne.

"Oh, you're funny," said Monsieur Jo. "You're incredible."

He was laughing, but he would rather have been dancing with Suzanne.

"The story of our dykes is incredible," said Joseph. "We'd thought of everything, but not of those crabs. Our dykes were in their way."

The laughter had subsided a little.

"They're tiny little crabs," said Suzanne. "They're black, rice-paddy colour, they were just made for us – leave it to us ..."

The laughter began again.

"On that score, it's true: leave it to us."

"These dykes were to hold back ..." said Monsieur Jo.

"To hold back the sea," said Suzanne. "You should know that us, we bought some sea – it's an idea no-one would ever have, right? It was my mother's idea."

The mother became serious again.

"Shut up or you'll get goddamn slapped," said the mother.

Monsieur Jo started in surprise. But Joseph jumped right in.

"We wound up in the soup, all right," said Joseph. "The story of our rice fields is falling-down funny, and there we are waiting like goddamn idiots for the sea to pull back, and we're rotting away. It was sea-soup on salty mud. When we bought it..."

Joseph lit a cigarette without offering one to Monsieur Jo. Monsieur Jo took out a pack of American cigarettes and offered them to the mother and Suzanne. The mother and Suzanne were listening, enthralled, to Joseph.

"When we bought it, we believed we'd be millionaires within the year," said Joseph. "It was a sure thing. We built a house, then we waited for everything to grow, then the sea rose, then everything was goddamn ruined, and now there we are waiting for the Messiah in the house, which isn't even finished."

"It rains inside, and there aren't any railings," said Suzanne.

The mother laughed again; she had forgotten she'd lashed out at Suzanne.

"Don't listen to them, Monsieur Jo," she said. "Maybe it doesn't have any railings, but it's a good house, I'd get a good price for it if I sold it – I'm sure I would get 30,000 francs."

"You can say that all you like," said Joseph. "Who would buy that tumbledown place? Crazy people like us," said Joseph.

Suzanne began to smile fiercely and gazed into the distance.

"It's true that we're crazy," said Suzanne ecstatically.

"Completely crazy," said Joseph.

NOTES

1. A *pagne* is a piece of native cotton cloth worn wrapped around the body as a dress, skirt or loincloth.

A word of Vietnamese origin, *rac* means a stretch or stream of water such as a canal, backwater or river. Here it refers to the river where "Paul" and his sister go swimming in an earlier sketch.

2. The corporal is a Malay labourer in *The Sea Wall*, where Marguerite Duras describes his wretched life with cold outrage. To build their roads through swamps and forests, the French authorities used chain gangs of "convicts" who were often political prisoners and poor peasants, whose wives were used as prostitutes by the native overseers. "The corporal said he had been flogged almost to death, but at least he had not starved"; when "his" road is finished, he and his family become homeless beggars living on garbage until he finds work on the mother's plantation. His one hopeless ambition had been to be a bus conductor on the highway he'd helped to build; instead, he gleefully ties himself to the family Citroën's mudguard with water for the leaky radiator, blinking in amazement to see flashing by "the road that had claimed six years of his life".

In *Marguerite Duras*, Laure Adler says that even today, *The Sea Wall* is admired in Vietnam for the honesty with which its author described the injustices of the French colonial period, and her compassion for "the children of the plain", who died year after year of sunstroke, cholera and worms, simply returning to the earth like "the drowned little monkeys at the mouth of the *rac*".

20th Century Press Notebook

Introduction

The second of the four *War Notebooks* is called the *20th Century Press Notebook* because of handwritten notations on its cover. It is one of the "two notebooks in the blue armoires at Neauphle-le-Château" mentioned by Marguerite Duras in the preamble to *The War*, and it was probably written between 1946 and 1948.

Of the forty-four lined pages of this small notebook with a sturdy cover of blue-grey paper, the first twelve are devoted to "Théodora," the only unfinished novel by Marguerite Duras. A fifth notebook entitled "Théodora, novel" has deliberately been omitted from the *War Notebooks* in spite of its chronological proximity to the texts presented here. The rough drafts of this narrative, written in 1947, form in fact a completely separate entity, which includes not only this fifth notebook but also about a hundred typed pages marked with several layers of successive corrections. In addition – which was not the case with the *War Notebooks* – Marguerite Duras clearly stated her refusal to publish the text in that form, which she considered irremediably flawed. She did, however, publish an excerpt from it in 1979 in *Les Nouvelles littéraires*, which she also included in the collection *Outside*, with this introduction: "I thought I had burned the novel *Théodora*. I found it in the blue armoires, unfinished, unfinishable. *Les Nouvelles littéraires* asked me for an article on hotels; I gave them an excerpt from *Théodora*."[1]

Even so, the figure of Théodora, a young woman characterized by her subversive taste for freedom, threads her way through some of the author's published work. Alissa, a central character in *Destroy, She Said*, may be considered an avatar of Théodora; above all, the character now baptized Théodora Kats in *Yann Andréa Steiner* establishes an explicit filiation with the *War Notebooks*, borrowing the principal characteristics of the daughter of Madame Cats described in the *Hundred-Page Notebook*. This same girl, named Jeanine in *The War* and called "the friend" of the narrator, was supposedly "deported to Ravensbrück with Marie-Louise, the sister of Robert {Antelme}".[2] In *Yann Andréa Steiner*, the dialogues between the title character and the narrator diverge from that initial assertion and endow Théodora with contradictory life stories, in the service of both remembrance and invention.

The subsequent pages of the notebook, numbered by Marguerite Duras, contain the beginning of what would become *The War*. The essential content of these pages filled with small, compact handwriting was retained in the published work – with the exception, chiefly, of the most virulent passages attacking the Catholic Church and the government of General de Gaulle. Marguerite Duras made annotations in the margins with a red felt-tip pen which indicate that she reread the manuscript several decades later. This text, which she referred to at that time as a "diary", was composed after the events it relates, and the manuscript reveals that the dates therein were quite probably added after the first version was written. Pages 132–34, greatly abridged and reworked, form part of the second fragment of "Did Not Die Deported" published anonymously in the {feminist} magazine *Sorcières* in 1976.

NOTES

1. *Outside* (Paris: Éditions P.O.L, 1984), p. 293.
2. *La Douleur* (Paris: Gallimard, coll. "Folio", 1993), p. 57.

Théodora

It was shortly after entering the hotel dining room that we noticed that Bernard was being punished. We could hardly help noticing that in particular, since the table closest to ours happened to be the one occupied by the governess and the children in her care. Théodora, who had arrived at the hotel three weeks after I did, was not as familiar as I was with the governess and her handling of the children. Under the circumstances, and even though I'd spoken to her about this, Théodora could not be as sensitive as I was to the punishments inflicted on Bernard by his governess. Still, we had all formed opinions of one another, and although we pretended to ignore one another completely, the willpower thus expended would alone have proven that we were far from indifferent. This situation stemmed from the fact (at least in the beginning) that we had not found any excuse to approach one another. After three weeks, this missing excuse had become something like one more excuse not to approach one another. There was no reason any more. We had become for one another the living proof of our lack of ingenuity. But this complete lack of interaction had not prevented me from noticing, for example, the children's perfect manners. At least at the table, where their behaviour was exemplary. And Bernard's punishments, which occurred four times a week without fail, intrigued me all the more in that his attitude at the table was perfect. So perfect that it seemed suspect to me, and not unrelated to the reason for the punishments the boy endured.

However, I did have an opinion. And the governess must have known that I had one. She did not know what it was. Nor did I know the reasons for the punishments. Still, we did have our opinions and we could not simply ignore them.

The punishments fell on Bernard with remarkable regularity. He endured them as an obligation, and appeared not to suffer from them at all. When Germaine, the maid, brought him his plate, he himself pushed it away. These punishments, the nature of which never varied, seemed pointless, since for three weeks their schedule had remained strictly the same, as did their form, as did the indifference with which the governess dispensed them and Bernard endured them.

Despite everything, though, it gave me pleasure to see, to confirm once more that Bernard, once more, was being punished. A pleasure no doubt minute but certain, to see that it was all continuing, for the longer it continued, the more likely it was to continue to continue. This kind of confirmation is always certain to bring pleasure, to bring a certain well-being, perhaps because it all usually ends badly. I was nearly certain that Bernard was always punished for a single invariable reason, and I told myself that it must be worth it. The reason might have been, simply – it wasn't impossible – to see when the governess would stop punishing him, when she would begin to flag. That particular reason was not my least favourite one. In the same way I have hoped that a myriad of things would continue in my life; among others, I experienced the war while hoping it would not end. Likewise, I had an old cat that had lasted two years beyond the average age for cats, which pleased me; perhaps they'd forgotten about that one, he's not going to have an ordinary death, I said to myself, not him. I took extremely, indecently good care of that cat, knowing perfectly well that he would die someday, of course, but I knew it the way one knows those things, at the same time hoping that perhaps ...

Although Bernard's punishments were of a different *order* and in reality depended only on his governess, whereas the end of the war and my old cat's death definitely depended on something else, these punishments of quite a different nature did bring me a bit of the same pleasure: not knowing how it would all end. I am aware that I will be disappointed. Because in the same way that the war ended, and my old cat died, these punishments will end. And no matter how they end, I'll be disappointed. Only, while I'm waiting, what fun! (I mean, while waiting for Théodora.) Whenever I notice that Bernard isn't touching his chocolate cake or apple tart, I smile at him in a certain way, the least obvious way possible, for even though the governess increasingly avoids looking at me, and especially when Bernard is being punished, I'm afraid she might see me smile. She knows I'm smiling because Bernard smiles back at me, almost imperceptibly, no doubt, but not to she who knows him well. If he is smiling at me – since he's well brought up and she has taught him that a boy must not take this kind of initiative with grown-ups – if he is smiling at me, she knows it's because I'm smiling at him. But not obviously enough for her to therefore point out to me the impropriety of my conduct. The best thing, for her, is to pretend to ignore my secret complicity with Bernard. For if she were to look at me, then it could only be sternly. Well, apparently, she is loath to do so, a point in her favour, which makes me believe she is playing her role reluctantly, and in short, that she is not altogether certain about the usefulness of her punishment of Bernard.

And so, I had my way of encouraging Bernard and supporting him, of urging him to carry on, of showing him my admiration and my faith in the success of his experiment.

Our complicity came to an end this evening, in a way that neither of us could have foreseen.

When we arrived this evening in the dining room, Théodora and I, I noticed that the governess was looking with singular persistence at Madame Mort's back. The latter did, in fact, happen to be in the former's immediate field of vision, and to make things even easier, Madame Mort {Madame Death} had her back to her. This openly curious stare might have made me believe, early in my stay at the hotel, that the governess was wondering for whom Madame Mort was in mourning. Very quickly, however, I realized that she must have known that Madame Mort was in mourning for her husband and that the Monsieur Théo who was accompanying her was his brother, and I thought that if she knew this, it was because she must have learned it from Germaine, who had enough generosity of soul to understand that curiosity about someone at a neighbouring table can become excessive, and even distressing, if it is prolonged, and that a chambermaid's duty is to satisfy such curiosity with the requisite discretion. Therefore, if she knew, like everyone in the hotel, that Madame Mort was plunged in the deepest mourning, and that in spite of what one might have hoped, she was not sharing Monsieur Théo's room – if she knew this and was nevertheless staring so obstinately at Madame Mort's back, it was because Bernard was once again being punished, and because once again she had noticed me noticing the apple tart untouched on the boy's plate.

I had spoken of all this, casually, to Théodora. This evening, my pleasure at seeing Bernard punished was increased by that of learning what Théodora would think about this, for, knowing Théodora as I did, I knew she could not be indifferent to the hint of grandeur in Bernard's endeavour. I anticipated the sort of pleasure she would take in it, which could not fail to affect the nature of mine. Théodora's arrival had brought a certain period to a close; one might call it that of my pure complicity with Bernard. I enjoyed in advance watching Théodora pass through the same stages as I had. And from now on it would be my pleasure to see what attitude someone like Théodora would take towards Bernard's mysterious punishments; it would have to be different from mine, but in any case could bring me nothing but pleasure. Because already for quite some time now, Théodora has been my joy. Whatever she does, whatever she does to me, none of her words, none of her actions, even if they are (to use the common phrase) directed against me, can bring me anything but joy.

Marie was not eating any of her apple tart, either. This development is so new that Marie emerges from the kind of background in which I have kept her until now. While Marie is not eating, the governess eats with particular attention, as does Odile. Théodora has not noticed anything yet, which makes it easier for me to observe the scene. Marie is not eating. She does not seem to know that anything is on her plate, even though the governess served her as usual; Marie now appears, however, to have forgotten completely about eating. In front of her, Bernard isn't eating either. For the first time I have not smiled at him, and he has not once looked at me. He is clearly jealous and feels forsaken because he has ceased to interest me.

Marie, motionless, stares at the dining-room chandelier. She is beautiful, and is at least eighteen years old. She must be a good fuck. Her eyes are green and shining, her dress is red, that's the situation. Between her red dress and her green eyes, there is a still, set harmony, like a question asked, which it falls to me to try to answer. She's so beautiful, Marie, that I wonder if she isn't more beautiful than the scene in progress, and might not carry off the prize. Now Théodora has noticed that Marie interests me. I do not forget Théodora, ever. But Marie is beautiful for me. "I, too, am beautiful; Théodora isn't the only one." That's true: not noticing Marie before this evening is my responsibility, Théodora has nothing to do with that, although her presence is not unrelated to Marie's new attitude. Théodora exists. As usual, she doesn't speak to me. It's been so long since we've had anything left to say to each other, except once in a while, and always on the same subject. I'm busy with Marie's eyes; Théodora can only acquiesce, she always does, nothing can change that. Marie does not acquiesce.

"You're not eating, Marie?" says the governess in a loud, firm voice.

Marie shifts her green gaze from the chandelier to the face of her governess.

She says, "No."

The governess is a trifle pale but not enough yet in my opinion.

"This is the first time you haven't eaten, Marie. Are you ill?"

Marie smiles at her governess. I am more or less sure that she is joining in Bernard's punishment only to please me, because she has noticed something: that it pleased me to see punishments refused. Her smile is assured.

"No, Mademoiselle, I feel fine."

Now Théodora is following the scene as I am, as oblivious of me as I am of her. The governess becomes visibly angry. Her hands tremble. She looks over – but we, we are so accustomed to being looked at that it doesn't make us lower our eyes.

"Marie, you will go upstairs to bed after dinner."

Marie's smile broadens. Her eyes travel back up to the chandelier and Marie says, "No."

I experience Marie's refusal, like her beauty, as being addressed to me. It isn't certain that everyone heard that "No." It was said quite softly, and at the moment when I'd already become unable to take my eyes off Marie's mouth – which means that I saw that "No" more than I heard it. If Marie had pronounced it distinctly, it would not have the same character; I would not have wondered if she'd been addressing only me, and would not have taken that refusal as a provocation meant for me. If that word had been spoken for everyone, Marie would not have emerged from it full blown as she just has with breasts, mouth, eyes, hair, multiple and varied shapes melded into a single one, ripe for me. Perhaps, as she said that "No", she doubted her right to do so, but once it was said, she must have been as proud as if she had accomplished a great feat. A minute ago, I had no idea there was a place in me for her; I feel as refreshed as after a spring shower. She's young, that one, she still believes it's worth it to refuse, she's like a plant seeking the sun. She is ripe for me.

Shortly after Marie replied to her governess, Madame Mort hurriedly left the dining room. No-one noticed her leaving, not even Bernard, who, as impassive as ever, is looking at Marie. If I noticed that departure, it was in the periphery of Marie's face. Without seeing Théodora, I sense her shadow beside me, the cold shadow of Théodora.

The governess is now disfigured by pallor.

"Marie, leave the table right now."

Marie looks at her governess and keeps her eyes riveted on her. The governess returns Marie's gaze, but her lips are quivering.

"No," says Marie.

Someone, it's Madame Bois, says to her little girl, "Don't look."

It's the thing to say, the most perfect thing to say. But in vain, since Madame Bois continues to look, the little girl continues to look. It had to be said, however.

The face of the governess is open, as torn open as genitals in a rape. It falls apart before our eyes, and while that defeat is accomplished and becomes this dazzling perfection, Marie becomes shrouded in mystery. She refuses without deigning to explain herself. She refuses everything. She would have refused not only to eat the apple tart and to obey her governess but everything anyone could have proposed to her. Once she was set on refusing, she would refuse everything. Théodora knows this. When I look at her, I know she knows this: she's laughing a laugh that is silent and endless, endless, endless.

The governess leaves. She rises, pushes her chair gently back and leaves, followed by Odile. Bernard appears to hesitate. It seems to me he's looking to Marie for guidance about what attitude to take. But Marie appears to have no idea that Bernard is still there. She has begun playing with her napkin ring.

Then Bernard stands up, a little disappointed not to have been the real stake in the game. Marie stares at her hands playing with the napkin ring; no-one can see her eyes any more. She is alone at the table.

"Eat the tart now," says Théodora. "If I were you, I'd go ahead and eat it."

Marie starts. Who spoke?

"Why?" says Marie. "I no longer want it, otherwise I'd have eaten it just now."

"Please excuse me," says Théodora.

Marie leaves the dining room. She's quite flushed, she seems about to cry. She walks out somewhat unsteadily.

"Go comfort her," says Théodora.

I leave. I look for Marie. If I have something to tell her it's right away. In a little while it will be too late. I find her sitting on a chaise longue in the courtyard, crying.

"Forgive Théodora, she didn't mean to hurt you. Perhaps she did so inadvertently?"

"If I refused to eat the apple tart," says Marie, "it's because I had my reasons, it's nobody else's business. I don't understand how she can ..."

"I assure you, she realizes that perfectly: she wanted to say only what she said and nothing else ..."

"I don't know who you are. Whether she realizes it or not has nothing to do with this, it can't possibly mean anything to me. We don't know one another ..."

"What shall I tell her you said?"

"I don't understand," says Marie.

"I came to apologize for her, and at her request. I don't know what to tell her when I return to the dining room."

"But really," says Marie, "you are most extraordinary – I don't know her."

"You cannot understand ..."

"It's true that she's so beautiful," says Marie dreamily. "Did she seem amused by all that, do you think?"

"Everything amuses her ... What shall I tell her you said?"

*

"She's funny, that kid," said Théodora.

She wanted to go up to the room right away. She lay down on the bed. She stretched out. She seemed to be tired.

"I do realize how idiotic this all is," I said.

"There's no end to it," said Théodora. "You think I hurt her feelings?"

Silence of our room. Silence of our life. The shutters are open. Night has fallen. Night. Night.

"Don't think about it," I said. "I do realize how idiotic this all is ... You must have hurt her in some way, but it's not important ..."

I asked Théodora to get undressed and go to bed. She did not answer.

Théodora's stillness, eyes closed, lying on the bed. Outside, pitch black. In the mirror my face is pale, pale.

"There's no end to it," says Théodora again.

First part: dining room – garden – flowers [offered] by T. to M. – the hero and Marie.

The War (Rough Draft)

Facing the fireplace. The telephone beside me. On the right, the door to the sitting room and the corridor; at the end of the corridor, the front door. He might come straight here, he'd ring the doorbell. "Who is it?" "It's me." Or he might telephone as soon as he arrives at a transit centre: "I'm back, I'm at the {Hôtel} Lutétia, for the paperwork." There would be no warning. He'd phone as soon as he arrived. Such things are possible. Some people are coming back, after all. He isn't a special case, there aren't any particular reasons why he shouldn't come back. There aren't any reasons why he should. He might come back. He'd ring the bell. "Who is it?" "It's me." Lots of other things like that are happening. They finally crossed the Rhine. They finally broke through the major stalemate at Avranches.¹ I finally made it through the war. It wouldn't be an extraordinary thing if he came back. Careful: it would not be extraordinary. "Hello?" "Who is it?" "It's me, Robert." It would be normal and not extraordinary. Be very careful not to make it into something extraordinary: the Extraordinary is unexpected. Be reasonable. I am reasonable. I'm waiting for Robert, who should be coming back.

The telephone: "Hello?" "Hello! Heard any news?" Two beats. First one: phones do ring; waiting for it to ring is not a waste of time; phones are meant to ring. Second one: shit. Desire to rip someone's throat out. "No news." "Nothing? No information?" "None." "You know Belsen was liberated yesterday afternoon?"

"I know." Silence. Am I going to ask yet again? That's it, too late, I'm asking: "So what do you think? I'm beginning to get worried." Silence. "You must wait, and above all, hang in there, don't get discouraged – you're not the only one, unfortunately ... I know a mother with four children who ..." Cut this off: "I know. I'm sorry, I have to go out. Goodbye." Done. I put the phone down.

I'm still sitting here. Mustn't move to much, it's a waste of energy. Saving every bit of strength for the ordeal. She said, "You know Belsen was liberated yesterday afternoon?" I hadn't known. Another camp liberated. She said, "[*illegible*] yesterday afternoon." She didn't say so, but I know that the lists will arrive tomorrow. Go downstairs, pick up a paper, pay for the paper, read the list. No. I hear a throbbing in my temples, getting worse. No, I won't read that list. I'll ask someone to read it and let me know in case ... First off, the system of lists – I've been using them for three weeks, and it's not the right way. Plus the more lists there are ... No, no list: the more lists there are, the fewer ... They'll keep appearing until ... Until the end. He won't be ... It's time to move. Stand up, take three steps, go to the window. The École de Médecine: still there, even if ... Passers-by in the streets; they'll still be walking ... At the instant when I hear the news – still passers-by ... It happens. A notification of death. They're already informing ... "Who's there?" "A social worker from the town hall." The mother with four children was notified. If this pounding in my temples keeps up ... Above all, I must get rid of this throbbing, it can be deadly. Death is inside me: it's own pounding in my temples, no mistake about that; must stop the pounding, stop the heart, calm it down – it won't calm down of its own accord, it needs help; must keep reason from breaking down any more, draining away; I put on my coat. Landing. Staircase. "Good afternoon, Madame Antelme." Concierge. She didn't seem any different. The street either. Outside, April carries on as if nothing were wrong. In the street, I'm asleep, hands jammed into pockets, legs moving forward. Avoid newspaper kiosks. Avoid transit centres. The Allies are advancing along all fronts. Even a few days ago, that was important. Now, not at all. I no longer read the news bulletins. Why bother? They'll advance until the end. Daylight, broad daylight on the Nazi mystery. April – it will have happened in April. The Allied armies surge across Germany. Berlin in flames. The Red Army continues its victorious advance in the south. Past Dresden. The Allies are advancing on all fronts; past the Rhine, that was bound to happen. The great day of the war: Remagen.[2] It began after that. Ever since Eisenhower was sickened by Buchenwald, three million women and I don't give a fuck how the war turns out. In a ditch, face turned towards the earth, legs bent, arms flung out, he's dying. I see. Everything. He starved to death. Through the skeletons of Buchenwald ... his skeleton. Warm weather. Perhaps he's beginning to rot. Along the road next to him pass the Allied armies advancing on all fronts. He's been dead for three weeks. That's it. I'm sure of it. The legs keep walking. Faster. His mouth sags open. It's evening. He thought of me before dying. The exquisite pleasure of pain. There are far too many people in the streets. I'd like to move across a great plain and be able to think freely. Just before dying he must have thought my name. All along the road, along every German road, others are lying more or less as he does. Thousands. Dozens, hundreds of thousands, and him. Him – one of the thousands of others. Him – distinct from those thousands for me alone in all the world, and completely distinct from them. I know everything you can know when you know nothing. They evacuated them, then at the last minute, they killed them. So. Generalities. The war, generality. The war. The necessities of war. The dead, necessities of war, generality.

He died saying my name. What other name would he have said? The war: generality. I don't live on generalities. Those who live on generalities have nothing in common with me. No-one has anything in common with me. The street. Some people laugh, especially the young. I have only enemies. It's evening, I'll have to go home. It's evening on the other side as well. In the ditch darkness is taking over, covering his mouth. Red sun over Paris. Six years of war are ending. Big deal, big story, they'll be talking about it for twenty years. Nazi Germany is crushed. The butchers, crushed. So is he, in the ditch. I am broken. Something broken. Impossible for me to stop walking. Dry as dry sand. Beside the ditch, the parapet of the Pont des Arts. The Seine. Just to the right of the ditch. Something separates them: darkness. The Pont des Arts. My victory. Nothing in the world belongs to me except that corpse in a ditch. Childhood, over. Innocence, over. It's evening. It's my end-of-the-world. Shit on everyone. My dying isn't directed against anyone. The simplicity of my death. I will have lived ... I don't care about that, I don't care about the moment of my death. In dying I don't rejoin him, I stop waiting for him. No fuss. I'll tell D.: "I'd best die – what would you do with me?" Craftily, I'll be dying while alive for him; afterwards death will bring only relief. I make this base calculation. Not strong enough to live for D. I have to go home. D. is waiting for me. Half past eight.

"Any news?" "None." No one asks how I am or says hello any more, they say, "Any news?" I say, "None." I sit on the sofa near the telephone. I don't say anything. I know D. is uneasy. When he's not looking at me he seems worried. It's already been a week. I catch him puttering around. "Say something," I tell D. Just last week he laughed and told me, "You're nuts, you haven't the right to worry like that." Now he tells me, "There's no reason ... Be sensible ..." He doesn't laugh any more but he smiles, and his face crinkles. And yet without D. I don't think I could keep going. We turn on the light in the sitting room. D. has already been here for an hour. It must be nine o'clock. We haven't had dinner yet. We don't talk. D. is sitting not far from me; I'm still sitting in the same place on the sofa. I stare fixedly out the black window. D. watches me. Sometimes he says, "Enough." Then I look at him. He smiles at me. Then I look at the window. Only last week he was taking my hand, kissing me, telling me impulsively, "Robert will come back, I promise." Now I know he's wondering if hope is still worth it. Once in a while I say, "I'm sorry." He smiles. An hour later I say, "How come we've had no news?" He tells me, "There are still thousands of men in camps the Allies haven't reached yet." "The Allies have reached them all, there are Americans and British everywhere." "How do you expect him to get word to you?" "They can write. The Bernards heard from their daughters." This goes on for a long time, until I ask D. to assure me that Robert will come back. "He'll come back," D. tells me. Then he says we ought to eat something. I go to the kitchen, I put potatoes in a saucepan, water in the saucepan, I turn on the gas, I put the saucepan on the flame. Then I bow my head, lean my forehead against the edge of the cooker, pushing harder and harder. I close my eyes. I don't move, leaning against the cooker. Silence. D. doesn't make a sound in the flat. The gas hums, that's all. Where? Where is he? Where can he be? Where, in the name of God where? The black ditch – dead for two weeks. His mouth sags open. Along the road, next to him, pass the Allied armies advancing on all fronts. Dead for two weeks. Two weeks of days and nights, abandoned in a ditch, the soles of his feet exposed. Rain on him, sun, the dust of the victorious armies. For two weeks. His hands open. Each hand dearer to me than life. Familiar to me. Familiar that way only to me. I shout, "D!" Footsteps, very slow, in the sitting room. D. appears. He comes into the kitchen. Around my shoulders I feel two firm, gentle hands that pull me away from the cooker. I huddle against D.

"It's awful," I say. "I know," says D. "No, you can't know." "I know," says D. "Just try. We can do anything …" "I can't do a thing any more." D.'s arms are around me. The tighter he holds me, the more comforting it is, much better than words. Sometimes, gripped in his arms, I might almost believe I feel better. Able to breathe for a minute. We sit down at the table. Two plates on the kitchen table. I get the bread from the cupboard. Three-day-old bread. Pause. "The bread's three days old," I tell D. "Everything's closed at this hour ..." We look at each other. "True enough," says D. We're thinking the same thing about the bread. We start eating. We sit down again. The piece of bread in my hand ... I look at it. I feel like vomiting. The dead bread. The bread he didn't eat. Not having bread is what killed him. My throat closes up – a needle couldn't get through. The bread, the taste of the bread he didn't eat. We didn't know until a month ago, and then the world was flooded with photographs: charnel houses. The light broke through onto mass graves of bones. We know their rations. While we were eating bread, they weren't. I'm not even going to discuss the Germans. Corpses thick on the ground, millions of corpses. Instead of wheat, crops of corpses: Take, eat, this is my body. There are still some who believe in that. In {the posh neighbourhood of} Auteuil, they still believe in it. Class warfare. The corpse class. The only relief: dead people of the world, unite! And get that guy down off his cross. The Christians, the only ones who don't share the hatred. During the Liberation, when it was throat-cutting time, they were already preaching leniency and the forgiving of sins. The little priest's bread: Take, eat, this is my body. The farm worker's bread. The maid's always-eaten-in-the-kitchen bread: "We have a maid who constantly eats more than her ration card! Imagine, madame! Such people are simply appalling." Hard-earned bread. Bakery bread bought by the capitalist papa for his dear little offspring who at this very moment is starting to take an interest in the war. The earthy bread of the Soviet partisan, all the trouble it cost him – in short the basic bread of the land of the Revolution. I look at the bread. "I'm not hungry." D. stops eating. "If you don't eat, I don't eat." I nibble so that D. will eat. Before leaving, D. says, "Promise me to ..." I promise. When D. said, "I have to go home," I wanted it to be over and done with, I wanted him already gone and then I wouldn't have to close the door behind him.

D. has left. The flat creaks beneath my feet. One by one, I turn off the lamps. I go to my room. I go very slowly. The important thing is to sleep. If I'm not careful I won't sleep. When I don't sleep at all things are much worse the next day. When I have slept, things aren't as bad in the morning for an hour. When I do fall asleep it's in the black ditch, near him lying dead.

Went to the centre at the Gare d'Orsay. I had considerable trouble gaining admission for the Tracing Service of *Libres*.[3] They insisted that it wasn't an official service. The BCRA is already there and doesn't want to relinquish its place to anyone.[4] To begin with I got us organised on the sly, with forged papers. We have managed to collect a lot of information about the transfers and whereabouts of camp survivors, which has appeared in our paper. A great deal of personal news. "You can tell the Such-and-such family that their son is alive; I saw him yesterday." But my four comrades and I were thrown out. "Everyone wants to be here, it's impossible. Only stalag secretariats are allowed here." I protest, saying that seventy-five thousand wives and relatives of prisoners and deportees read our paper. "It's unfortunate, but regulations forbid the operation here of any unofficial services." "Our paper isn't like all the others, it's the only one that publishes special issues of lists ..." "That's not a sufficient reason." I'm talking to a senior official in the repatriation service of the Frenay ministry.[5] Apparently preoccupied, he's distant and worried. "I'm sorry," he says. I say, "I won't go without a fight," and I head for the main offices. "Where are you going?" "I'm going to try to stay." I attempt to slip through a line of prisoners of war that's blocking the corridor. He looks at me and says, "As you like, but be careful – those (he points at them) haven't been disinfected yet. In any case, if you're still here this evening, I'm sorry but I'll have to evict you." We've [spotted] a small deal table that we place at the beginning of the "circuit". We question the prisoners. Many come to us. We gather hundreds of pieces of information. I work steadily, without looking up, without thinking of anything. Now and then, an officer (easily recognizable: young, starched khaki shirt, pouter-pigeon chest) comes over to ask who we are. "Just what is this tracing service? Do you have a pass?" I present my forged passes. Next there's a woman from the repatriation service. "What do you want with them?" "We're asking for news of their comrades who are still in Germany." "And what do you do with that?" She's a perky young platinum blonde, navy-blue suit, matching shoes, sheer stockings, manicured nails. "We publish it in *Libres*, the newspaper for prisoners and deportees." "*Libres?* You're not from the ministry?" "No." "Do you have the authority to do this?" she says coolly. "We're taking the authority. It's simple." Off she goes. We keep asking our questions. Our task is made easier, unfortunately, by the two and a half hours it takes the prisoners to get to identity verification, the first office in the circuit. It will take the deportees even longer, since they have no papers. An officer comes over: forty-five, sweating in his jacket, very curt this time. "What is all this?" We explain yet again. "There is already a similar service in the circuit." Boldly, I ask: "How do you get the news to the families? We hear it will take at least three months before everyone will have been able to write ..." He looks at me and laughs haughtily. "You don't understand. I'm talking about information on Nazi atrocities. We are compiling dossiers." He moves away, then returns. "How do you know they're telling you the truth? It's very dangerous, what you're doing. You must know ... The militiamen ..." I don't reply. He goes away. A half-hour later a general heads directly for our table, trailed by the first officer, the second officer and the young woman. "Your papers?" I present them. "Unsatisfactory. You may work standing up, but I do not want to see this table again." I object: it takes up hardly any room. "The ministry has expressly forbidden the use of tables in the main hall." They call two scouts over to remove the table. We work standing up.

The radio occasionally blasts music that varies between swing and patriotic tunes. The line of prisoners grows longer. Now and then I go to the ticket window at the far end of the room. "Still no deportees?" "No deportees." Women in uniform. Repatriation service. They talk about the prisoners, referring to them only as "the poor boys, the poor boys ..." They address one another as Mademoiselle de Thingummy, Madame de Butt-Hole. They're smiling. Their work is just so hard. It's suffocating in here. They're really very, very busy. Some officers come over occasionally to see them; they swap English cigarettes and idle banter. "Indefatigable, Mademoiselle de [*illegible*]?" "As you see, Captain ..." The main hall [rumbles] with footsteps. And they keep coming. Trucks stream in from Le Bourget. In groups of fifty, the prisoners arrive, and then – quick, {an army song on} the loudspeaker: "*C'est la route qui va, qui va, qui va ...*" When it's a larger group, they put on the "Marseillaise". [Hiccups of silence] between the songs. The young men look around the main hall. All smiling. Repatriation officials herd them along: "Alright, my friends, form a queue." They queue, still smiling. The first ones to get there say, "Long wait," but nicely, and still smiling. When asked for information, the men stop smiling and try to remember. The officers call them "my friends"; the women, "those poor boys", or "my friends" to their faces. At the Gare de l'Est, pointing to her stripes, one of these "ladies" scolded a soldier from the Legion: "So, my friend – we're not saluting? Can't you see I'm a captain?" The soldier looked at her. "Me, when I see a skirt, I don't salute her, I fuck her." A prolonged "Ohhh!" greeted those words. "How rude!" The lady beat a dignified retreat.

April. I went to see S., the head of the centre, to sort things out. We are allowed to stay, but at the tail end of the circuit, over by the left luggage. Really pleased. As long as there are no deportees I can handle it. (Some are turning up at the Lutétia, but only rarely at Orsay.) A few isolated cases. At which point I leave the circuit, my colleagues understand that. I return only after the deportees are gone. When I do return, my comrades signal across the room: "Nothing." I sit down again. In the evening I take the lists to the paper. And go home. Every evening: "I'm not going back to Orsay tomorrow."

But I do believe that tomorrow I won't be going back there. First convoy of deportees from Weimar. 20 April. I receive a phone call at home that morning: they won't arrive until the afternoon. No courage. Whenever I pass by Orsay I run away. I run from newspapers. Outside the Orsay centre the wives of prisoners of war clump into a compact mass. White barriers separate them from the prisoners. They call out, asking for news of this or that person. Occasionally the soldiers stop. A few of them know something. Women are there at seven in the morning. Some stay until three in the morning – and come back later that day. They're not allowed into the centre. The prisoners arrive in an orderly way. At night they arrive in big lorries, and emerge into bright light. The women scream, clap; the men stop, dazed, speechless. Sometimes they reply, usually they just go inside.

At first I would ask many of them, "Do you know any political deportees?" No. Most of them knew STO workers.[6] No-one knew any political deportees and they didn't really understand the difference. They'd seen some at the transit centre "in a terrible state". I admire the women who stay and never stop asking {their questions}. I asked D. to come to the centre to see the first deportees from Weimar. After breakfast, I feel like running away again. "Antelme? Oh, yes ..." They won't tell me. They'll look at me in a way that ... I'm working badly. All these names I add up, names of prisoners of war, are not his. Every five minutes I feel like packing it in, putting down the pencil, abandoning my questions, leaving the centre. Each lorry stopping out in the street: them. No. At around half past two I get up; I'd like to know when they're arriving. I go looking in the main hall for someone to ask. Ten or so women are in a corner of the room listening to a tall woman, a

general in a navy-blue suit with the cross of Lorraine on the lapel.
She has blue-rinsed white hair, curled with tongs. She gestures
as she speaks; the girls watch. They seem spent, and afraid. Their
bundles and suitcases are sitting around, and there's a small child
lying on one bundle. Their dresses are filthy. But what's remarkable is that their faces are distorted – by fatigue, or fear? And
they're quite dirty, young. Two or three of them have huge bellies,
pregnant fit to burst. Standing nearby, another woman officer
watches the general speak. "What's going on?" She looks at me,
lowers her eyes discreetly: "{STO} Volunteers." The general tells
them to stand up. They do, and follow her. They look frightened
because people jeered at them outside the centre. I heard some
volunteers being booed one night; the men hadn't expected it and
smiled at first, then gradually they understood and took on that
same stricken look. The general now turns to the young woman
in uniform: "What should we do with them?" She points at the
huddled group. "I don't know," says the other officer. The general
must have informed them that they were scum. Some of them are
crying. The pregnant ones are staring vacantly. They're all working girls, with big hands scarred by German machinery. Two of
them may be prostitutes, but they, too, must have worked with
machines. They're standing there, as the general had asked, looking at her. An officer comes up: "What's all this?" "Volunteers."
The general's voice is shrill: "Sit down." Obediently, they sit down
again. That's not enough. "And keep quiet," says the general
sternly. "Understood? Don't think you're going to just walk away
…" The general has quite a refined voice. Her delicate hand with
its red fingernails threatens and [condemns] the volunteers with
their grease-stained hands. Machines. German machines. The
volunteers don't reply. The man approaches the huddled group
to study them with quiet curiosity. Casually, in front of the volunteers, he asks the general, "Have you any orders?" "No," she says,
"do you?" "I heard something about six months' detention." The
general nods her lovely curly head: "It would serve them right."

The senior officer blows puffs of cigarette smoke over the bunch of volunteers following the conversation open-mouthed, watching with haggard eyes. "Right!" says the senior officer, a horseman, pirouetting elegantly, Camel in hand, and off he goes. The volunteers watch everyone and look for some sign of the fate that awaits them. No sign. I snag the general as she's leaving: "Do you know when the convoy from Weimar is arriving?" She looks me up and down. "Three o'clock." Another once-over and then, a delicate, threatening finger: "But I warn you, it's not worth your getting in the way here, only generals and prefects will be coming." I look at the general. "Why? What about the others?" I wasn't being careful, my tone must not have been appropriate to use with a lady of such quality. She draws herself up: "Oh-ohoh. I detest that sort of attitude! Peddle your complaints elsewhere, missy." She's so indignant that she reports this to a small group of women, also in uniform, who listen, take offence and look my way. I approach one of them. I hear myself say, "So she's not waiting for anyone, that woman?" I get a scandalized look: "She has so much to do, her nerves are in a state." I return to the Tracing Service at the end of the circuit.

Shortly afterwards, I go back to the main hall. D. is waiting for me there with a forged pass.

Around three o'clock there's a rumour. "They're here!" I leave the circuit to go stand at the entrance to a small corridor opposite the main hall. I wait. I know that Robert A. won't be among them. D. is beside me. His job is to find out from the deportees if they've seen Robert Antelme. He's pale. He pays no attention to me. There's a great hubbub in the main hall. The uniformed women are busy with the volunteers, making them sit on the floor somewhere out of the way. The main hall is empty. No prisoners of war are arriving at the moment. Some officers bustle about. I hear: "The minister!" I recognize Frenay among the officers. I'm still in the same place, at the mouth of the little corridor. I watch the main entrance. I know Robert Antelme hasn't a chance of being among them.

Something's wrong: I'm shaking. I'm cold. I lean against the wall. Two scouts emerge abruptly from the entryway, carrying a man. His arms are wrapped around the scouts' necks. The scouts carry him with their arms crossed beneath his thighs. The man's {head} is shaved, he's in civilian clothes, and he seems in great pain. He's a strange colour. He must be crying. You can't call him thin – it's something else: there's hardly anything left of him. And yet he's alive. He looks at nothing – not the minister, not the room, not anything. He grimaces. He's the first deportee from Weimar to arrive at the centre. Without realizing it, I've moved forward, into the middle of the hall, with my back to the loudspeaker. Two more scouts appear, supporting an old man, who is followed by about ten other men. They are guided to garden benches that have been brought in. The minister goes over to them. The old man is weeping. He's very old, at least he must be – it's impossible to tell. Suddenly I see D. sitting next to the old man. I feel very cold. My teeth are chattering. Someone comes over to me: "Don't stay there, it's making you sick, there's no point." I know him, he's a guy from the centre. I stay. D. has started talking to the old man. I go over everything rapidly: there's one chance in ten thousand that he knows Robert Antelme. But I've heard they have lists of the survivors of Buchenwald. So. Aside from the {skeletal deportee} and the weeping old man, the others don't seem too badly off. The minister is sitting with them, along with some senior officers. D. talks to the old man for quite a while. I look only at D.'s face. He seems to be taking too long. So I go towards the bench, into D.'s field of vision. He notices, looks at me and shakes his head. I gather that he's saying, "Doesn't know him." I go away. I'm very tired. I feel like leaving the centre and taking a rest. I'm sure that I could manage to sleep this afternoon. Now the uniformed women are bringing the deportees some mess tins. They eat, and while they eat, they answer {questions}. But what's striking is that they don't seem interested in what's said to them. The next day I'll read in the papers that the group included General Challe; his son Hubert Challe (who would die that night), a former cadet at Saint-Cyr; General Audibert; Ferrières, the head of the State Tobacco Department; Julien Cain, the director of the Bibliothèque Nationale; General Heurteaux; Professor Suard of the faculty of medicine in Angers; Professor Richet; Claude Bourdet {a writer and journalist}; the father of Teitgen, the Minister of Information; Maurice Nègre {an agricultural engineer}; Marcel Paul {a union activist} and others.

I go home towards five in the afternoon, walking along the Seine. It's lovely weather, a beautiful sunny day. Once I've left the embankment and turned onto the rue du Bac, I've left the centre far behind. I'm going home, I'm eager to be home. Maybe he will return. I'm very tired. I'm very dirty, I spent part of the night at the centre. I intend to take a bath when I get home. I must wash; not washing doesn't solve anything. But I'm cold. I don't feel like washing. It must be at least a week since I last washed. I think about myself: I've never met a woman more cowardly than I am.

I think about the wives and mothers I know who are waiting for deportees. None is as cowardly as that. Absolutely none. I am very tired. I know some who are quite brave. The fortitude of S., R.'s wife, I'd call simply extraordinary. Although I am a coward, I know it. My cowardice is so bad that no-one dares discuss it around me. My colleagues in the service speak to me as if I were sick in the head. So do M. and A. Me, I know I'm not sick. I'm cowardly. D. tells me so sometimes, "One never, ever, has the right to destroy oneself like that." He often tells me, "You're a sick woman, you're crazy." When D. also says to me, "Take a look at yourself: you don't look like anything any more," I can't understand. Not for one second do I grasp the need to have courage. Maybe being brave would be my way of being a coward. Why would I have courage? Suzy is brave for her little boy. Why would I husband my strength, for what? If he's dead, what good is courage? There's no battle out there for me to fight. The one I do fight is invisible. I struggle against a vision: the black ditch, the corpse stone-dead for two weeks. And it depends – there are moments when the vision takes over. I don't care to live if he's no longer alive. That's all. "You must hold on," Madame Cats tells me. "Me, I remain steady; you have to, for him." I feel sorry for Madame Cats. Why fight it? In the name of what? I have no dignity. My dignity – can go to hell. No shame at all any more. My shame has been suspended. "When you think back on it," says D., "you'll be ashamed." There's just one [thing]: we're talking about me. People who wait with dignity – I despise them. My dignity is waiting too, like the rest, and there's no rush for its return. If he's dead, my dignity can't do a thing about it. What's my dignity compared to that?

People are out in the streets as usual. Queues in front of shops. There are already a few cherries. I buy a paper. The Russians are in Strasbourg and perhaps even farther along, on the outskirts of Berlin. I'm waiting for the fall of Berlin too. Everyone, the whole world, is waiting for that. All governments agree. The heart of Germany, the papers say. And the wives of deportees: "Now they'll see what's what." And my concierge. When {the heart of Germany} stops beating, it will be all over. The streets are full of murderers. People dream the dreams of murderers. I dream about an ideal city, its burnt ruins flooded with German blood. I think I smell this blood; it's redder than ox blood, more like pig blood, and wouldn't coagulate but flows a long way, and on the banks of these rivers, there would be weeping women whose butts I would kick, sending them nose-diving into their own men's blood. People who at this moment, today, feel pity for Germany, or rather, feel no hatred for it, make me pity them in turn. Most especially the holier-than-thou bunch.

One of them recently brought a German child to the centre, explaining with a smile, "He's a little orphan." So proud. Leading him by the hand. Of course, he wasn't wrong (the disgrace of people who are never wrong). Of course he had to take him in: this poor little child wasn't to blame. The holier-than-thou types always find an occasion for charity. His little German Good Deed. If I had that kid I'd probably take care of him, not kill him. But why remind us that there are still children in Germany? Why remind us of that now? I want my hatred complete and untouched. My black bread. Not long ago a girl said to me, "Germans? There are eighty million of 'em. Well, eighty million bullets can't be hard to find, right?" Anyone who hasn't dreamed that blood-thirsty dream about Germany at least one night in his life, in this month of April 1945 (Christian era), is feebleminded. Between the volunteers impregnated by the Nazis and the priestling bringing back the German boy, I'm with the volunteers. First off, the little priest, he'll never be a volunteer, he was a war prisoner, and then, no question, the clerical life pays well enough so that he doesn't have to choose – and he can easily forgive every sin: he's never committed any, he's real careful about this. That he could believe he has the right to forgive – no.

More news: Monty has crossed the Elbe, it seems; Monty's aims aren't as clear as Patton's. Patton charges ahead, reaches Nürnberg. Monty's supposed to have reached Hamburg. Rousset's wife phoned me: "They're in Hamburg. They won't say anything about the Hamburg Neuengamme camp for several days."

She's been very worried lately, and rightly so. In these last days, the Germans are shooting people. Halle has been cleaned out, Chemnitz taken, and they've swept on towards Dresden. Patch is cleaning out Nürnberg. Georges Bidault is talking with President Truman and Stettinius about the San Francisco conference.[7] Who cares? I'm tired, tired. Under the heading "Wurtemberg

Occupied", Michel [*illegible*] says in *Libération Soir*: "We'll never
hear of Vaihingen again. On every map the delicate green of forests
will sweep all the way down to the Enz ... The watchmaker died at
Stalingrad ... The barber served in Paris, the village idiot occupied
Athens." Now the high street is hopelessly empty, its cobblestones
belly-up like dead fish. "Regarding deportees: 140,000 prisoners of
war have been repatriated, but so far, few deportees ... Despite all
the ministerial services' efforts, the question requires action on a
grander scale. The prisoners wait hours in the Tuileries gardens."
{And:} "Cinema Night will be a particularly brilliant affair this
year." I feel like holing up in my flat. I'm tired. They say one in
five hundred will come back. 600,000 political deportees. 350,000
Jews. So 6,000 will return. He might be among them. It's been
a month; he could have sent word. It seems to me I've waited
long enough. I'm tired. I don't know if it's the arrival of those
deportees from Buchenwald – I can't wait any more. This evening
I'm not waiting for anything.

I'm very tired. An open bakery. Maybe I should buy some
bread for D. It's not worth it any more. I won't wash, I don't
need to wash. It must be seven o'clock. D. won't come before half
past eight. I'll go home. Perhaps I shouldn't waste my {bread}
coupons. I remember {the refrain}: "It's criminal to waste food
coupons these days." Most people are waiting. But some aren't
waiting for anything. Others have stopped waiting, because he
came home, because they've received word, because he's dead.
Two evenings ago, returning from the centre, I went to the rue
Bonaparte to alert a family. I rang, I delivered my message: "I'm
from the Orsay centre. Your son will return, he's in good health,
we've seen one of his friends." [I'd hurried up] the stairs, I was
out of breath. Holding the door open with one hand, the lady
heard me out. "We knew that," she said. "We had a letter from
him five days ago. Thank you anyway." She invited me in. No.
I went slowly downstairs. D. was right there waiting for me at
home. "Well?" "They knew, he'd written. So, they can write." D.

didn't answer. That was the day before yesterday. Two days ago. In a way, every day I wait less. Here's my street. The dairy shop is packed. There's no point in going there. Every time I see my building, every time, I tell myself, "Maybe a letter came while I was out." If one had, my concierge would be waiting for me in front of the door. Her lodge is dark. I knock anyway: "Who is it?" "Me." "There's nothing, Madame Antelme." She opens her door each time. This evening, she has a favour to ask. "Listen, Madame Antelme? I wanted to tell you: you should go see Madame Bordes, she's in a bad way over her sons, won't leave her bed any more." Am I going to go there now? No. "I'll go tomorrow morning. Tell her there's no reason for her to worry herself sick. Today it was Stalag VII-A that came back. It's too early for III-A." Madame Fossé puts on her cape: "I'll go. Pitiful, she is; nothing for it – won't leave her bed any more. Doesn't read the papers. Can't make head or tail of 'em." I go upstairs. Madame Bordes is an old woman, the school concierge, a widow who raised six children. I'll go tomorrow morning. This whole business has hit Madame Fossé hard. I used to go to see her occasionally, the last time was only three weeks ago. "Sit yourself down, Madame Antelme." I don't go there any more. Whenever I see her, though, I'm tempted – just a little – to stop off. "No need to say it, I know what it's like." When I tell her, "I have no-one to be there for," she replies, "How well I know, Madame Antelme." Madame Fossé had her first husband taken a prisoner of war in 1914–18. He died a prisoner. "That day I just set out blindly with my two brats, wanted to kill myself and them too. Walked like that with them all night, and then the feeling passed. Told myself I shouldn't. I went back to the factory." She has told me that story ten times but since Robert's arrest, tactfully, she hasn't mentioned it. I go home. I'm not expecting anything. I'm cold. I go to wash my hands. The water is frigid. I go to sit once more on the sofa, near the phone. I'm cold. I hear the street bustling down below. It's the end of the war. I don't know if I'm tired. I believe I am. For some time now, I haven't truly slept. I wake up, and then I know I've been asleep. In a ditch for two weeks now, day and night. He said my name. I should do something. I stand up and go to the window, lean my forehead against the glass. Night falls. Below, the Saint-Bênoit is lit up. The Saint-Bênoit, literary café. The world eats, and always will. They have a secret menu for those who can {afford it}. "Madame Bordes – won't leave her bed any more." Madame Bordes doesn't eat anymore. 350,000 men and women are waiting, and bread makes them feel like vomiting. Two weeks in that ditch. It isn't normal to wait like this. Women waiting behind closed doors for their lovers: "If he's not here by eleven, it's because he has betrayed me ..." Mothers waiting for the child due home from school who is two hours late: "He must have been run over" – and they clutch their bellies because the thought gives them shooting pains. But in the next few hours, these women will know. Madame Bordes has been waiting for almost three weeks now. If her sons don't return, she'll never know anything. I'll never know anything. I know that he was hungry for months and died without having eaten, that he didn't have a morsel of bread to ease his hunger before dying. Not even once. The last cravings of the dying.

Since 7 April we've had a choice. Perhaps he's among the two thousand shot dead in Belsen the day before the Americans arrived. At Mittel Glattbach they found fifteen hundred in a charnel house, "rotting in the sunshine". Everywhere, huge columns on all the roads, where they drop like flies. Today: "The 20,000 survivors of Buchenwald salute the 51,000 dead of Buchenwald" (*Libres*, 24 April, 1945). We have a choice. It's no ordinary wait. *They've* been waiting for months. Hunger ate into their hope. Their hope had become a fantasy. Shot the day before the Allies arrived. Hope had kept them alive, but it was useless: machine-gun fire on the very eve of their liberation. An hour later, the Allies arrived to find their bodies still warm. Why? The Germans shot them, and then left. The Germans are in their own country, you can't reach out to stay their hands and say, "Don't shoot them, it's not worth it …" Time is different for them: they're losing the war, fleeing. What can they do at the last moment? Bursts of machine-gun fire, the way you break dishes in a tantrum. I'm no longer angry at them, you can't call it that any more. For a while I was able to feel anger towards them; now I cannot tell the difference between my love for him and my hatred for them.

It's a single image with two sides: on the one, him facing the German, a [bullet hole] in his chest, twelve months' hope drowning in his eyes at this very moment, in a moment; on the other, the eyes of the German aiming at him. That's the image – two sides between which I must choose: him crumpling into the ditch; the German swinging the machine gun back onto his shoulder and walking off. I don't know whether I should concentrate on taking him in my arms and let the German run away (for ever), saving his skin, or whether I should grab the German and with my fingers dig out those eyes that never looked into his – thus abandoning {Robert} to his ditch. Everything, every image, matches {that conundrum}. I have only one head, I can't think of everything any more. For three weeks, I've been thinking {the Germans} should be kept from killing them. No-one has dealt with that. We could have sent teams of parachutists to "secure" the camps for the twenty-four hours before the Allies' arrival. Jacques Auvray began trying to arrange that in August 1944. It wasn't possible, because Frenay didn't want any such initiative to come from a Resistance movement. Yet he, the Minister for Prisoners of War and Deportees, had no way of doing it himself. It wasn't possible. That's what interests me, in the end. I don't understand why; I can't think of everything. It wasn't done, that's all. They'll be shot down to the last concentration camp. There's no way to prevent it. Sometimes, behind the German, I see Frenay, but it doesn't last.

*

I'm tired. The only thing that does me good is leaning my head against the gas cooker, or the windowpane. I cannot carry my head around any more. My arms and legs are heavy but not as heavy as my head. It's no longer a head, it's an abscess. The cool windowpane. D. will be here in an hour. I close my eyes. If he did come back we'd go to the seaside. That's what he'd like best. I think I'm going to die anyway. If he comes back I'll still die. If he rang the bell: "Who is it?" "Me, Robert." All I could do would be open the door and then die. If he comes back we'll go to the beach. It will be summer, the height of summer. Between the moment when I'll open the door and the one when we're at the beach, I'll have died. Surviving somehow, I see a green ocean, a pale orange beach; inside my head I feel the salt air; I don't know where he is while I'm looking at the sea but he's alive. Somewhere on this earth he is breathing; I can stretch out on the beach and relax. When he returns we'll go to the shore. That's what he'll like the best. He loves the sea. Plus it will do him good. He'll be standing on the beach looking at the sea, and it will be enough for me to look at him looking at the sea. I'm not asking anything for myself. As long as he's looking at the sea, so am I. My head against the windowpane. My cheeks become wet. I might well be crying. Out of the six hundred thousand, here's one who's crying. That's him by the sea. In Germany the nights were cold. There on the beach he'll be in shirtsleeves and he'll talk with D. I'll watch them from a distance. Absorbed in their conversation, they won't be thinking of me. Anyway, I'll be dead. Killed by his return. Impossible for it to be otherwise. That's my secret. D. doesn't know this. One way or another I will die, whether he returns or not. My health isn't good. Many times in my life I've had to wait as I'm waiting for him. But him – I've chosen to wait for him. That's my business.

I return to the couch, I lie down. D. will arrive. He rings the doorbell. "Nothing?" "Nothing." He sits down next to the sofa. I say, "I don't think there's much hope left." D. looks exasperated, he doesn't reply. I continue: "Tomorrow is 22 April. Twenty per cent of the camps have been freed. I've seen Sorel at the centre, he told me that about one in five hundred will come back." I know that D. no longer has the strength to answer me, but I continue. The doorbell rings. D. looks at me: "I'll get it." I stay on the sofa. I hear the door opening. It's Robert's brother-in-law. "Well?" "Nothing." He sits down, he tries to smile, he looks at me, then he looks at D. "Nothing ...?" "Nothing." He nods, reflects, then says, "If you ask me, it's a question of communication. They can't write."

D.: "Marguerite is crazy. Practically speaking – let's be practical – Robert isn't in Besançon, right? There's no normal postal service in Germany, right?"

Michel: "The Americans have other things to do, unfortunately."

Me: "Well, we've definitely had news from people who were in Buchenwald. There's a chance he was in the 17 August convoy that reached Buchenwald."

D.: "And what tells you he stayed there?"

Me: "If he left on a transport, there's not much hope."

Michel: "No-one's told you that he left at the last minute; he might have been transferred elsewhere earlier in the year."

D.: "If Marguerite keeps this up, when Robert comes back ..."

I'm tired. I'd like M. and D. to go. I lie down. I hear them talking, then after a while, the conversation flags, with some long pauses. I couldn't care less what they're talking about. Whatever happens will happen. I'm tired ... Suddenly D. grips my shoulder: "What's the matter with you?" "I don't know." Michel is standing next to him: "Why are you sleeping like that?" "I'm tired, I'd like you to go." They continue talking. I go back to sleep. Then D. again. "What is it?" I ask where M. is. He's gone. D. fetches a thermometer. I've got a slight fever. "It's fatigue, I wore myself out at the centre."

NOTES

1. During the Battle of Normandy, in Operation Cobra, the Americans ended several weeks of stalemate by breaking through the German defences on the western flank of the Normandy beachhead. On 30 July, 1944, the Fourth Armoured Division seized the strategic prize of Avranches, and Patton's Third Army began pouring through the Avranches corridor to fan out through northwestern France.

2. On 7 March, 1945, the US Ninth Armoured Division captured the Ludendorff Bridge at Remagen and established the first Allied bridgehead across the Rhine, a watershed event in the Allies' push eastward across Germany.

3. Marguerite Duras was a journalist at *Libres* (*Free*), a newspaper in which she passed on whatever relevant information she could glean to those waiting for their loved ones to return. *Libres* was the newspaper of the MPNGD (National Movement of Prisoners of War and Deportees), a Resistance movement founded by François Mitterrand.

4. In June 1940, General de Gaulle entrusted the creation of the London-based Bureau Central de Renseignement et d'Action (Central Bureau for Intelligence and Action) to André Dewavrin, alias Colonel Passy. The BCRA operated its own missions in France and coordinated intelligence from all the Resistance networks there, providing vital information about German military operations to the Allies.

5. Henri Frenay was a conservative Catholic army officer who turned in disillusionment from the Vichy regime to become one of the first and most important leaders of the Resistance. He was a founder of the movement Combat in 1941; in 1944 De Gaulle appointed him Minister for Prisoners, Deportees, and Refugees, and Frenay served in De Gaulle 's first provisional government after the war.

6. By early 1942, Germany needed more foreign labour for its war effort. Many thousands of French workers were sent to Germany, mostly prisoners of war at first, then volunteers enticed by promises of good pay and decent food. By February 1943 the Germans had introduced the Service du Travail Obligatoire Compulsory Labour Service, an organized deportation of French

workers, with the complicity of the Vichy regime – the only European government that legally compelled its own citizens to serve the Nazi war machine. France was the second-largest contributor of unskilled labour and the largest contributor of skilled labour to the German wartime economy.

7. The United Nations Conference on International Organization, known informally as the San Francisco Conference (25 April–26 June, 1945), was attended by delegations from the nations that had signed the 1942 Declaration of the United Nations (a statement of the Allies' objectives in World War II). The conference concluded with the signing of the Charter of the United Nations.

US Secretary of State Edward Stettinius, Foreign Secretary Anthony Eden of Great Britain and French Foreign Minister Georges Bidault, an important Resistance leader, headed their respective national delegations to the conference.

Hundred-Page Notebook

Introduction

The third of the *Wartime Notebooks*, called the *Hundred-Page Notebook*, is a small exercise book of lined paper with a blue cover. Only the first thirty-two pages were filled and numbered by Marguerite Duras, probably at about the same time as the second notebook was written, somewhere around 1947. These thirty-two pages – in the second of the two "notebooks in the blue armoires at Neauphle-le-Château" mentioned in the author's preface – contain the end of what will be the central text of *The War*.

Pages 150–55 were reused in the second fragment of "Did Not Die Deported", published in the second issue of the magazine *Sorcières* in 1976. In its published form, the text contains a series of chronological references: "Saturday 26 April"; "Sunday 27"; "Tuesday 29 April".

The War (Rough Draft)

Sunday, 22 April, 1945. Dionys slept in the sitting room. I wake up. Again, no-one telephoned last night. I have to go see Madame Bordes. I make myself some strong coffee and take a corydrane tablet {a combination of aspirin and amphetamine}. My head is spinning and I feel nauseous. I'll feel better; mornings, after the coffee and the corydrane, it passes. I go into the sitting room: "It's Sunday, there's no post." D. asks me where I'm going. I'm going to see Madame Bordes. I make him some coffee, I take it to him in bed. He looks at me, giving me a sweet, sweet smile. "Thanks, Marguerite darling." I say "No." "Come on, now." I say "No." I can't bear hearing my name. After the corydrane, I perspire heavily and my temperature drops. I go downstairs. I buy the paper. Today I'm not going to the printer's. Another photo of Belsen: scrawny bodies lined up in a very long pit. The heart of Berlin, within 3 miles {of the front}. "The Russian communiqué is unusually frank." M. René Pleven announces a reorganization of the wage scale, higher farm prices. Mr Churchill says, "We haven't long to wait now." {The Russians and the Allies} may meet up today. Debû-Bridel rails against the elections that will take place without the deportees and prisoners of war. Page two of the *Front National*[1] says that a thousand deportees were burned alive in a barn on the morning of 13 April, near Magdeburg. In *Art and War*, Frédéric Noël says, "Some people imagine that war produces revolutions in the arts, while in reality wars affect other dimensions of life."

Simpson takes twenty thousand prisoners. Monty has linked up with Eisenhower. Berlin is in flames: "From his command post, Stalin must see a wondrous and terrible sight." "There have been thirty-seven alerts in the past twenty-four hours."

I arrive to see Madame Bordes. Her {youngest} son is in the front hall: "Mama won't leave her bed any more." The daughter is crying on a couch. The concierge's lodge is dirty and untidy. "We're in a fix," says the son. "She won't leave her bed any more." I enter the bedroom where Madame Bordes is lying. In a loud voice I say, "Well, Madame Bordes?" She looks at me with red eyes. "So, there it is," she says weakly. The son and daughter come into the room. The neck of her nightgown reveals how thin and wrinkled she is. Madame Bordes has had six children.

Her sleeves are rolled up, uncovering her dry, knobby elbows. She usually wears a small chignon; today her hair hangs loose. "Making herself sick," says the son. "Can't taste anything now," says Madame Bordes. "They won't be coming back." Then the tears brim over and run down her cheeks. She doesn't feel them. "There's no reason to get yourself into a state," I say. "The III-A hasn't returned yet." Madame Bordes punches the sheet with her fist. "You already told me that a week ago but Marcel, he saw some III-A at the centre." She knows two of her sons are in the III-A, but she doesn't know where the III-A is. Her young son spends his nights in the centres trying to find out. "I'm not making this up," I say. "Read the paper and you'll see ..." "The papers don't explain clearly," says Madame Bordes. I tell her it won't do her any good to make herself ill. "I can't go on," she whimpers. "Not knowing – that's the terrible thing. I can't go on."

I sit down on the edge of her bed. She's stubborn, she won't look at me any more and weeps. "That's the terrible part," says the son. "We don't know anything ..." Mewling, Madame Bordes tells me, "You say he's just not back yet but that's all there is in the streets and none of them's mine! I can't go on." I cannot think what to do. They know I work for the Tracing Service. If I handle this right, she'll be up and about for another three days – yet again. I want to go home. It is rather worrisome, though, that they haven't written yet. I'm lying: the III-A must have been liberated two days ago. "I just know I'll never see them again," says Madame Bordes. She weeps in spasms, she's done for. Out there on the roads, in the columns: "I can't go on." He stops; machine-gun fire. Here, Madame Bordes "won't leave her bed any more". Here, the closer we come to victory, the emptier Madame Bordes feels, but she'll get up. She has to get up: there's no point in her staying in bed, no point at all. I also feel like leaving her on her own, it's her business. But her young son is looking at me. I take the paper and read the list of those coming back [*illegible*]. The three of them listen. I explain. I go back to the paper. I re-explain. Madame Bordes has stopped crying; she listens open-mouthed. "You see," says the son. The daughter smiles: "She's awful ..." "It's not that," says Madame Bordes. "But when you don't know ..." I leave them, go back upstairs. Before that, I go to get some bread. A woman comes up to me. It's the dairy-shop owner. "Madame Antelme, please, have you heard anything about III-A?" "No, but I could find out." "Because my mother ... she's beginning to wonder," says Madame Gérard. "She's falling apart." I'll tell her this afternoon; yes, she can count on me. I get the bread, I go upstairs. D. is playing the piano. I sit down on the sofa. D. is oblivious.

I don't dare tell him not to play the piano. It gives me a headache. Still, it's strange: no news. The troop movements in Germany ... They've got other things to do. Thousands of men are waiting; others advance towards the Russians. Berlin is on fire. A thousand cities razed. Thousands of civilians are fleeing. Fifty men take off every minute from the airfields. Fifty passengers, fifty prisoners. Not him, not yet. Here we're busy with local elections. We're also repatriating {prisoners of war}. There had been talk of commandeering civilian cars and flats, but they didn't dare, for fear of causing offence. After all, they couldn't go that far. Still, it was the perfect occasion, the only one in centuries. De Gaulle isn't that keen on it. De Gaulle has never spoken of his political deportees save as a sideshow – his North African Front comes first. On 3 April, De Gaulle said, "The days of tears are over. The days of glory have returned." He also said, "Among all the places on earth where destiny has chosen to deliver its judgements, Paris has long been a symbol. It was so when the city of Saint Geneviève, with Attila in retreat, announced the victory of the Catalonic Fields.² It was so when Joan of Arc ... It was so when Henri IV ... It was so when the National Assembly of the Three Estates proclaimed the Declaration of the Rights of Man. It was so when the surrender of Paris in January 1871 sanctioned the triumph of Prussian Germany ... It was so again during the famous days of September 1914 ... It was so in 1940 ..." (Speech of 3 April, 1945.)

He skipped 1848 {the February Revolution that overthrew King Louis Philippe}. In 1871 {the year of the Paris Commune} he saw only one thing: the consecration of Prussian Germany. And that's what we've got in power. France is caught in a reactionary Catholic grip. That's what *reaction* is: reacting against the people's impulsive belief in their own strength. De Gaulle bleeds the people of their strength. Popular uprisings nauseate him, offend his delicate sensibility. He believes in God, in his works and pomps and vanities. It pains him not to be able to speak openly of this in his speeches. The difference between De Gaulle and Hitler, it's that De Gaulle believes in transubstantiation. He speaks straight to the heart of Catholics. Hitler believes in power from above. De Gaulle believes in the Power Above. And that's what we've got in power. No difference, except in the nature of the founding myth. Beyond the Rhine, Aryanism. Here, the Good Lord. Fortunately, he didn't declare himself: "After Saint Geneviève, after Joan of Arc, myself, Saint de Gaulle." All he knew how to do was to send the people to be butchered. "The days of tears are over. The days of glory have returned ..." He doesn't dare talk about the concentration camps and clearly recoils from mingling the people's tears with victory for fear of diminishing it, of weakening its meaning. He is the one who demands that local elections be held now. He is a regular army officer.

At this moment the people are paying. He doesn't notice. The people are made for paying. Berlin is burning. The German people are paying. That's normal. The people, a generality. The thousands of Frenchmen rotting in the sunshine: a generality. Discrimination takes place on high, not down below. Throughout history, the people have been the ones who have paid. De Gaulle refuses to remind them of this. Glorifying the people's suffering is dangerous and risks reassuring and emboldening them (see 1871). Later he will say, "The dictatorship of popular sovereignty entails risks that must be tempered by the responsibility of one man." He loathes blood, it offends his temperament. Catholics cannot bear blood. De Gaulle is a Catholic general, meaning that his role is to spill blood but under orders. Popular uprisings make him puke. Speaking about the word *revolution*, another damn idiot, the Reverend Father Panici, ventured to remark several days ago in Notre-Dame: "Popular uprising, general strike, barricades etc. All that would make a lovely film ... But is that more spectacle than revolution? Is there any real, profound, lasting change there? Look at 1789, 1830, 1848.[3] After a period of violence and some political upheaval ... the people grow weary: they have to go back to work and earn a living ..." {One must} discourage the people. He also said, "When it's a question of hierarchy, the Church does not hesitate: it approves." De Gaulle has declared a day of national mourning for the death of Roosevelt. No national mourning for the five hundred thousand deportees shot and starved to death. We must treat America with tact and consideration. Roosevelt, he's not some generality, he's an officer, a leader. There's a protocol among leaders. Day of national mourning: France in mourning for Roosevelt. We don't go into mourning for the people.

I can't go on. I tell myself: something's got to happen – it's just not possible ... I should describe this waiting by talking about myself in the third person. Compared to this waiting, I no longer exist. There are more images going through my head than there are along the roads of Germany. Every minute, bursts of machine-gun fire inside my head. But I'm still here, they're not fatal. Shot down along the way, shot, shot. Dead with an empty belly. Hunger, Hunger wheeling in his head like a vulture. Impossible to give him anything. I can hold bread out into the empty air. I don't even know any more if he needs bread. If he's dead – useless. I bought some honey, sugar, rice, pasta. I tell myself, if he's dead, I'll burn it all; no-one else ... But nothing can diminish the way his hunger burns me. People die of cancer, a car accident. Of hunger as well: you're dying of hunger – and they finish you off. What hunger has done is capped off with a bullet through the heart. I'd like to be able to give him my life and I'm unable to give him a piece of bread. I can't go on – this isn't what anyone would call thinking. Everything is in a state of suspended animation. Madame Bordes isn't thinking any more. Madame Bordes is me. We're interchangeable. "Every absurdity," D. tells me, "every bit of goddamned nonsense – you'll have spouted them all ..." Along with Madame Bordes. There are currently people who do think. "We must think over what's happening." D. tells me, "You should try to read ... One should be able to read no matter what happens." I tried to read. I don't understand a thing any more. Words no longer form a logical chain. Sometimes I suspect that they do but in a different experience of time. Sometimes, quite simply, I believe that they don't, that they never did. A different chain (my chain, I'm in chains) holds me fast: maybe he's been dead for a fortnight, already crawling with vermin in that ditch; dead without having tasted a morsel of bread, with a bullet – in the back of the neck? Through the heart? A shot right in the eye? His mouth pale against the German earth … and I'm still waiting because nothing is certain, he might yet be alive, might die from one moment to the next, from moment to moment possibility comes and goes – he might be in the column, advancing step by step, head bowed, so tired that perhaps he doesn't take that next step, he stops … Was that a fortnight ago? Six months? A little while ago? A second ago? The second after? There's no room in me for the first line of the best book in the world. The most beautiful book is useless, it lags far behind; me, I'm at the front lines of waiting. Madame Bordes is at the front lines of a battle without weapons, bloodshed or glory. Behind Madame Bordes civilization lies in ashes: thought, enlightenment, reason. The wisdom of centuries, gathered from every corner of the world, would not explode in a heartbeat the way her heart explodes with every beat. Madame Bordes disdains all hypotheses, all consolation; what she wants to know is whether the men of III-A have returned. Sometimes her heart and head are invaded by upheavals, analyses, syntheses, wrenching turmoil, bright hopes, crushed expectations, precipices around which thought wanders shivering and dazed, unable to make sense of anything. "Every possible absurdity – you'll have spouted it all." That's our business. This is our business, and ours alone: you who judge us, just go along home. If I were told, "You'll be fucked by ninety soldiers and he'll receive a piece of bread," I'd ask to be fucked by a hundred and eighty soldiers so he'd get two pieces of bread. If someone told Madame Bordes, the school concierge, "Scream 'Long live Hitler' in the middle of the street at one in the morning and {your sons} will get a piece of bread," Madame Bordes would ask to do it every night. To us, these aren't idiotic suppositions, and we're ready to believe that, too. Calculations like those – I make them three hundred times a day. A finger for a piece of bread; two fingers for two pieces. Ten years of my life to give him two more. Anything is always possible since we know nothing. Alive or dead? Not only {is anything possible} at every second of the day, but at every second of the day, *that question* arises, and we have no idea how to answer it.

Still on the sofa by the telephone. It's Sunday. Today Berlin will fall. It's really the end. The papers are saying how we'll know: the sirens will sound one last time. The last time of the war. People are saying, I'm going to get roaring drunk, or, I'll dance a jig, or, I'll stay out all night, but most of all they say, I'm going to get plastered, and how. I don't go to the centre anymore, I'll never go again. They're arriving at the Lutétia. They're arriving at the Gare de l'Est. The Gare du Nord. It's over. Not only am I never going back to the centre, I'm not budging at all. I think so, but I thought so yesterday, too, then at ten in the evening I went out and took the metro to D.'s place. D. opened the door and wrapped his arms around me. "Anything new since a little while ago?" "Nothing, I can't stand it." I left, I didn't even want to go in. I'd wanted to see D.'s face, make sure nothing strange was apparent there, no fresh worry since that morning. So I left. I'd gone to see him because at half past ten that evening, I'd been stricken with fear. Suddenly. Fear. "But don't you see that he'll never come back?" More than that. Ice in the heart. I found myself downstairs, driven outdoors. Once outside, I told myself, "I've got time to get there and back before the last metro." Panic. Flight: that's what it is. Sweating all over. Something new in this waiting. I'd looked up abruptly and the flat had changed completely – even the lamplight wasn't the same. Something was threatening. On all sides. Abruptly, I was sure, sure, sure. He's dead. Dead. Dead. Dead. Today's the twenty-seventh of April today's the twenty-seventh of April to-day's the twenty-seventh of April. Dead Dead Dead. The silence. The silence. Silence. New, there's something new. I stood up and went to the middle of the room. It happened in an instant. What's happening to me? Black night at the windows is watching me.

I draw the curtains. It's still watching me. What's happening to me ... The signs – the room is full of black and white signs, black and white. No more throbbing temples. It's not that anymore. I feel my face change, change, fall slowly apart. No-one is there. I'm going to pieces, coming undone, changing. I'm frightened. Shivers down my spine. Where am I? Where? Where is she? What's happening to her? My head has stopped pounding. I don't feel my heart any more. The horror rises slowly, like the sea. I'm drowning. A small part of me is left, a wafer: my head. I'm not waiting any more. I'm afraid. It's over. Where are you? How can I find out? I don't know where he is. I'm with him. Where? With him. Where with him? I don't know, with him. Where? I don't know any more. What's this place called? What *is* this place? In fact, just what is this whole business? What business? What's it about? Robert Antelme – who's he? You're waiting for a dead man, yes, of course you are, a dead man. No more pain. I am just about to understand: you and that man have nothing in common. He's dead, I mean, it's so obvious ... Might as well wait for someone else. You don't exist any more. Once you no longer exist, why wait for Robert Antelme? Another would do just as well, anyone at all if you'd like. Nothing left in common between you and that man. Who is Robert Antelme? Has he ever existed? What makes him Robert and not someone else? In fact, talk about that a little. What are you waiting for like that? What makes you wait for him and no-one else? Why the hell have you been beating your own brains out for a fortnight? Who are you? What's going on in this room? Who *I* am? D. knows who I am. Where's D.? I can see him and ask him to explain ... I must see him. Because now there's something new.

Tuesday, 24 April. The phone's ringing. It's dark. I turn on the light, check the alarm clock. Half past five. I hear: "Hello? What?" It's D., sleeping in the next room, who answers. This is it. This is it. I hear: "What? What are you saying? Yes, this is the place, Robert Antelme, yes." A pause. I'm next to Dionys, who's holding the phone. I try to grab the receiver. D. tries to hang on to it. There's more ... "What news?" Silence. I try to wrestle the phone away. This is hard, impossible. "And, so? Some friends?" D. turns from the receiver to me: "It's friends of Robert's who've arrived at the Gaumont centre." I say, "It's not true." Then: "And Robert?" D. listens to the receiver. I try to snatch the phone away. D. says nothing, he listens, he's got the phone. We're fighting over the receiver. "You don't know anything more?" He turns to me: "They left him two days ago." I've stopped trying to get the receiver. I'm on the floor by the phone. Something has given way. He was alive two days ago. I give in to it. It's bursting, coming out my mouth, nose, eyes. It has to come out. D. has put the phone down. "Marguerite, Marguerite darling." She doesn't answer. She's busy. Leave her alone. It's coming out everywhere as water. "Alive, alive." Someone replies: "Marguerite, my dear, my dear." Two days ago, as alive as you and me, oh yes. "It isn't possible, ..." Someone replies: "Marguerite darling, my dear." "Leave me alone, leave me alone." It comes out in whimpers, too, it comes out any way it likes. It's coming out. She lets it happen. "Oh, he's so incredible! I knew it ..." D. picks me up and says, "Alright, let's go there. They're at the Gaumont, they're waiting for us. Let's make ourselves some coffee." D. said, let's make ourselves some coffee, but it was so that I'll have some coffee. D. under the electric ceiling light in the kitchen, laughing. D.'s extraordinary laughter. He keeps saying, "Ha! You thought they'd get him! But he's sharp, Robert ... Probably hid at the last moment ... Us thinking he couldn't take care of himself because he seemed so ..." D. is in the bathroom, washing. He says, "Because he seemed so ..." She's leaning against the kitchen-cupboard door. Seemed so ... he doesn't seem like everyone else, it's true. He's so absentminded. He's a funny one, really. He always seems so up in the clouds but he must have been way ahead of them ... You can't let that fool you. She's still leaning against the kitchen cupboard. D. from the bathroom: "You're getting the coffee ready?" "Yes." She puts the water over the gas flame. She grinds the coffee. D. repeats: "We have to move fast. He'll be getting here in two days."

D. comes in. The coffee's ready. The taste of hot coffee: he's alive. I dress quickly. I've taken a corydrane tablet. Still some fever, I'm dripping with perspiration. I'll have to deal with that. The streets are empty. D. walks quickly. We get to the Gaumont Cinema, now a transit centre. They'd told us to ask for Hélène D. We ask for her. She comes over. She laughs. I laugh. But I'm cold. Where are they? At the hotel. She takes us there.

The hotel is old. All lit up, bustling with assistants in white and {deportees in} stripes. "They've been arriving all night long," we're told. Here's the room. The woman leaves. I tell D.: "Knock." My heart is pounding so, I won't be able to go in. Just when D. is about to knock, I ask him to wait a moment. Then he knocks. Inside the room are two people at the foot of a bed. A man and a woman. The woman's eyes are red. They're both looking at the bed. They don't say anything. They're relatives. Two "zebras" are in the bed: one's asleep, he's about twenty; the other smiles at me. I ask: "You're Perrotti?" "That's me." "I'm Antelme's wife." He's quite pale. "Well?" "We left him two days ago." "How was he?" Perrotti looks at D. "In better shape than lots of others." The young man has awakened: "Antelme? Oh, yes. We were going to escape with him." I've sat down near the bed. They don't seem in any hurry to talk. I say, "They were shooting people?" The two zebras look at each other, don't answer right away. "Well, they'd stopped shooting." D. speaks up: "You're sure?" Perrotti says: "The day we left, they hadn't shot anyone for two days." The {two deportees} talk to each other: the young man asks, "How do you know?" "The Russian kapo told me." Me: "What did he tell you?" "He told me by the by that they'd been ordered to stop shooting." The young guy: "It depended on the day – there were days they shot people, others they didn't." Perrotti looks at him, at me, at D., and smiles: "Please forgive us, we're really tired." D. is staring at Perrotti: "How come Robert isn't with you?" "We looked for him so we could escape together when the train left, but we couldn't find him." "We looked hard, though," says the young guy. "How come you didn't find him?" asks D. "It was dark," says Perrotti. "And then there were still a lot of us in spite of ..." I see: the train, the station in the middle of the night. They didn't find him because he'd been shot: "You looked carefully for him?" "Well, that is ..." They look at each other. "Oh, yes!" says the young guy. "I mean, we even called his name, although it was dangerous." "He's a good comrade," says Perrotti. "We looked for him. He used to give talks about France ..." The young guy: "Should've been there, he could really mesmerize an audience." Me: "If you didn't find him it's because he wasn't there any more, because he'd been shot." D. goes over to the bed, gesturing brusquely, almost as pale as Perrotti: "When did you last see him?" They look at each other. I hear the woman's voice: "They're tired ..." We're interrogating them as if they were criminals, not letting up for a moment. "Anyway, me, I saw him," says the young guy. "I'm sure of it." He stares vacantly and repeats, "I'm sure of it." But he isn't sure about anything. I hear D.: "Try to remember when you saw him last." Perrotti: "I saw him in the column, you remember, on the right: it was still daylight, an hour before we reached the station." The young guy: "Were we ever exhausted! Me, in any case, I saw him after {his} escape, I'm sure about that at least, since we'd agreed to leave at the station ..." Me: "What? His escape?" Perrotti: "Yes. He tried to escape but they caught him ..." I repeat, "What? Didn't they shoot people who ran away? You're not telling the truth." Perrotti seems to lose heart. "I mean, we've told you he'll come back, we saw him ..." D. breaks in, tells me: "Be quiet." Then he takes over: "When did he escape?" They look at each other: "Was it the day before?" "I think so," says the young guy. Me: "How did they shoot the people?" "Be quiet," says D. Then: "Make an effort, we're very sorry, but try to remember ..."

Perrotti smiles: "I understand, sure. We're tired ..." Silence for a minute. Then, the young guy: "I'm certain I saw him in the column after he tried to escape ... Now I'm certain of it." Perrotti: "When?" "With Girard on the right, I'm sure of it." I repeat: "How did you know when they were shooting people?" Perrotti: "Don't worry, we'd have found out – the SS did their shooting at the rear {of the column}, then pals would pass the news along, we always knew who ..." D.: "What we'd like to figure out is why you didn't find him." "It was dark," says Perrotti. "Maybe he'd escaped," says the young guy. "In any case, you did see him after his escape." "Definitely," says Perrotti. "Absolutely," says the young guy. "What did they do to him?" "Well, he got beaten ... Philippe'll tell you better than I can, he was his pal." Me: "How come they didn't shoot him?" "The Americans were so close, they hadn't time any more." "Plus it depended," says the young guy. "Where did they go?" "We don't know. But they wouldn't have had to go far ..." "Oh, no!" says the young guy. "The Americans were all around." Me: "Was it before or after his escape that you agreed to escape together at the station?" Silence. They look at each other. D.: "If you talked to him afterwards, it's very important, you understand. That's a little more proof ..." They don't know any more. They no longer recall. They try their best: "Don't remember." We leave. "I'm completely reassured," says D. I say, "I'm very worried." D. insists that Robert will arrive. "If he's not here in three days ..."

Another period of waiting begins.

24 April, half past eleven {in the morning}. Another telephone call: "It's François.[4] Philippe's back; he saw Robert ten days ago. Philippe escaped. Robert was alright." I explain: "I saw Perrotti. It seems Robert escaped and was recaptured. What does Philippe know?" François: "That's true, he did try to escape, he was caught by some children ..." Me: "When did he last see him?" Silence. "They escaped together. He was by the side of the road ... He was

beaten. Philippe was far enough away, the Germans didn't see him. He waited. He didn't hear any shots." Silence. "He's sure?" "He's sure." "That's not much. He didn't see him after that?" Silence. "No, because he'd escaped." Me: "That was when?" (I know François has figured all this out.) "It was the thirteenth." Me: "What should I think?" François: "No question, he'll be back." "Were they shooting people in the column?" A pause. "It depended ... Come to the printer's." "No. I'm tired. What does Philippe think?" Silence. "There's no doubt, he should be here within forty-eight hours." Me: "How is he?" "Exhausted. He says that Robert was still hanging on and in better shape than he was." "Does he have any idea where the train was going?" "No, no idea." "You're not just trying to keep my spirits up?" "No – come to the printer's." "No, I'm not coming. And if he doesn't arrive in forty-eight hours?" "What do you want me to tell you?" "Why in forty-eight hours?" "Because by this time, they've been liberated. According to Philippe they were liberated between the fourteenth and the twenty-fifth, definitely. That's the only possible timetable."

Perrotti escaped on the twelfth. He came back on the twenty-fourth. Philippe escaped on the thirteenth. He came back on the twenty-fourth. So it takes eleven to twelve days. Robert should be here the day after tomorrow. Perhaps tomorrow.

Wednesday 25
Thursday 26
Friday 27
Saturday 28
Sunday 29
Monday 30
Tuesday 1

Wednesday 2
Thursday 3

Wednesday 25. Nothing.

Thursday 26. Nothing. D. called the doctor. I have a temperature, it isn't serious. The flu, says the doctor. He gave me a sedative. Madame Cats and D. are sitting beside me. It's dark out. Ten in the evening. Riby phoned. I didn't know him. He asked for Robert. He was in the column, he escaped after Perrotti and got back before him.

Friday 27. Nothing during the night. D. brings me *Combat*.[5] The first session of the San Francisco conference: "Molotov impassible, Bidault concerned, Eden a dreamer ... Much was said there about justice, to the great satisfaction of the lesser powers." At the last minute, the Russians have captured a metro station {in Berlin}. Stettin and Brno have fallen.

The Americans are on the Danube. I tell D.: "All Germany is in their hands." D. is cautious. "In theory, but practically speaking, it's difficult to occupy a country." "What can {the Germans} do with {their prisoners}? What did they do with them at the last minute?" I figure that those who've come back from the column are those who escaped. And the others? I don't dare ask D. anymore. We fight almost every day. D. gets angry. I'm harassing him. Sometimes he tries to "change the subject". That's not possible. He says: "Still, what [days] these are ..." "Yes," I say. When Madame Cats is there, I don't dare say much; she's had no news of her daughter. She tells me: "They'll come back, my dear." I say: "Yes." She stops me smoking, so I smoke at night. She's adamant about my not smoking. It's funny. I go along with her. "The doctor said so." She's insistent, it's not normal, she's incredibly tenacious. Sometimes she says, "I can feel myself becoming horrible, pay no attention." She's sixty, she's still quite strong but she has a bad heart. She makes me remain lying down and heats up some

American milk for me. Occasionally, after she's gone, I tell D.: "Madame Cats is awful."

D. explains to me that it's the only thing that does her some good. If I were truly ill, I believe Madame Cats wouldn't think so much about her daughter. It's extraordinary. She arrives at nine in the morning and leaves in the evening. All day she stays by me while I'm lying down, and she won't let me smoke. It's been like that for three days. Sometimes she says, "I'm an old woman, it's not important to me. You're the one who should be receiving news." While she's heating the American milk, she shouts from the kitchen, "If you smoke, I'll know it from the smell!" When D. is there, that's when he smokes and he gives me a puff. This morning she noticed; D. tried to joke about it but I thought she was going to cry. When we're alone in the afternoons we don't say anything to each other. Sometimes she puts her thumb and index finger up to her eyes and presses on them; that's when things have become too much for her. The rest of the time she tries to smile. She tells me: "Don't think, try to sleep." And sometimes she forgets all about me. Her eyes glaze over from staring outside; she nods, and speaks: "I'll never see her again, never see her again." Then she shakes her head for a long time. Her daughter was a cripple, she had a gammy leg. "I know they killed cripples. How could she have walked, poor thing ..." (Madame Cats waited six months, from April to November. In November she learned that her daughter had been dead since March.) I don't talk about Robert with her. It's not worthwhile; all she does is to say, "I'm sure they'll come back." And then she says, "I'm sure I'll never see her again." It's not worth asking her anything at all. The days are long. Towards five o'clock there's some sunlight in the sitting room. Towards five o'clock. Sometimes a phone call. Madame Cats takes it. She says, "No, nothing yet." Then: "She's resting." Then she puts the phone down. She has given instructions at her place to phone her here, and she left a letter addressed to her daughter with the concierge of the building where the daughter

lived, because "she would go directly home – she doesn't know
that I'm in France" (Madame Cats is Belgian). She has also left
a letter with her own concierge, because "if she were to arrive,
she would need to know where to find me." That letter says, "I
am at the home of Marguerite Antelme, the telephone number
is ..." She has also left letters at the train stations, the transit
centres, at the homes of her cousins and her sister, because
"you never know: instead of going home, she might go straight
there." She has bought 5o tins of American milk, 20 pounds of
sugar, 20 pounds of jam, some calcium, phosphates, alcohol, eau
de cologne, rice, potatoes, a rubber doughnut cushion and draw
sheets. She says, "All her underwear is washed, mended, ironed,"
and also, "I had her black suit lined and I fixed her coat pockets,"
and, "I'd put everything in a big trunk with mothballs, and the
day before yesterday I aired everything, it's all ready," and, "I've
had new taps put on her shoes and darned her stockings," and, "I
don't think I've forgotten anything, it's all ready – except that I'll
need to buy more sugar: they need lots of sugar for the heart, yes,
they all have weak hearts." And also, "I won't see her again. With
her gammy leg, they'll have gassed her."

When the conversation turns to the Germans, Madame Cats
says, "I wish every last one of them were gone, even the children;
I'd kill them myself if I could." I saw Madame Cats about a fortnight ago and she hadn't changed her mind. "If one showed up
at my office in Brussels," she told me, "I'd throw my paperweight
in his face. I'm still strong – I'm sure I'd kill him." Madame Cats
says these things calmly; I believe she could do what she says.
She's good and bad, uncompromising. She says to me, "How
much sugar do you have?" I say, "I have no sugar, I've got time."
"That's not wise, Marguerite: at the last minute you won't be able
to find any." Then she returns to her thoughts. So do I. Perrotti,
Philippe, Riby. He should have arrived today, though. He was
beaten. Philippe didn't hear a shot. If he waited, it's because they
usually shot them. Perhaps they shot him a bit farther off, and

Philippe wouldn't have heard. Philippe is the last person to have seen him. Perrotti looked for him at the train: he says he saw him but that's not certain, he didn't seem so sure about it. Whereas Philippe is sure he saw him because they'd arranged to escape together. But Perrotti didn't see him. He looked for him at the station; he didn't find him. Yet he, too, is sure that he wasn't shot. I have to wait. I reconstruct – but there's a hole: between the moment when Philippe *didn't* hear a gunshot and the train station, what happened to him? I must be reasonable and try to understand. A black hole. I do my best; no light dawns.

27 April. I get up. Madame Cats has left. No-one telephoned last night. He was still alive on the fourteenth, maybe the fifteenth. I dress, I stay close to the phone. D. insists that I go out to eat at the restaurant with him. Maybe he's at a transit centre waiting to leave. The restaurant is full. But in that case, why doesn't he write? People are talking about the end of the war, about Berlin, teasing one another about the sirens. "What if the last German planes bomb Paris?" I'm not hungry. He's back in that ditch. I'm not hungry. "They will never pay sufficiently for this," people are saying about the German atrocities. Well, I've had enough. I want to die. No, I'm not hungry. Since he's dead, I want to die. The people talk, talk and eat. It's not their fault: "I know one of them who came back from Belsen. Horrible!" "I know one who ..." Cut off from the world, even from D. If I don't get a letter this evening or a phone call this afternoon, then he's dead. D. looks at me. He can look at me all he wants. He's dead. I could tell D. a million times, he wouldn't believe me, but *I know*. I also feel a bit sorry for D. Everybody's reading the papers. The Red Army in the heart of Berlin, Stettin taken, Brno taken. *Pravda* writes: the bell has tolled for Germany. The ring of fire and steel tightens around Berlin. It's over. He won't be here for the peace. If he's not here for the peace, what will I do? What can I do? I'm not hungry. The Italian partisans have captured Mussolini at Faenza. All northern Italy is in their hands. Mussolini has been caught; that's all they

know. The earth turns, the papers turn, the German people are crushed to a pulp. Germany is pulp. So is he. {The Communist daily} *L'Humanité* says that Pétain is returning in a sleeper, while the deportees are returning in cattle trucks. *Le Monde* is talking about the future and the "Gaullist order". The future. A future will emerge from this adventure. Thorez⁶ is also talking about the future, saying that we'll have to work, that the refusal of sacrifice is more costly than combat, and that a wait-and-see policy is a deadly poison. Yes. *Le Monde* says we're lucky that France didn't collapse into anarchy in September 1944, when {Paris was liberated and there for the taking, and} there was an obvious temptation to go for broke. It says that "reforms should be well thought out," and that only De Gaulle ... It's true, we'll be voting. Thorez speaks of the sovereignty of the people; *Le Monde*, of order. Nothing about the people. When he comes back, I'll explain to him what *Le Monde* is, what it represents for us at this point, what it means to us – this future envisioned by *Le Monde*. He'll need to know this. He won't puzzle it out on his own. As soon as he's back, we'll set it out for him, this temporizing role of *Le Monde*: three-franc paper, mouthpiece of the governmental "soul", the {conservative} *Le Temps* reborn, the moment has come to restore order – resurfacing intact after six years of silence, with three times as much paper as *L'Humanité* at its disposal BECAUSE *L'Humanité* made the mistake of selling clandestinely at the cost of the people's blood. If he comes back, we'll tell him. What a joy. To tell him that and everything else. I've saved all the papers for him. If he returns I'll eat with him. Before, no. No. The moment has come to settle up. Everyone's paying. I'm paying. I won't eat. In Germany, the mother of the little sixteen-year-old German who lay dying on 17 August, 1944, alone on a pile of stones on the Quai des Arts, is paying as well. He must have been dumped in the river. We're paying for a "criminal" waiting game. Our dark past. Our sad childhood. Our threatened future. De Gaulle is in power. Perhaps he saved our honour; people believed that for four years. Now

that he's out in the daylight, there's something frightening about
him. He begrudges the people any praise. The people are being
stifled. He talks about the French as if he were Louis XVI, and
the Gaullists have now revealed their true colours. What's terrible
is that in April 1945 there are so many differences between me and
the person next to me at the table. Unanimity doesn't exist. A few
hundred thousand French lie rotting on German soil, but they
don't rally anyone, they haven't tipped the Gaullist balance one
inch. The elections will take place anyway, says De Gaulle, because I said so, because nothing can interfere with order: "For as
long as I'm here, the firm will soldier on." De Gaulle will never
get over the fact that after these six years of war, France still leans
towards socialism. He's paying too, like us. Not once will he speak
directly to those who are paying now; when he addresses "his"
French people, his sheep, it's always to distract them from their
pain – and this because the people's hope is rooted in their pain.
At this moment, the person next to me reading *Le Monde* isn't
waiting for anything. What a sad ending. Something broken in
hatred – in anger – in joy. "I'll get falling-down drunk." "Me, I
won't do a thing." We are the only ones waiting for something:
news. The rest of the world's phoney expectation, waiting for
peace. In France millions are waiting. Only the Americans know
what has happened to their people. The French, the Germans,
the Russians will never know. American communications are reli-
able. The American war machine moved to the continent with its
news pipelines, tanks with transmitters, and all manner of links
and channels. No American will have vanished, lost completely.
The parents of the little gypsy children in Buchenwald will never
learn if they were gassed, had their throats cut by the Official
Slaughterers of Jewish Children (in German), were burned or rotted out in the open. Millions of Soviet partisans have disappeared.
I'm waiting. No news pipeline, simply the constantly yearning
soul of this part of the world, where the dead pile up in a higgledy-
piggledy heap of bones: Russians, Czechs, Frenchmen, Germans,

Italians, Belgians, Dutchmen, Greeks. America has seen the giant crematoria smoking. The mother of the German sixteen-year-old will never, ever, know: I was the only one in the world to know and I can't help thinking of a grey-haired old woman who will wait, grieving, for the rest of her life. Perhaps someone saw {Robert} in that ditch, when his hands reached out for the last time and his eyes wept blood – someone who will never learn who he was, and whom I will never know. Only the American and British dead get identification tags; that's the advantage of going abroad. Here at home, in our old Europe, we've shown less foresight. That's where the wind of Socialism swept through, and where the cancer of Fascism took root. Europe, the [fucking nuisance] of the world. The pride of belonging to that race, a pride I can't use for anything because there isn't *anything* I can use for anything, as long as I don't know whether he's alive or dead. And yet, there's a trace of pride in Madame Cats' pain and mine. We are of the same race as the people of the crematoria, the gassed of Majdenek. The egalitarian function of the crematoria of Buchenwald, and their hunger. The proletarian truth of the mass graves of Belsen. In those graves, we have our share of blood. We've never seen men so equal, so alike as the skeletons of Belsen, so amazingly identical. America can't take credit for a single one of those skeletons: they are all European, and in the vanguard of this war. The four hundred thousand skeletons of German Communists who died in Dora between 1933 and 1938 are in the great European common grave; the extra-continental nations have no place there – only the peoples of Europe claim them. That is the sole foundation from which a European man can think. When the Americans tell us: "There isn't one American now, be he a barber in Chicago or a dirt farmer in Kentucky, who doesn't know what happened in the German concentration camps," they're trying *at the same time* to lavish consolation on us, to reassure us and to dazzle us with the admirable workings of the American war machine. What I mean by that is their reassurance of the Kentucky farmer who hadn't really known why his son had been taken away and sent to the European front.

But when you tell him that Italian partisans executed Mussolini and parked him on some meat hooks so that all Milan could have a look, the American will not feel that intense joy, that fraternal satisfaction we derive from this image. That the Italian people were capable of this gives us hope, one peculiar to us Europeans – even though it was these same Italians who bombed us during the exodus of 1940 – because we see there the beginnings of one of those characteristically European reversals.

28 April. Those waiting for peace aren't waiting, not really. I don't even think about the peace: I'd like to know where he is, to know *something*. No news since Riby. To me peace still seems like a distant pay-off I don't dare believe is near. I live from hour to hour, I last from morning to afternoon. Still nothing. The waiting is settling in. I see peace as a twilight that will fall over the dead. Then there will be no more reasons not to have news, they'll all drop away. Peace: darkest night. As well as the beginning of forgetting. Paris is lit up at night. I found myself the other day on the Place Saint-Germain-des-Prés: it was completely illuminated, as if by a spotlight. Les Deux Magots was packed. Heads swam above the cigarette smoke inside. It was still too cold to sit out on the pavement. The street was deserted. Peace seemed possible to me, and I hurried home. I glimpsed a possible future taking shape. I'm a wreck, there's no place for me anywhere, I'm nowhere else, just with him – somewhere inaccessible to those who have no-one over there. I'm left hanging in suspense over an unlikely outcome, and things affect me only as signs. The lamp post on the square is a sign. To me it has lost all other meaning. Nothing is real any more, to those of us who wait. Everyone else grows impatient, on the other hand: soldiers, civilians – they want to go home. You hear this over and over: "What are they waiting for to sign the

peace?" And every time I hear that, I know the threat is growing.

Today we learn that Hitler is dying. Himmler said so on the German radio in a last appeal, while offering to surrender unconditionally. My concierge comes upstairs and says, "Did you ever hear the like? We won't get to skin that bastard alive." "There's no justice." "It's too much, not to have his hide, it's too much." "We've been robbed." That finishes spoiling the peace, rotting the harvest on the stalk. The one most responsible among all those responsible is escaping from us. That completes as well the incredible sense of the dismemberment of Germany. Berlin is burning, defended only by the "thirty suicide battalions", and at its heart, Hitler puts a revolver bullet in his brain. Hitler is dead.

The news hasn't been confirmed. Some believe it, others don't. But uncertainty hovers. The entire world is thinking of Hitler.

"Still."

"Still – what?"

"What he must have gone through! Have you thought about the last three hours of his life ... Never since the world began has any man ever led an event of such importance to its conclusion."

"What do you imagine he was thinking of before he died?"

"Of himself, perhaps; of his life, for the first time."

"Let's be rigorously objective about this."

"No."

28–29 April. Himmler declares in his message that "Hitler is dying" and that "he will not last forty-eight hours after the announcement of unconditional surrender". That would be a mortal blow to him. The United States and Britain said they would accept the surrender only with the USSR. Himmler sent his offer of capitulation to the San Francisco Conference. At the last minute, *Combat* announces that the offer of surrender has been addressed to Russia as well. The Italians don't want to hand Mussolini over to the Allies. The press is unanimous in their opposition. The newspaper *Avanti* writes: "The Italian people were Mussolini's first victim, and he should die by their hand." {The Italian Fascist politician} Farinacci was judged by a people's tribunal and executed in a city square (unnamed) in the presence "of a considerable crowd". In San Francisco: difficult hours; Europe is in the minority there. Stettinius presides. "Witnessing the behaviour of the Great Powers, the lesser powers can hold their heads up once again" (*Combat*, 28 April). Meaning France and Italy and …

Peace has not yet been secured, and already there is talk of the "afterpeace". That's normal. *They* won't be here for it, or for the peace, either. There are so many of them, so very many, and you can't bring back the dead: there is no resurrection, just that single one in all of world history, and it's still an endless source of astonishment. Impossible: no matter what you say or do, you cannot make a German Communist who died in Dora in 1939 amid the rise of Fascism understand that he shares in this victory. Thälmann[7] did know this before he was shot. Much has been written about death. It's the chief inspiration for artistic endeavour. The face of death discovered in Germany, on the scale of eleven million human beings, confounds art. Everything comes up against this crime and struggles against this giant dimension no cross could bear. Something new has happened. Someone quoted to me a certain man of letters opining that he is very "moved", and has become melancholy, and has much "food for thought". I think of all our poets, of all the poets in the world, who are now waiting for peace so that they may sing of this crime. One problem. The people, more simply, confront this issue when it's time to eat bread, to work. For the poet who is able *not* to write, the issue becomes more difficult, a question of life and death. All thoughts, all beliefs are under attack and defend themselves. If this crime is not "understood" collectively, then humanity will not be worthy of having lived through it. A man who died in Belsen was not entombed in "the purple shroud wherein the dead gods sleep". He knew why he died: to save a justice in its birth throes, and whatever his "political position", he died to throw off a yoke of servitude. He died all alone – save for that collective soul and class consciousness with which he removed a bolt from a railroad one night, somewhere in Europe, without any uniform, any witness, any leaders. He was on his own. He had no part in the immortal glory of soldiers. There are no more soldiers. A people is breaking free of nineteen centuries of bondage. There are no more soldiers or civilians: now they are one and the same.

NOTES

1. Created in May 1941, the Communist-led Front National de l'Indépendance de la France was a vital Resistance movement whose armed wing was the Francs-Tireurs et Partisans Français. The FN itself engaged in sabotage, provided logistical support to Resistance members and published its own newspaper, *Front National*.

2. When the Huns threatened Paris in 451, Saint Geneviève rallied its citizens to save the city. Franks, Burgundians, Visigoths, Bretons and Saxons were among those who fought in the decisive battle of the Catalonic Fields (between Troyes and Châlons-sur-Marne), where the Roman emperor Valentinian III defeated Attila the Hun.

3. In 1789 the French Revolution surprised King Louis XVI; in 1830 the July Revolution overthrew King Charles X; in 1848 the February Revolution overthrew King Louis-Philippe and established the Second Republic.

4. In her biography of Marguerite Duras, Laure Adler tells the "legendary" story (with variations) of how François Mitterrand, whose nom de guerre was Morland, helped to save the life of Robert Antelme, who was on the brink of death when he finally was found in Germany by his friends.

5. Founded in 1941 by Henri Frenay and Claude Bourdet, among others, the Resistance movement Combat published a clandestine newspaper of the

same name. Georges Bidault was recruited by the great Resistance leader Jean Moulin to set up an underground press and organize this paper, on which Albert Camus served as editor in chief and editorial writer between 1944 and 1947.

6. Maurice Thorez was an important pre-war French politician, a leading Communist, and a founder – along with Blum, Daladier – and others – of the left-wing Popular Front, which was distinguished by its interest in social reform. When the Communist Party was banned by the French government after the Nazi-Soviet pact of July 1939, Thorez fled to the Soviet Union. In the summer of 1944, in recognition of the Communists' contribution to the Liberation, De Gaulle allowed Thorez to return to France, where he later became deputy prime minister (1946–7).

7. Ernst Thälmann, a founding member and leader of the German Communist Party, ran against Hitler in the presidential election of 1932. Thälmann was imprisoned in March 1933, during the Nazi pogrom against left-wing opponents of the regime after the Reichstag fire. On 18 August, 1944, he was executed in Buchenwald.

Beige Notebook

Introduction

The work of editing the *Wartime Notebooks* was most crucial by far in the preparation of this last of the four, which was probably written over a rather long period, between around 1946 and 1949. To this *Beige Notebook* – with reinforced cloth covers – belong ninety-two pages of material, a few of which are partially or entirely filled with a child's drawings. Most of the pages have come loose from their binding, and some (the number is difficult to determine) have been lost. In addition, the composition is rather discontinuous and does not respect the order of the remaining bound pages. To facilitate their reading, and rather than seeking to recreate a hypothetical order of composition, we juxtaposed fragments linked to particular themes or to the same published work. Certain fragments, quite short and difficult to decipher, were omitted.

The inspiration of the *Beige Notebook* is very largely autobiographical; at the same time, almost all of the texts it contains were later rewritten and published, most of the time as works of fiction. This notebook thus presents an unusual opportunity to observe the way in which Marguerite Duras, from the beginning of her writing career, drew on the stories of her own life as material for fiction.

Marguerite Duras excerpted several passages from the *Beige Notebook* for the {feminist} journal *Sorcières* (1976); three of these contributions are included here: "The Thin Yellow Children"

{"The children of the plain", page 178}, "The Horror of Such Love" and the first fragment of "Did Not Die Deported". Other, longer pieces would later be integrated within the novels or novellas of the early 1950s: *The Sea Wall*, *The Sailor from Gibraltar*, *Madame Dodin*. Finally, the notebook contains writings that do not appear among her published works: autobiographical texts on the return of Robert Antelme; a vacation in Italy in the summer of 1946; her pregnancy and the birth of her son Jean; political commitment; reading; writing; daily life on the rue Saint-Benoît. That Marguerite Duras reread these pages is confirmed by many marginal annotations in her handwriting made with a red felt-tip pen, notes that refer to themes or titles of her works ("Deportation"; "War"; "Sea Wall"; "Dodin"; "Sailor"; "Sorcières") or to the abandonment of the text in question ("not used").

The Sea Wall (Rough Draft)

When her children ate, she would hover in front of them and watch, following their every move; she would have liked Suzanne to grow some more and Joseph too, if possible.

"Have some of the wading bird, Suzanne. That condensed milk, that won't nourish you ..."

"Plus it rots your teeth," said Joseph. "Look at me – it rotted all my teeth, even left me with a goddamn lot of trouble."

"When we have money, you'll get yourself a bridge and no-one will notice a thing," the mother said to Joseph. "Take some of the wading bird, Suzanne dear."

The mother became very gentle with them when she wanted to make them eat.

Suzanne was coaxed into taking a piece of the waterfowl. The mother prepared a coffee for Joseph, who was adjusting his acetylene lamp. After setting it down, he lighted it and went out onto the veranda to see if the angle of the beam was correct.

"Shit," said Joseph, "he's croaked."

The mother and Suzanne went out to join Joseph. The acetylene lamp cast its beam on the embankment by the river, where the horse lay on its side. Its nostrils almost touched the grey water; it must have simply collapsed in one go.

"You should have a closer look," said the mother.

Suzanne went back inside. She couldn't bear to look at the

dead horse. She huddled in one of the rattan armchairs, tucked her legs up under her and stared at the acetylene lamp.

"Poor beast," said the mother. Then she called out, "Well?"

"He's still breathing," yelled Joseph from the yard.

"Could we do something?" said the mother. "Suzanne, go fetch the old checked blanket from the car."

Suzanne went down below the bungalow to get the blanket.

"I'm not going there!" she shouted to Joseph. "Come get it!"

Joseph returned, took the blanket, spread it over the horse and went out to meet the trackers who were arriving.

"Poor beast," continued the mother, "it's terrible."

There were many children on the plain. They perched on the buffaloes. They fished at the edges of the river's backwater. There were always plenty of them playing in the river. When boats came down the *rac*, you saw them aboard those as well. As the sun went home to bed, so did the children, off to their corners in the straw huts, to lie on the bare floors of bamboo slats. Approaching hamlets up on the mountain, one also encountered children venturing outside their village: children, goats and the first mango trees. There were plenty of stray dogs as well, wandering from village to village, covering 12 or 13 miles a day, searching through garbage for something to eat. Skinny dogs, long in the leg, chicken thieves, whom the Malays drove off with stones or killed to eat them. These dogs were the children's natural companions. Wherever there were children, there were dogs: the children did not chase them away. Every woman had a child a year, so it was the same with the children as it was with the rice, the [*illegible*] and the tigers, and the rains, the floods, the epidemics. The children flourished on the big plain: there were crowds of them, herds. The women began bearing them in their bellies, carried them afterwards on their backs, then launched them on their own, and never did a child prevent its mother from going to set out rice seedlings, sow the fall seeds and walk the 37 miles to Ram to buy the year's *pagnes*. When a child was quite young, the mother carried it on her back in a kind of hammock, tied at the waist and shoulders; the child rode from place to place on the mother and the mother, at mealtimes, would chew rice and stuff the child with the paste of chewed rice, mouth to mouth. And when this happened in front of a Westerner, the Westerner would turn away in disgust, and the mother would laugh because they'd been doing that on the plain for a thousand years, and disgust was irrelevent. The plain was steeped in poverty; no-one mourned children when they died, no-one made them graves, and they buried them right in the ground, in the plain: the children returned to the plain like the wild forest mangoes, like the fruits of the mangrove trees. Many of them died every year, a great many. They died of the cholera brought on by green mangoes, but how can one keep children from climbing mango trees? And every year there were hordes of them perched in the mango trees, and then a certain number would die, and the next year others would take their places beneath those same mango trees. And lots of them would drown; still others caught worms from the dogs, filling up with worms and dying suffocated. The [*illegible*] who came down from the mountain rubbed the children with saffron {to protect them from mosquitoes}, but still some of them died, in enormous numbers. Some of them had to die, after all. The plain gave only its quota of rice and fish and [*illegible*]. Supposing that the children hadn't died any more, they would have become like a poison, the plain would have been invaded by children as if by locusts, and perhaps people would have been forced to kill them. When one asked a woman how many children she'd had, she counted on her fingers the dead children and those still alive, and every time there were many more dead than alive. All these children learned how to talk, to sing, to laugh, to swim, to fight, all on their own, among themselves, without help from the parents, and once they were grown they were like their parents, hardworking, cheerful and brave.

*

The mother had always had a few of these children at the bungalow. She'd taken many of them under her wing. They were usually
orphans or children who'd been given to her. A beggar woman
had given her a little girl who'd caught worms from the dogs; that
little girl died like the horse did, of the great misery of the plain,
of that fine and fatal equilibrium of this plain. The mother and
Suzanne had wept over that little girl. And in Suzanne's life, that
day had been a day of anger and injustice.

What the mother would have liked would have been to build
great barriers against the flood tides that scorched the crops. Not
only for herself but for the entire plain, to see the arable land
stretch far beyond its present limits; she would have liked to see
more villages spring up along both sides of the *rac*, and see large
paddy junks on that waterway sailing the open sea all the way to
Siam. The mother went to the city several times to ask the Land
Office to please come and evaluate the condition of the plain. The
Land Office representatives had come and then they had left, and
that had been three years ago. And the sea, making itself at home,
would come in and scorch the crops. She didn't know what to
do with herself in this country, the mother, and she was burning
herself out with impatience.

Joseph had met her at the cinema. She had smoked American
cigarettes throughout the entire film and since she hadn't had a
lighter with her, Joseph had lit her cigarettes for her and smoked
the ones she'd offered him. They had left the theatre together.
And from that day on, Joseph had left Carmen and had not been
back to see her at the Hôtel Moderne for eight days and nights.

That's how the mother, who had finished what she'd had to
do, was forced to wait eight days for Joseph's return. Neither the
mother nor Suzanne could drive the car, and they'd had to wait
for Joseph to return and take them back to the plain.

The first two days, the mother had not stopped crying, and she'd taken so many pills that she'd slept all day long. She had paid no attention to Suzanne, leaving her to her own devices. Suzanne had spent her mornings with Carmen, and the rest of the time in the {well-to-do white district called} Hauts Quartiers.

Now she made a habit of going to the Hauts Quartiers. She never strolled there any more. She would leave the hotel at around five o'clock and go directly to a cinema. Then she would leave the first cinema and head straight for another one. After which, she would come right back to the hotel. The mother had given her a little money, and with Carmen's contribution she had enough to buy a ticket in the orchestra seats where she would be less conspicuous. She was through with feeling ashamed. Suzanne thought a great deal about Joseph; she believed that Joseph was through with them, and she knew she didn't count for much in her brother's life. The mother was no help to her at all. Carmen was the only one who talked to her, asked her what she had done and gave her money. Suzanne didn't like Carmen, but she accepted her money all the same. Every evening, Carmen would ask her if she had met anyone, and Suzanne would say no. The next day, Carmen would give her more money. Suzanne felt no gratitude towards Carmen. When she returned in the evening, Carmen would kiss her, take her to her own room and ask her if she had "met anyone" or seen Joseph. Suzanne had not seen Joseph. Carmen wasn't the least bit distressed that Joseph had left her, but what she would have liked was to reassure the mother.

"She hasn't got up yet," Carmen would say. "What Joseph's doing, that had to happen, but she's like a young girl, she doesn't want to understand."

Suzanne would leave Carmen and go to see the mother.

Instead of a bed, Carmen's room had a divan covered with hand-painted cushions. There were Harlequins and Pierrots on the walls. On the dressing table with its triple mirrors, there was a pot of artificial flowers. Suzanne had a true horror of that room, because she knew that it was where everything with Joseph had begun.

Suzanne knew what it was all about. Joseph had told her that it meant being completely naked with a completely naked woman and in the same bed. Suzanne saw Carmen completely naked and she did not understand Joseph. And now he was again completely naked lying with a completely naked woman. And that made a huge difference between herself and Joseph.

It was always the same thing. The mother, awake, lying on the bed in a chemise, would be waiting for Joseph in the dim light.

"So, you saw him?" the mother would ask.

"Didn't see him," Suzanne would reply.

Since the mother was letting Suzanne go into the Hauts Quartiers in the hope that Joseph would turn up, she would then start crying and ask for a pill.

"You'd be better off coming down to dinner," Suzanne would say, "than taking your stupid pills."

The mother insisted. She had never yet felt so afraid of having an epileptic fit and dying as at that moment. It was probably staying alone in her room all day that was giving her such ideas. Suzanne felt a dull, pent-up anger at her mother for waiting like that for Joseph. Suzanne repeated what Carmen kept saying.

"Sooner or later," said Suzanne, "it had to happen. That's no reason to make yourself sick."

The mother said that she knew this, but that it was still terrible to lose Joseph that way, so suddenly.

Suzanne went to the window, sat down by the casement, and watched the river that spread its wide and shining waters in the distance, beyond the bustling city. The mother fell asleep. Suzanne thought about the films she had seen.

It was at the hotel that she was supposed to meet the thread salesman from Calcutta. He was passing through, staying at the hotel. He was looking to get married and wanted the woman to be [young,] French and a virgin.

He had confided in Carmen, who told him immediately about Suzanne.

He was a man of about forty, who had travelled several times around the world.

The Horror of Such Love
(Rough Draft)

I was told: "Your child is dead." It was an hour after the birth; I'd caught a glimpse of the child. The next day, I asked, "What was he like?" I was told: "He's blond, a bit sandy-haired; he has your high brows, he looks like you." "Is he still there?" "Yes, he'll be there until tomorrow." "Is he cold?" R. replied, "I haven't touched him but he must be, he's very pale." Then he hesitated. "He's beautiful: that's because of death, too." I asked to see him. R. told me no. I asked the mother superior. She told me: "It's not worth it." I did not insist. They had explained where he was: in a little room next to the delivery room, to the left as you went in. The next day I was alone with R. It was quite hot. I was lying on my back; my heart was very tired, I wasn't supposed to move. I wasn't moving. "What's his mouth like?" "He has your mouth," R. said. And every hour: "Is he still there?" "I don't know." I couldn't read. I looked at the open window, at the foliage of the acacias growing on the embankments of the railway line encircling the city.

In the evening, Sister Marguerite came to see me. "He's an angel, you should be content." "What will they do with him?" "I don't know," said Sister Marguerite. "I want to know." "When they're that little we burn them." "Is he still there?" "He's still there." "So they're burned?" "Yes." "It's quick?" "I don't know." "I don't want him to be burned." "There's nothing to be done about it." The next day, the mother superior came: "Do you want to give your flowers to the Holy Virgin?" I said, "No." The sister looked at me:

she was seventy years old, withered by the daily work of running a clinic; she was terrifying, she had a belly I imagined as black and dried out, full of shrivelled roots. She returned the following day. "Do you want to take Communion?" I said, "No." Then she looked at me. Her face was horrible, it was the face of wickedness, the Devil's face. "So: it doesn't want Communion and it's feeling sorry for itself because its child is dead." She left and slammed the door. People addressed her as "Reverend Mother". (She is one of the three or four people I've met whom I would have liked to gut. To gut. The word is staggering. To gut. The word was made for her, for her belly bloated with black ink.)

It was very hot. It was between the fifteenth and thirty-first of May. Summertime. I told R.: "I don't want any more visits. Just you." Lying down, still facing the acacias. I was so empty that the skin of my belly was sticking to my back. The child had come out. We were no longer together. He had died a separate death. An hour, a day, a week ago, a death apart, dead to a life we had lived nine months together and through a death he had just died separately. My belly had collapsed heavily, plop, into itself, like a worn-out cloth, a rag, a pall, a slab, a door, a void, that belly. It had gloriously carried in an adorable bulge that flourishing seed, a submarine fruit (a child is a green fruit that, like a green fruit, makes your mouth water) that had lived only in the dark, viscous and velvety warmth of my flesh and had been killed by daylight, by the death blow of its solitude in space. So small and already so much, ever since he had died apart. "Where is he?" I kept saying to R. "Has he been burned?" "I don't know." People were saying, "It's not so terrible at birth. Better that than to lose them at six months." I didn't answer people. Was it terrible? I believe that it was. Precisely that coincidence between his "coming into the world" and his death. Nothing. I had nothing left. That emptiness was terrible. I had not had a child, not even for an hour: forced to imagine everything. Motionless, I imagined.

This one, who is here now and sleeping, this one laughed a little while ago, he laughed at a giraffe someone had just given him. He laughed and that made a sound. It was windy, and a tiny bit of the sound of that tiny laugh reached me. Then I raised the hood of his pram a little more and gave him back his giraffe so he would laugh again. He laughed again and I plunged my head under the pram's hood to capture all the sound of the laugh. Of my child's laugh. I put my ear to this shell to hear the sound of the sea. The idea that this laughter was blowing away with the wind was unbearable. I caught it. I'm the one who got it. Sometimes when he yawns, I inhale his mouth, the breath of his yawn. I am not a crazy mother. I am not living only on that laughter, that breath. I need many other things, solitude, a man. No. I know what a child is worth. "If he dies," I thought, "that laugh – I will have gotten it." It's because I lost a child, it's because I know they can die that I'm like this. I measure the full horror of the possibility of such love. Motherhood mellows you, they say. Rubbish. Since having my child I've turned nasty. At long last I'm certain about that horror, at last I've grasped it, at last believers have become complete strangers to me.

Holiday with D.

It was a beautiful afternoon. It was August. Oh, that month, that terrible month you know is the hottest one, the heart of the year – that peak – that calvary of beauty – that Via Dolorosa, the month of August. The balcony of the studio flat overlooked the valley, a gigantic valley over 60 miles long, almost 20 miles wide, and two-thirds of a mile deep spreading forests, lakes, fields and clearings out beneath our balcony in a cosmic, aerial view for us, moving D. to say, "Our Mother Earth is green." On the balcony we'd feel the razor-sharp wind that almost never stopped whipping past, day and night, blowing, blowing. Enough to drive you crazy. I was telling D.: "In Carcassonne, in the seventeenth century, they used to adjourn trials after three days of wind. It influenced the juries." That afternoon – a lull. (The calm before the crime, before death.) We were reading down in the garden, D. and I, on a mat, in front of the valley. Then, having had enough of reading, D. went to watch the ants at the base of the linden and I went to adjust the rubber hose on the cellar tap and I began to water the garden path then I got undressed and I watered myself then said to D., "Come and get watered." D. didn't want to, then the grass, then the wall [...]

Memories of Italy

He was, however, separate from me. I loaned myself to him so that he could make himself. In my flesh bathed his, nascent but distinct, with his youth, nervousness, freshness, independence, the anger of a sea creature struggling towards the surface. His independence was deep inside me, so naked, so striking, that I felt as if torn apart by the truth, stripped bare, like a woman screwing, his truth. That is how the virility of maternity feels. None of the most acknowledged aspects of virility can touch that one, if by virility one means the brutal exercise of a freedom. I brutally exercised my freedom in the face of that complete freedom rooting around deep inside me. I felt that freedom live, and my own, just as free, outside, containing it.

(Now when I reread those lines, he is here, outside me, a few yards away, asleep. His freedom is no less complete, nor is mine. My life is linked to his, dependent on it down to the slightest details. If he dies, the beauty of the world dies and it will be pitch dark on my earth. In other words, if he dies, I die to the world. That's why I don't fear his death more than I do death. That's why, just when I am the most fettered, I am the most free. My revolt, my rebellious power, has never been as violent. Since such a love, such an amorous imprisonment, is within the realm of possibility, while at the same time this possibility contains the death of the object of that imprisonment, in this case I would want God to exist in order to embody this possibility, and so that I could curse him. Because the object of my love is more important to me than myself – not only in my own eyes but in itself, embedding itself more preciously in the world, with a greater value. I'm not the one who imparts that precious worth to him, but it's important to me that he live. People who have no children and who speak of death make me laugh. Like virgins and priests who imagine love. They have an imaginary experience of death. Alive, they imagine themselves struck down by death, whereas the dead cannot enjoy that death. With a child, though, one lives out that idea every day and if it should actually happen, you enjoy your death alive, you are among the living dead.)

And I became afraid that it was too late for anything at all, even for having that child. It was then that I thought of the evening between Pisa and Florence, of that evening and our stay in Bocca di Magra, because it was there, in the sun, in the luminous haze of the beach, beside the sea, in mid-August, that for the first time in my life the feeling of death inside me vanished. Just as if, amid that light and those colours, the slow fog of the idea of death that always darkens my life had suddenly ceased, and left me free. Then I felt, on my burning skin, the cool shivering of my blood and organs – I really felt that, because I had come out of the water and sat down in the sun and, profoundly refreshed by my dip, at the same time I felt that coolness pearling in my armpits in a very light sweat; I felt my flesh cooled by my swim and well protected by my skin, and even though that skin was burning, I wasn't hot. My sweat began to bead among the hairs in my armpits, and then – below my ribs, in a hollow still throbbing from my swim (looking down, I saw my heartbeat on the skin of my abdomen) – hunger struck. That was when my life was so precise, so well delineated, there, crushed beneath the sun yet fighting and demanding and carrying on, that the idea of death became acceptable, as a reality as implacable as my own. And then I told myself that as long as

I could live such moments and feel myself so strongly, bathed in such a light, I could gladly grow old.

And then Ginetta called to me: "Let's have a sunbath." We climbed up the dunes and went deep into the reeds, the two of us. The others – Elio, Robert, Dionys, Anne-Marie, Menta, Baptista and the rest – stayed on the beach. The reeds were so dense that they muffled almost all sound. Ginetta spread her towel out in a nice snug bare spot, and took off her bathing suit. I did the same, placing my towel beside hers and shedding my suit. It was the first time I had seen Ginetta stark naked. I found her very beautiful.

"You're very beautiful, Ginetta." She said, "I don't know about that, but Elio tells me so." She was very long, very long, the way certain animals are long: the antelope, the panther, certain breeds of dogs, long-legged bitches with hollow flanks and long necks, bred for hunting and racing. She had an almost flat belly, barely curved, and firm breasts, rather small for her body, and suspended in a unique way, with equal tension on all sides as if they had roots reaching all the way to the shoulders, down to the top of the abdomen, even into the armpits, widespread roots. When she lay on her towel, her arms behind her head, you saw almost nothing of her breasts except their brown tips. They barely made a bulge above her ribs. She told me that she found me beautiful, too, and then we fell silent. Above the reeds, the snowy flanks of the marble quarries of Carrara sparkled with whiteness. On the other side, we saw Monte Marcello, above the hill overlooking the mouth of the Magra River, Monte Marcello wrapped in its vines and fig trees, way atop its dark slopes of pines. Elio, Robert, Dionys, Baptista and Gino were playing ball, and we heard their laughter along with the soft sound of the August sea, flattened by the heat. Listening to Elio like that, lying near Ginetta's naked body, I thought about their love, not through time but in space, about how that love of Elio's had taken root in and was feeding every day on that woman. It was a terrifying love, which terrified us perhaps because it was always so present, every minute, so present and definitive that it was frightening the way the absolute is frightening, because it forced you to believe in love and because, far from impoverishing you (since you, you were not living a great love like that), far from depressing you, it made you hope for more than you'd ever expected from love until then, and made you wonder (that's the word, I believe, wonder, meaning to stand bereft of reason before a marvel) at the fact that two beings, a man and a woman, could take in each other an interest so overwhelming, inexhaustible and daily resurgent that each represented, for the other, the whole world. Not that Elio or Ginetta devoted all their time to loving each other – far from it, they're on the contrary people very busy with life, absorbed in various occupations, but each is for the other the springboard that launches them into every day, strengthened by that elan they find only in one another. You might tell me that it was a stroke of luck, witnessing such a love, in a setting like Bocca di Magra. I believe it was a stroke of luck.

Hearing Elio's voice, Ginetta smiled. "He's like a child," she said. Then shortly afterward she said, "I'm forty-one years old." She was brushing away flies with a hand she'd freed from beneath her head, a long brown hand with pale fingernails. Through the slits of her eyelids, you could see her pupils staring at the reeds. And since she was brown from the sun, those pupils seemed much greener than usual – exactly the colour of the sea when the {south-west wind called the} *libeccio* blows. "And Elio, he's thirty-eight," she said. The sea breeze could not penetrate the reeds, and the heat was terrific. Ginetta and I felt the sweat gradually trickling from our pinned-up hair past our eyelids, and from the creases of our drawn-up knees, and beading on our upper lips, where it was cool and salty when we licked them. Ginetta sat up, reached into her bathing cap, pulled out two lemon halves, and handed one to me; she lay down again and we squeezed the lemons over our open mouths. "It's very good," said Ginetta. There was more to it than that, but I knew what she meant. I felt quite friendly towards her, for saying that. The sun was beating down on us almost unbearably, but it was such a violent way of feeling our physical being that this burning was a pleasant pain. We were thinking about the sea 15 yards away and into which, running to avoid searing our feet on the sand, we would be jumping in a moment. But we could still wait, and bear a bit more broiling sunshine. It was a terrible burning and now and then, unable to endure it any more in the same spot, we would turn over, passing our palms soothingly over our bellies and thighs. I knew that Ginetta was thinking about her approaching old age (worse than her death), the time when their love would lose some of its splendour, and I knew that at that moment, she accepted this, vanquished by the reality of the sun, of this August noon in which she lay, every bit as real. So powerful was this radiant reality that it forced a halt on the way to death. And if death was at the end of this reality, it was acceptable. That's what Ginetta was feeling, the same as I was feeling, at that moment. Drop by drop the lemon juice slipped down our throats to land on our raw hunger, reviving it, making us take the measure of its strength, its depth. After the taste of salt in our naked, sea-washed mouths, the lemon made our mouths water with saliva that seemed as cool as a spring in that heat, and the lemon was quite ideally the very fruit of that particular kind of sun, and that particular moment. These lemons of the Carrara plain are enormous, they have a thick peel that keeps them cool in the sun, they're as juicy as oranges, but they have a harsh flavour, a pure acidity, and they don't have that refreshing taste our lemons do.

The others kept playing, shouting when someone managed to catch the ball, or missed it, louder when someone missed it or took too much time returning it to his partner who, frozen in expectation, was searing the soles of his feet. Elio and Baptista were shouting the most. Dionys, somewhat less, and Robert hardly at all. Menta was also shouting with Anne-Marie; they were refereeing, cheering or booing the players. We had scrambled back into our suits – it wasn't possible to stay in that sun – and passed through the reeds to arrive at the top of the dune. Ginetta let out a hoarse, wild cry the way she always did when she had come over from her side of the Magra to ours in a boat (a dog, Gibraltar, came along). Elio turned around: "Hey, Ginetta!" We ran into the sea. Ginetta swam a long way out. Me, I swam a few strokes, near the shore; I was one of the less-accomplished swimmers. The sea was blue, even there, right under our eyes, and there were no waves but a very gentle swell, the breathing of a deep sleep. The others left their game and huddled on their towels on the sand. I stopped swimming and looked at them, at Dionys and Robert. Robert was looking at me; he blinked behind his spectacles, smiled at me and jerked his head upwards in little nods, as if to say: "And what about you? How's it going? You, you're so tiny in the sea, and look at you! Managing to swim and live – sometimes I forget to watch little old you and finding you again, that makes me happy." And I was looking too, at him, and thinking, "He's there because he didn't die in the concentration camp." I knew he knew that I'd been thinking this, every day, for a year. And that at that moment I was thinking: "There he is laughing away, he doesn't know a thing; me, I know." When he weighed his 84 pounds and I would take him in my arms and help him pee and go caca, when he had a fever of 105.8, and down at his coccyx, his backbone was showing, and when day and night, there were six of us waiting for a sign of hope, he had no idea what was happening.

He was curious about everything. Dionys would read him *L'Humanité*. He'd ask us if we were doing alright. He didn't know that he was dying. He was happy. He didn't feel the fever, he'd say, "I feel stronger," and it was the fever, he was just wasting away with fever, and when he tried to lift the little spoon to eat his gruel, his hand drooped from the weight. And he'd got to the point where the blanket felt too heavy and was hurting him. And now, there he is laughing on the beach in the sunshine.

He's in Italy, that's right, having sunbaths, playing ball, he's a Communist, he talks with Elio and Dionys about the Marxist justification of tourism in a revolutionary period. Yes indeed, he eats *pasta chuta* – {pasta with fresh tomatoes, black pepper, sea salt and chives} – he drinks Chianti, he climbs up to San Marcello in no time. Only Dionys and I know these things, know what he does – the others don't, and he least of all. Dionys and I, watching him in action, we kept reviewing the past, and behind his back, we'd fall about laughing. And even though things weren't going well between Dionys and me, on that point, we were in perfect complicity. We laughed ourselves silly, with looks that said, "You believe it? We fooled him!"

It was the only thing we agreed on. On everything else, we didn't. It isn't time yet to say those things, anyway I couldn't say them clearly, because, beside the fact that I don't have clear ideas about anything, on that subject I had even fewer. What made the shadow that lay between Dionys and me at that time even worse was that he claimed to know perfectly why it was there but said he wasn't going to explain it, he refused, accusing me of bad faith because I knew just as well as he did "what was going on" but was pretending I didn't. I don't believe that this was really that important, that it seriously affected our memories of that trip. At the time, it wasn't that important, at least I don't think so; I don't know if Dionys agrees with me. We haven't talked about it, because shortly after our return, I was expecting the baby. It's his nature to have views on the subject, though; Dionys certainly has some, but I don't know what they are.

The baby came and temporarily swept everything away. This morning, as a matter of fact, in that harsh and implacable light, I felt that the baby was a solution. No, Dionys would say, there is no solution to a problem except the one that follows from the very conditions of the problem. And yet, this morning, I felt that the baby was a solution even for Dionys; {I felt this} on his behalf and no matter what he thinks about it. I don't mean that this child will replace anything whatsoever, and in particular what is past, between us, the madness of the first months. No. It's a soothing solution. When a couple is breaking up, when everything falls apart, at one of life's moments of greatest doubt, when love is dying on itself and there's no way of telling how life will regain its savour, and when, after having four arms and legs you find yourself crippled by the amputation of the other – this flower grows in your womb. So you stop driving yourself goddamn crazy trying to find out if you exist. You exist because of this community. And then you feel free to leave each other, without this leaving the mortal taste of death in your mouths. More precisely, you are free. The past is not destroyed down to its roots. Free from the past. Even though it was all going badly at that point, Dionys carried the same weight, his life and death had the same meaning in me, and I could watch him swim with the emotion of four years earlier. With even greater emotion, probably, because I was not discovering it but rediscovering it, and he was swimming bathed for me in my knowledge of him, of all that I knew he'd done during four years before going swimming that day.

One day, I thought he'd drowned. A terrible *libeccio* was blowing the way it does every August. Even in just over 2 feet of water, the waves would knock you down. The entire sea was rearing up, white, rugged with waves three times the height of a man. Everyone had decided that we shouldn't swim; at most, we'd go to a large flat area sheltered by the quay at the mouth of the Magra, to be splashed by the waves. Dionys had decided to go swimming. It's his nature to trust other people only moderately and simply to be nice but never with conviction. Everyone had argued against it. Dionys had finally given in.

And after deciding that, he was furious about deciding that. He looked longingly at the sea. I knew what he was thinking: that he'd let himself be persuaded, which was beneath him, and that I was the one who'd prevented him, I was the obstacle to his living as he pleased. The sea was alone in its uproar. In the brilliant

sunshine, colours were bright after the previous night's storm and
the air was cool: it was weather for going along the beach all the
way to Marina di Carrara while looking at the sea. Robert, Anne-
Marie and I had decided to do that. After accompanying us for a
little while, Dionys sat down on the sand, intending to stay there,
he said, to look at the sea. This was halfway between Marina di
Carrara and the quay where the others were, Elio, Ginetta, Menta
and Baptista. And we knew that Dionys was planning to swim
without any interference while we were gone. We had stopped
in front of a line of rocks 20 yards out from the shore and against
which the sea was breaking with all its strength. A veritable wall
of spray shot up from the rocks and drained endlessly away with
a mighty noise. At their base the sea struck muffled sounds like
blows, then plumed up into the sun and evaporated. Dionys said
he wanted to stay there to watch. "You're not going to watch
that for two hours," Robert said. Dionys said that yes, indeed, he
wanted to, that it was by watching the same spectacle, ceaselessly
renewed, that one managed to pass from curiosity to interest, that
seeing was precisely that. He said this, and lay down, determined
to stay. We were standing around him, looking sometimes at the
sea, sometimes at his body stretched out on the sand. And we
saw his body in the sea. Just as completely as fire, the sea would
have devoured him. It was quite simply unimaginable that he
could make it out of there. Seeing how powerfully the waves were
crashing against the rocks, we imagined that force attacking him
head-on, at chest height, bowling him over and holding him down,
implacably and with the weight of a massive slab of water, until
he was dead, then releasing him, and then him coming back in
the cresting tangle of frothing waves like a mat of crushed reeds.
Because the sea that morning was inhumanly high and you might
as well have bathed in flames in a huge oven, attacked a raging
bull, a pack of ravening wolves, hurled yourself alone against an
oncoming tank, setting flesh against steel. And yet no-one said
anything. We could tell from the look in his eye that Dionys had

reached that stubborn limit where he became completely un-
reasonable and would, if we opposed him even the least bit more,
head without any hesitation straight for death. Tight-lipped, he
stared at the rocks, disdaining us absolutely. At that moment we
hated him, all the while measuring, as never before, what it would
be like to lose him, and what that whole admirable valley of sunlight, fruits and snowy marble, and our lives, would be like once
the sea had swallowed him up. By staying, however, we would be
displaying such unbearable, dishonourable, unforgivable tactless-
ness (just as if, by preventing him from satisfying his desire to go
swimming that morning, we had kept him from making love with
a woman for whom he'd felt an insane desire, and all because of
some odious formalism, for example because the woman would
have ruined him, just as if – in short – we had prevented him from
living, by denying him the adventure of risking danger, claiming
concern for his safety whereas, by not running the risk, he would
find his life impossible to live, etc.) that without discussing it, or
saying anything to him to let him know anyway what that silence
meant, we went off to Marina. To tell the truth, we weren't sure
he would go swimming. I said to Robert, "You think he'll go
swimming?" "He's not crazy," said Robert.

I don't remember Marina di Carrara very well. Before reaching
it, we passed a holiday camp run by Alfa Romeo. All the little
children were eating, standing up, near a long table. Marina was
criss-crossed by clanging and crowded streetcars, hurtling beneath a torrid sun down the middle of dusty avenues lined with
flowering oleanders in front of bombed-out houses. All I will say
is, once again it looked like Africa, just like Sarzana on market day.
Naked children white with dust surrounded stalls of watermelons
and cotton goods; there wasn't one tree, one blade of grass on
the dust-whitened square. It was noon. Large awnings of white
canvas shaded cafeterias and their terraces sprinkled {with water
to settle the dust}; a peddler thundered into a mic in praise of
his elastic bands, while the little black-eyed Italian children with

their skinny legs pinched one another, shrieked or napped in the shade of the stalls, in the dust. Now and then a girl would come out of a house, and one of them came from the cafeteria where we were going to have lunch: she was fresh, pink and brown, dressed in black, dazzling and moist like a fruit of water and night pulled from the water still dripping with coolness and night. Or it was as if the dense darkness of the cool houses of Marina – while the sun outside was scorching colours, sounds, the very earth rising in a fiery white dust – had harboured a kind of equatorial undersea vegetation, the mere sight of which flooded you with coolness and desire in the burning sun, and made you feel the value of that sunshine in which bloomed a darkness so rich, so heavy, so fertile, so brimming with beauty. And when we entered the restaurant, the girl's eyes gleamed in silence, black and wet; she stood in the shade of the awnings, her mouth half-opened on her teeth, her mouth like the virgin interior of an oyster, moistened, her lips like the edges of a fresh wound ready to bleed, and they would have made, those lips alone, the manhood of every fellow who saw them parting in a smile rise up naked and deadly, while she simply stood there, completely, as completely as a plant, unself-conscious, her hand resting on the white table laden with a heavy dish of tomatoes shining with oil and as red as the girl's lips, red with the cold fire of dark shadows after the sun.

I was saying that Marina resembled Sarzana, and as I said it I believed that Dionys was already cold and dead, floating on the crest of the waves. I felt the sun on my life but the whole inside of my body was drenched in an icy stream. Robert bought a bottle of Chianti. He seemed reassured. Anne-Marie bought some chocolate. We were on the main avenue of Marina. Streetcars were still going by. I went to have a coffee in a bar, under a parasol. The coffee was quite good and it was nice on that terrace. Anne-Marie and Robert came to join me carrying the Chianti and the chocolate, and I said to myself it wasn't worth the bother because Dionys was dead. They ordered a Cinzano and I, another coffee, and they told me what they'd seen and what they should have bought in the grocery. They were so emphatic about it all that I realized they were trying to reassure me about Dionys, to prove to me that if they'd been really worried, they wouldn't have been thinking about such things. But I told myself: "If they've bought the Chianti, it's to reassure me," and I didn't believe in it any more. We took the streetcar back and at the last stop, by the edge of a pine forest, we returned to the beach. To the right, we walked past a wood of olive trees for a while; they were very old, with squat, twisted trunks, gnarled and distorted, but their foliage was light, young. Afterward we came to the thick stand of reeds. There was no wind; the sun was directly over the plain, and all the villages in the Carrara Mountains – when we turned around, which we couldn't help doing – stood out whitely in the valleys against the mountainsides. I was waiting for the moment when we'd reach the wall of rocks. The sea was still terrifying, whipped up by a vain and bitter fury. Anne-Marie and Robert were talking about Marina and the bombings of the coast, especially around Marina. Strewn all over the beach, little mollusks were dying, torn from the sea; they were drying out in the sun and collapsing in small sticky puddles of bright green. Death was everywhere. The air smelled of death; the scent of pines, iodine, rain – it was the smell of death. I looked at the quay in the distance and thought that my life extended that far, after which, I would not be able to return to the hotel. We reached the wall of rocks; Dionys wasn't there. On the beach, there was the imprint of his body lying down. "He'll have gone back to the hotel," said Robert.

But afterward, Anne-Marie and he didn't chat any more and they looked off into the distance, on the beach. I had ceased to exist. Everyone has experienced that, has seen an empty beach when they were expecting to find someone there. We've all seen that, the empty beach and the empty sea and that's all, the sun overhead, and in the distance, mountains, villages bright and bustling in the sunshine, orchards as far as the eye can see, laden with fruit. Who hasn't seen that? The empty sea, the empty beach, the sun and *all* the rest. Empty. There where you expected to find someone, nothing, only the imprint of a body on the sand, and beside it, the sea. Beside it, the sea. Unfathomable. As far as the eye can see, the sea. You make the connection between the sea and the imprint of the body on the sand, and it's horror. The insuperable thing. To go on living with the idea of that precious body lost in the sea of inhuman scale, of mathematical, diabolical proportions, buffeted by the whims of the water, in the depths of the night. The body you've touched, loved, felt beneath your fingers. A second death, that.

So Dionys wasn't where we'd left him but a little farther on, near the quay. He had dug himself a hole in the sand and was waiting quietly for us, he said, but actually somewhat impatiently, because we'd taken so long. And I – I didn't say one word more than the others. "Hello," we said, and Dionys stood up; we went along the beach and then returned to the hotel via the path leading through the Jews' Camp (more about that later). I was quite calm, and I was discovering that, listening to Dionys talk and knowing he was there, walking beside me, I asked for nothing more, nothing. He was still cross with me because of my attitude that morning and he directed a few pointed remarks at me, but it was as if he were speaking from a million miles away or in ancient times. Besides, I listened only to the sound of his voice, and if he'd cursed me I would have heard only the tone of his voice, I would have felt only the contours, the weight, the sound of it in the sun. I was a cave to receive that voice, nothing more – I was no longer of this earth, not that I would have been any happier, but I was experiencing a kind of cosmic moment, a sort of ascesis, if you will, in which nothing of life could reach me any more save the very idea of life, and not its earthly manifestations. Dionys was pictured, so to speak, and nothing would ever disfigure [that image] again.

That's how I knew, once I'd had that experience because of him, that I was attached to him, at my core. Not that I loved him, for the experience was no proof of love, because passion adjusts to death, which it subordinates to itself. No: that I was attached to him. And that it was important. I remained in that state all day and through a strange contagion, Robert was, in my eyes, possessed of the same eternity as Dionys. And at noon, al fresco, I let them drink all the Cinzano they wanted, and they were astonished. They were astonished and I smiled at their astonishment; they were little children and I was like a believer before the heathen, or someone who believes in eternal life before some children oblivious to everything, except their games.

It was like this for months after Robert returned from Germany. I would look at him and be fulfilled. He would eat a lamb chop and then suck the bone, eyes lowered, entirely absorbed in finding every scrap of meat. After which he'd eat a second chop and then a third, without looking up. He was sitting near a window in the drawing room, all surrounded with cushions, in his slippers, his cane by his side, his legs as scrawny as crutches in his trousers, and when the sun shone, you could see through his hands. He'd come back from far, far away, a place from which one almost never returns. You know, behind him there was an abyss of pain: death was behind him, he was coming back from it, you could see this, he was clawing his way out of death, hauling himself along by clinging to his chop bone like a drowning man clutching a wreck he didn't dare let go of yet, not yet, in those first days, when he didn't waste one crumb of bread. Me, I would watch him, every-one did, a stranger would have watched him too because that was an unforgettable sight, the spectacle of blind life. Of life scorned, crushed, humiliated, spat upon, beaten, a life supposedly mortally wounded at its root, and then there in the deepest density of the body, a trickle of life still ran, the withered tree isn't dead: at its foot, a bud. And it starts up again. And the sign of its new start is hunger, more than hunger, blind, stubborn devouring, the gulping of a newborn at the breast. After careful thought, I do not believe that anything in the realm of strength and beauty has ever stunned me like the sight of Robert eating for the first time three weeks after his return. The doctor kept him on gruel for three weeks when he was gripped by fever, not knowing what he had.

All food simply raced through him, without nourishing him, and he would choke on a teaspoon of gruel: after swallowing it he would sit up straight in his bed, supported by us, gasping for air. After three weeks, the doctor said we had to give him everything to eat, to put him in front of food. And then he began to be hungry: as soon as he'd eaten and his hunger could feed on itself, it became gigantic, frightening. We'd leave him with the food, *alone, in the dim light of the drawing room*, and in silence, in a silence more pious and sacred than that of any religious service, he would eat. We avoided distracting or speaking to him at such moments, and walked on tiptoe. We would set the dish down in front of him and leave him and he would function. During that initial period he had no marked preferences for any dish, he was a chasm of hunger: an enormous call came from his wasted entrails, such a powerful, rumbling voice, an order that he obeyed, humble, servile, just as blind as a plant. Once he feels hungry, the doctor said, it means life is starting up again. I watched him. I watched Dionys sleep, warm and breathing, tanned, alive, beneath the arbours of muscat grapes, on that afternoon following his death within me. For a month I watched Robert, unable to become accustomed to it, or tired of it. When the dishes didn't arrive quickly enough he would sob, he'd say that no-one understood him. "Is he hungry?" the doctor would ask. We'd laugh. And when he sobbed with hunger, we'd hide to laugh our fill. All those things left their mark on me and this morning, when I awoke, they weighed on me, not that I'd thought about them specifically but they were there, they furnished me – the way my furniture furnishes my bedroom without me seeing it all every instant: these things are there, profoundly there. I don't think they're not there; they are there.

It's my life, it's what I cannot share or remove. These things *were* in the rumbling of the rubbish bin on the pavement, in the light beaming through the foundations of the {new} École de Médecine as well, and had a part in the meaning of a man's footsteps as he walked alone in a silent street. Ever since I saw Robert eat after his return, since that deathly fear, next to which all vanity, ambitions, all plans were literally swept away [...]

Among all cities I love these, the ones that resemble Sarzana, Marina di Carrara, Aden and certain Corsican cities, Bonifacio, Pontevecchio, Toulon as well, the treeless cities (Florence, too, the most striking thing is that there isn't a single tree in Florence) with the torrid squares that, from noon until three, empty out, close up, are completely dead. Such cities are usually dirty, smelling of onion, horse manure and, since they're by the sea, fish. The houses there are old, badly constructed, poor, crowded; the entryways and corridors smell musty, there are no gardens, and on the square a fountain dispenses a trickle of water. Shop displays are rare, and set in windows: there are slippers, pastries, caramels, postcards, work smocks. Everything's crumbling in these cities; the pavement is potholed, the sweeper naps from one to three o'clock, there's only one sweeper for the whole city because the municipality is poor, and there's trash in the gutters. These cities are swept by the sea wind that rises towards three in the afternoon, and then, on those empty squares, dust flies up in clouds; the dust of these cities is fine, salty, smelling of urine, and it's everywhere, covering the box trees in the priest's garden (the only plants in the city), powdering the little children's feet.

When it rains at the end of August, these cities smell like no other: the dust of five months of summer and all sorts of rotting rubbish swells and exhales its odours of wet hides. These cities weren't made to please, they're markets that provision the surrounding countryside. On their outskirts camp travelling picture-shows, funfairs. To me these cities are the most erotic in the world. Cities of shadow, of sunlight. Contrasting shadow. Shadow is erotic.

It's of these cities, I tell myself, that Gaston the sweeper is dreaming.

Did Not Die Deported

You had to see him eat. That man ate like no man ever eats. Or beast, either. Or anything, any species, not even the tiger, or the shark that goes miles and miles with its mouth open and, through a maddening excess of hydrochloric acid in its stomach, swallows twelve times its own volume in food. No, he ate with patience and passion.

At first he could not eat like that. I mean right after his return, because his stomach was so shrunken that the weight of the food would have torn it open, or if it hadn't burst, it would have pressed against his heart, which on the contrary, in the cavern of his emaciation, was now dilated and pumping so fast you could have counted its pulsations, unable to say that it was beating in the proper sense of the word, for it trembled like a hunted animal consumed by terror. No, he could not have eaten without dying of it. Yet, he had to eat: he could no longer go without eating without dying of that.

That was the problem. He was hungry. When he arrived, he embraced his friends. He went all around his flat. He was smiling. In other words, his cheeks puckered and unstuck themselves a little from his jawbone. Then he sat down in the drawing room. That's when he started looking at the {cherry} clafoutis sitting on a console table. Then he stopped smiling. "What's that?" "It's a clafoutis." Then, "Can I have some?" "Let's wait for the doctor." But in a moment: "I really can't have any?" Then he asked us about what had happened while he was gone. But it was over: now he had eyes only for the clafoutis. When the doctor entered the drawing room, Robert was on the sofa. The doctor stopped short and stood with his hand on the doorknob, turning pale. But he did come into the room and go up to Robert, he didn't leave, as we might have feared he would.

The doctor did not allow him any clafoutis. But he told the rest of us that if Robert was craving some clafoutis, that probably meant there was still a little hope. We removed the clafoutis without him noticing it. Then the struggle began. Against death. We had to tackle death gently, with delicacy, tact, finesse. It surrounded him on all sides, but, but, nevertheless, there was still a way to reach him – it wasn't large, this opening for communication with him, but life was in him after all, barely a scrap (but a scrap of life, it's got colour and a name after all: life). Death attacked. 103.1 degrees the first day. Then 104. Then 105.8. Death was getting winded. 105.8. The heart was quivering like a violin string. Still 105.8. But it was quivering. The heart, we thought – the heart will stop. Still 105.8. Death was striking staggering blows. But the heart was deaf. It isn't possible, the heart will stop. No.

Gruel, the doctor had said, by teaspoons. But one teaspoon of gruel choked him – he would cling to our hands, sucking air, and fall back onto his bed. Yet he'd swallow it.

Six or seven times a day we gave him gruel. Six or seven times a day he asked to make caca. We'd lift him by grasping him under his knees and arms. He must have weighed about 83 pounds: skin, bones, heart, liver, intestines, brain, lungs, everything. Eighty-three pounds on a frame just under 5 feet 10 inches tall. We'd set him down on a commode pan, its edges covered with a small cushion so he wouldn't wound himself, because at his joints, where there was nothing over the bare bone but skin, this skin was damaged and raw. (The elbows of the seventeen-year-old Jewish girl from the Faubourg du Temple were sticking through the skin of her arms and the joint was outside instead of inside, no doubt because she was young, with delicate skin. She wasn't in pain; the thing had happened gradually, without suffering: the joint stuck out, naked, clean, and the skin had hardened around the edges without forming a wound. There was no pain in her abdomen, either, where they had cut out, one by one, at lengthy intervals, all her reproductive organs, the better to study the ensuing premature ageing.) Once seated on his commode, Robert would release his shit in a single spurt, in an enormous, unexpected, disproportionate gurgling. What the heart could keep from doing, the anus could not, and it let go all at once. Everything was letting go, even the fingers couldn't hold on to their nails, letting them go as well; only the heart held on to its contents. The heart. And the head, haggard but sublime, alone, it rose from this charnel house, it emerged, remembered, recounted, related, recognized, demanded. It was attached to the body by the neck as heads usually are, but this neck was so wasted (the fingers of a single hand could encircle it), so withered, that you'd wonder how life got through there, *how*, when even a teaspoon of gruel could barely squeeze through, blocking the passage. (At the base, the beginning of the neck, there was a right angle, and on top, below the head and jaws, he was choking. Through his skin you could see the vertebrae, carotid arteries, nerves, pharynx, as on anatomy models, beneath that skin now like cigarette paper, still covering everything after so long. Yet blood did pass through this neck.)

So he would make his shit. It was a gummy shit, dark green, and it bubbled. No-one had ever seen the like before. Sometimes, when he'd done it and we were putting him back to bed, eyes closed, prostrate from the exhaustion following the ejection of shit like that, I would lean my forehead against the closed blinds of his room (when I'd been waiting for his return, it was on the gas cooker that I'd pressed my forehead to try not to think about anything any more) in an effort to suppress the despair filling me at the sight of that unbelievable shit coming out of his body. For seventeen days, that shit looked the same. That shit and the way he made it were inhuman. That's what separated him from us more than the fever, more than the thinness, the fingers without nails, the marks of blows. Even though we gave him only gruel, the shit stayed dark green. That clear, golden-yellow gruel, a gruel for pink-lipped infants – it came back out of him dark green and bubbling like marsh slime. Have you ever seen shit that seethed? That shit did. When the commode was closed, you could hear the rising bubbles bursting at the surface. That shit was as phlegmy and viscous as a big gob of spit. And as soon as it came out of him, the room filled with the odour of sludge, an odour not like that of putrefaction, of corpses (was there still enough matter in his body to make a corpse?), but more like the smell of a vegetal humus, of dead leaves in overgrown underbrush. It was indeed a dark odour, dense, like the reflection of that dense night from which he was emerging – one we would never know. (I'd lean against the blinds and the street, before my eyes, would carry on. And since they didn't know what was going on in the bedroom, I felt like telling them that in this room above them a man was shitting like that, a shit so different from the one they knew that it would change them forever.) Obviously, he had grubbed through trash bins, eaten dandelions, water from machines, but that didn't explain it. We looked for other reasons. Maybe he was eating himself, while we watched; perhaps he was digesting his liver, his spleen. How could we tell? How could we tell what that belly still contained of pain, of the unknown?

I repeat, seventeen days without that shit becoming one bit more human, resembling something familiar. Each of the seven times he went daily we would inhale it, we'd look at it, but without recognizing it. We carefully hid it from him to avoid horrifying him. Same thing with his legs, his body, which we shielded from his own eyes and which we *could not become accustomed* to, and which was unbelievable, unbelievable because he was *still alive* (that was the unbelievable thing). When people entered his room for the first time and saw his form under the sheet, they *could* not bear the sight, they looked away.

All that to tell you how he was.

After seventeen days death got tired. The shit stopped bubbling, became liquid, remained green, but had a more human smell, the smell of a man's shit (more delightful to us than the perfumes of spring, that shit smell we finally recognized).

And one day the fever dropped. After he'd received 12 litres of saline solution, one morning, the fever dropped. Lying on his nine pillows (one for the head, two for the forearms, two for the hands, two for the upper arms, two for the feet, because all that could no longer support itself, carry its own weight, which had to be cushioned by the duvet), motionless, he listened to the fever leaving him. The fever returned but fell again, returned again, a bit lower, but fell again and lower still, and one morning – "I'm hungry," he said.

We witnessed this mystery.

And one day the doctor told us: "Try to give him food. Let's start. Everything, give him everything."

Perhaps it was some of his spleen that was coming out of his body, or some of his heart. Because after all what was it? Those who wince at this very moment, reading this, those whom it nauseates – I shit on them, I hope one day they encounter a man whose body will empty out like that through its anus, and I hope that man is the most beautiful and beloved and desirable thing they have. Their lover. I wish that kind of devastation on them.

The Sailor from Gibraltar
(Rough Draft)

Spending a few days here in Rocca, I knew old Eolo. I was afraid of finding myself alone. I wanted to stay in a place where I'd know somebody, even one man. I know what I'm like – I would have fled a place where I knew no-one, after two days I would have gone back to Paris. In Rocca, I already knew old Eolo.

"She knows you're going to leave her?" asked the girl softly.

I found it natural to be telling her my story. It was a very ordinary story, quite simple, one anybody could hear and understand.

"I told her, but she doesn't believe it."

What made me believe that I had reached a decision was the cautious way I was handling it, my constant wariness.

"Maybe you've often told her, without having the courage to do it."

"I'd never told her. I've been thinking about it for four years [*illegible*]. This is the first time I've told her."

"Maybe you aren't [*illegible*] going to do it. If it hasn't happened yet, you can't tell until the last minute whether you'll do it."

She was quite serious. We were talking like friends and not like a man with a woman.

"I will do it," I said. "It's very simple. I don't even have to actually do anything. She'll pack her bags, she'll take the train. Me, I'll stay here. For what I want to do, I don't even need to lift a finger."

"And if she cries? If she begs you to come with her on the train?"

"She's a brave woman," I said. "She won't cry."

The girl thought for a moment.

"I see," she said, "what kind of person she is."

"And if she cries I won't go away with her, I'll stay in the sea, three days if I have to, so I don't have to see her. For me, it's a very important decision."

The girl looked at me with great friendliness.

"Shall we dance? It will do you good."

Around here, the girls had breasts like [marble].

"And you?" I asked. "What do you do?"

"I'm a servant," she said, "in a writer's house. I'm married to a sailor. It was all over between us a long time ago but we can't get divorced. So I take life as it comes."

The look she gave me told me that if I wanted to, she'd be glad to sleep with me. Not to please me but because she liked that.

She chose the place herself.

"What's your name?" I asked.

"Candida," she replied with a laugh. As if the name were only for me.

"Why? You have lots of lovers …"

Her face clouded over for just an instant.

"I'll be a servant all my life," she said, "and all my life I'll be married to that sailor. A divorce costs lots of money. So what else is there for me to do?"

"And when there's one you like better than the others, you keep him?"

"I keep him, of course, and I do everything I can to keep him."

"And when you can't manage it, you beg, you cry?"

"I beg, I cry, every time," she said laughingly, "and that [keeps me busy] for at least two months. Until I meet another one. I always have to have another one."

The next day I rose early and went to the beach. It was just as hot as in Florence but that wasn't important anymore here, in Rocca. Quite the contrary.

After lunch, which I had with Jacqueline, I went off by myself to take a dip in the Magra. Jacqueline left for the beach. I swam for a long time, until one o'clock. Eolo had loaned me his boat and I used it as a diving platform. I swam along the opposite shore, and I saw the dance hall and the place where we had been together, Candida and I. I was pleased to have met her. Not many houses sat along the banks of the Magra, but there were large and very well-kept orchards that each included a small private dock. As the morning wore on, the traffic on the river increased. Boats were going in all directions. They were covered with tarpaulins that concealed their cargo. Peaches and lemons, probably.

I was greatly enjoying my swim. The evening I had spent with Candida had done me good, somewhat in the way my encounters with the driver of the van and Eolo had. While I swam I thought about her again, about Candida, and I told myself that I must try to get to know other people like her and the driver. And then, for the first time since that driver had told me about her, I felt like seeing that Americana. It was obviously a slight feeling, very slight, not insurmountable, and it left me completely free. But there were no reasons not to indulge that feeling. I had recovered my curiosity about people, and that's why I felt like seeing what that Americana everyone was talking about was made of.

"I'll go out to the beach," I thought. "That's where everybody will be at this hour."

I returned the boat to Eolo and left for the beach. As I arrived

I could tell right away that she wasn't there. Since everyone said that she was extraordinarily beautiful, it was easy to see that she wasn't there.

I looked at her one last time. In her eyes, beneath her [*illegible*], I saw concern; it was true that I hadn't touched her since Florence.

"Hello," she said.

"Hello." She walked away without {another} word to me. I half-closed my eyes. I'll have to explain things to her, I thought, but I couldn't say anything. I had given her enough explanations that very morning. Then it was suddenly so hot that I forgot about her.

I was refreshed by my swim in the Magra. I had walked in the heat to reach the beach, but that coolness still lingered. The sand and the sea – everything was shining around me as brightly as gold dust. My eyelids were still at half-mast. The sun-drenched colours stung my eyes whenever I opened them. I [did] that several times: I closed my eyes for a long minute and opened them abruptly: the images were so strong that they slammed into my brain. In closing my eyes, I was bringing the sea into my head and it filled me up for several seconds. The feeling of defeat that had been bothering me until the previous evening disappeared. I had no qualms about my decision to leave the Registry Office and Jacqueline, and I did not understand why it had cost me such effort for so many days.

Beneath that sun, bathed in those colours turning me inside-out like a glove, I felt myself to be quite precisely of no importance whatsoever.

I was beginning to perspire, to feel the sweat pearling in my armpits.

I was well aware that one could not allow oneself to just drift along. But at the same time, I thought that in a pinch, one could be content with that. One could be content with anything beneath that sun, accept anything, even dying. I had always been quite frightened of diseases, germs, death. At the ministry, whenever I completed a death certificate with a final line where, at the heading "deceased", I would put a date, I would wash my hands. Even if the guy had died in Guinea, I'd wash my hands. To wash his death off me. I recalled that mania and began to smile. I was an idiot but I found myself likeable. Suddenly I tapped my thigh ... Fraternity. This moment deserved a celebration. I must offer a treat, I thought, to this likeable idiot that I am.

I had a craving for something. For what, exactly?

I thought about it; my stomach was always gurgling. I had an excellent stomach. I was in excellent health.

I realized all at once what I was craving. An aperitif. Something that would take hold of my stomach and exasperate that liberating gurgling. I thought – and that required all my strength – about which aperitif I craved.

I considered the lot. I wavered between a pastis and a Cinzano.

I was seized with an insane hope. I had never liked Pernod. I'd sampled it two or three times but without pleasure. On the other hand I did enjoy Cinzano. And then all of a sudden, I understood pastis, the incomparable delight of drinking a pastis, and without needing to taste it I began to love it. I sat up: Now I've gone and gotten too much sun, I thought, trying find an explanation for this new craving and my exaggerated joy in it.

I swivelled my head around and clamped my hands to my temples. How can you tell if you're suffering from sunstroke? Aside from my craving, I felt quite normal. Nothing hurt.

"Just calm down," I told myself. "Trying to understand what's happening to you – that's what will make you crazy."

I gave up and stretched out motionless again, prostrated by my craving for Pernod.

Jacqueline came over to me.

"What's the matter?"

"Nothing," I said. "It's the sun."

*

Her face with its closed eyes bespoke time the way others do freshness and innocence. Until that moment only the faces of certain
men had made that same impression on me. And, I repeat, certain
landscapes, certain cities.

It wasn't just her beauty. Otherwise it was impossible. This
beauty that really was immense, truly distinctive, must have
helped her acquire a great knowledge of the world. She was said
to be quite rich, and certainly wealth must have flowed to her
as do rivers to the sea. But, and I was sure of this from the first
minute, she had once been poor. She must never have forgotten
it. Money did not cloud her view of the world in any way.

I was convinced that she accepted being rich with a certain sorrow.
Wealth had demanded of her an increased watchfulness. But
now that had become part of her, like a phantom consciousness,
and gave her entire being a kind of rare gravity. People born to
wealth, I had noticed, all had something in common: the neglect
of detail, and thus of nuance. They had all somewhat given me
the impression of having more or less begun to die. I had always
[found] the living face of a rich man deader than the face of a dead
workman.

She was a sort of landscape, that woman. Hers was not a natural
beauty. She must have formed herself with the passage of time
and history. Everyone had a history, no doubt, but she, because of
her beauty, must have had an exceptional one. That was definitely
it. She had about her, not only in her face but in her long, naked
body as well, a kind of wakeful peace that, while not essentially
different from the serenity of women, resembled the equanimity
of men of wisdom and experience.

Rue Saint-Benoît: *Madame Dodin* (Rough Draft)

When I awoke, I did not immediately look at the alarm clock. I did not open my eyes. But my window was open and I heard someone coming along the street, walking with a quick, even step. Then, when this someone had reached the end of the block, someone else turned into the street. As the first person's footsteps were fading, those of the second one grew louder until they passed my window, resounding sharply in the empty street, for by then the first person was gone.

So I understood that morning had arrived and that people were already leaving for work.

Saint-Germain-des-Prés tolled six times. I opened my eyes. There was a pale grey light. I don't know from which direction the sun rises, but it must be behind the {new} École de Médecine. Light was coming through the reinforced concrete foundations {of the construction work there}. It was neither a colour, nor daylight; it was light. You could have said that it was grey, grey through the concrete columns. Everything else was in shadow, and in my bed, I myself was in dense shadow at the far end of my bedroom, and I saw the medical school standing out like a screen. I could not go back to sleep, or keep my eyes closed. Sometimes you wake up like that, for no reason, and can't fall asleep again. I looked at the medical school and while I looked at it, I was listening. Footsteps were relaying one another in the street. They hammered at the silence, they filled it completely: they completely filled the resonant space from the boulevard Saint-Germain to the rue Jacob. I also heard a clear, bright sound, of rushing water. It was a gutter draining. Rain was falling. Not a hard rain, but steady, settled in. I realized that those people going by were walking in the rain. I raised my head from the pillow and turned towards the open window. That way I was able to hear the rain. It was a very faint rustling: soft, diffuse. As I was listening, I was looking: it was a soft rustling, in the grey light. People were still passing by.

I could not go back to sleep. Suddenly, I couldn't. I was more awake than at any other moment of the day. I remembered being awakened like that, at dawn, and it was always an exceptional awakening, clear, gliding through the motionless body washed by sleep and unconcerned with rising, and you think and you feel, you listen and you see into yourself and outside as if through a windowpane.

The concierge dragged the big dustbin from the small inner courtyard of the block of flats out to the street. The noise of the dustbin on the flagstones of the entryway was a dull rumbling, quite loud: in the street it became sharp and metallic, with a pause when the concierge slid the bin over the step between the entryway and the pavement. The sound was metallic and grey in the grey light.

I then thought quite intensely about Madame Fossé, my concierge. I very often hear her take out the dustbin, not every morning but still, perhaps once a week. It's a chore she detests. When I heard her at it, I imagined her grumpy face straining with the effort. She says it's taxing work, beyond her strength now – she's sixty-nine – and that if the tenants emptied their bins every day the way they're supposed to, the one in the courtyard wouldn't be so heavy, but that they don't give a damn, and don't empty them until they can't stuff another thing inside. I remembered that the concierge had told me this quite often, and I'd reply that in the long run, it must come to the same thing, given that all the tenants didn't empty their bins every day. But my concierge cannot understand this, or doesn't want to. She says that the dustbin is heavy, too heavy for her. If you ask me, I believe it's a moral question with her. What she finds unbearable is having in the courtyard, so close to her lodge, a bin filling up with several-days-old refuse that stinks, and having to drag it, and smelling its stench while she's dragging it. She says that when you look at those tenants, so well dressed, and so rich (when you consider the rent they pay), you would never believe they'd be disgusting enough to put up with rotting refuse in their homes and for several days, too. And so each morning, when she drags out the dustbin, my concierge once again bitterly ponders – or rather, relives, in the sense of "revives" – an aspect of human nature she feels she alone understands, one that makes her all the more bitter in that she alone perceives it and cannot share it with anyone. And because of her station in life (which requires her to endure the performance of that disgusting chore or lose her job), finding herself forced in the end to empty that refuse, which stinks because it suits the tenants to empty it when they damn well please, makes her re-experience each morning the horror of her station in life. She has been dragging out that bin now for four years and for four years she's been complaining about the way she's treated by the tenants, whom she has never managed to convince of the real horror she feels at the thought that they despise her enough not to make an effort she claims is trifling: taking their refuse out every day.

When I heard her this morning and imagined her face distorted by effort and disgust, a face she must avert from the bin as she drags it along, I thought that this was the deeply moving face of a fierce and impregnable dignity. For, I repeat, she has never managed to become accustomed to the task. And in this grey light, in this tenacious rain, this morning, that was quite obvious to me. It was a violent hour, and that's still not the right word; "a strong hour" would be better, I believe: an hour that has strength, because it is virgin, dawning, the hour when the sun has not yet risen but soon will, when that immense event is imminent. That is where the hour's strength lies, for the hour is one of hope and possesses all its features, containing more promises than the nascent day will keep, since as the day goes by, this hope will sink once more into the following night, but while the day is yet unborn, this hope is intact and filled with the mystery of the coming day, which keeps the flame of life alight in man.

One ought to be able to say these things, and say them so well, so adequately, that attempting to repeat that feat would be useless, and although what I'm saying here is colossally absurd – for it's like saying that there can be a success compared to which all others, be they ever so much more valid, would collapse of their own accord, constrained by the first one – I have learned to look at things, to listen to them, and to assign myself in this business only the importance of "the other". That lone man walking briskly who inhabits the street more completely and evocatively, with more real and impressive presence, than a tragic hero upon the stage – I listen to him, the representative of a community. I am listening, in my selfhood, to an entire city, wide awake and restless, for that man concerns me not as a particular individual with specific experiences and sensibilities but as a member of that community to which we both belong, on the same footing. What is extraordinary is that this man walking along is anyone at all; I am anyone at all, listening to {someone} walking; and this anonymity exists with a great strength, filling me with joy, with love, with hope.

Nothing has happened but this: a man passes on the pavement and I awaken at that moment, cleansed by sleep, new, receptive, and then – his steps pass over my body, marking it and filling the conch shell I am with their resonance. This happens regularly, just like the rumbling of the dustbin. And even though I know Madame Fossé, I now rediscover her, apart from the specific relationship we may have: she is any elderly woman at all, dragging out a dustbin at six in the morning, cursing, embittered, terrible; her wrinkled old face is savage and indignant, and she bends to her task so that she can eat until she dies, after sixty years of toil. After sixty years of service, she found herself once more dragging her dustbin out into the rain this morning, alone, anonymous and bottling up inside herself what she'd like to scream in the world's face: that it horrifies her. One ought to be able to describe that: a man walking alone in an empty street, at dawn, when you have just awakened, when daylight is barely filtering through concrete construction work, while at the same time an elderly concierge drags, from her courtyard to the street, a bin full of reeking refuse, and you hear the sound of the bin and the man's footsteps, while you are in your bed, relaxed, warm, at peace.

[...] existence so perfect it might be lived instead of your own: sometimes I would wish this, and that afterwards men would abandon the vanity of writing. I know what Dionys will say: that I've been reading too much Hemingway lately. I'll show him my text and he'll say, "You've been reading Hemingway again, haven't you?" And he'll walk off, leaving me in despair. I'll tell him: "It's true that I read *Green Hills of Africa*. But you know, what I've written here ... Do you think I wouldn't have been able to write it just as well, one day?" Besides, the story about the dustbin – if there is a story there – belongs to me: it's a slow and static story, one that brings me a joy and sadness that have nothing to do with the blazing emotions of Hemingway's heroes. The day will come when I give Dionys a definitive reply. I've been trying to come up with one for four years now, without success. Dionys is always the one who produces the definitive pronouncement about me. I'd have to go into this at considerable length, and explain that although I believe in his definitive statements, and his alone, Dionys doesn't believe in mine. I've never said anything definitive to him about someone we know, because I don't believe anything definitive can be said about something that by virtue of its fluid nature can disprove your affirmation at any moment. Robert, however, is a constant temptation, one Dionys himself cannot resist. Because in his life, with his slightest actions, words and deepest thoughts as well as the way he strolls down a street, Robert embodies such harmony that you must inevitably search for his secret. The other day, I said that Robert operated through tropisms, and I'm not displeased with that turn of phrase. Dionys says that it's not enough, though; he's on the hunt as well. Regarding Robert, it's irresistible. You ought to be able to keep quiet, but instinctively you seek to express how you feel watching him eat, shave or simply sleep.

In the summer, Madame Fossé, my concierge, takes out, as she does every morning, her big dustbin. But at that hour in the summer, it's daylight, and the proprietress of L'Abbaye, the residential hotel over the road from my block of flats, is standing on her doorstep. So they chat. And at that hour, the street is so quiet that from my bed, when I am awake, I hear their words distinctly. It's always my concierge who begins: she doesn't say good morning, she complains about the dustbins. "After all, the tenants really go too far," she says. And Mademoiselle Ginsbourg invariably replies that indeed they do. Because of Mademoiselle Ginsbourg's presence, in the summertime, Madame Fossé's suffering is more bearable, since at the most critical moment she finds an echo in Mademoiselle Ginsbourg. After she has complained, her voice softens, and she usually talks about what kind of day it will be. She says, "That sky's overcast, going to be stormy." Or else, "That's sky's clear, going to be fine." Mademoiselle Ginsbourg agrees or adds a few touches, saying, "It'll clear around noon," or else, "Won't necessarily be fine, sky's clouded up over there ..." She must point in the direction she means, but I don't know which one.

Sometimes, when the man who sweeps the streets has started doing the rue Saint-Benoît a little earlier than usual, or when Madame Fossé is running a bit late, he happens to be sweeping in front of number 5 while Madame Fossé and Mademoiselle Ginsbourg are talking on their doorsteps, so he joins in the conversation, at the urging of Madame Fossé. Then the conversation takes a more general and philosophical turn, dealing with their respective jobs, the advantages and disadvantages entailed. The sweeper says his profession is a difficult one in the winter, especially when it snows. More briefly, Madame Fossé says his profession, street-sweeping, is a profession, whereas hers is not. She tells him that when he has finished his work, he has finished his work, that outside of his work hours he can do as he likes, but that she, on the contrary, never finishes here, that even at night, she's still a concierge, that she's constantly awakened by the front doorbell, that she cannot have a holiday because even if she managed to find someone to sit in her lodge, no-one, on the other hand, would take over emptying the dustbin in her place, that it looks easy, being a concierge, but that it's a rotten job, especially concerning the dustbins, etc. She's a concierge at night, during the day, every minute of her life. She doesn't explain what she means very well. She doesn't do a lot of work, but she's in the position of concierge day and night. She monitors the footsteps on the stairs day and night. It's a position so tightly superimposed on her own human condition that if you think about it, it's nightmarish, it coincides so perfectly that it's dehumanizing. The obsession. The horror. The sticky glue of nightmares. No escape.

She never explains herself at length on this subject. Mademoiselle Ginsbourg rarely joins any conversation with the sweeper, whose political opinions she does not share. Since they all speak from where they are standing – i.e. at their front doors and in the middle of the road – they raise their voices, which reach me easily. In the summer, when the pink and saffron-yellow sunlight peeks through the scaffolding around the École de Médecine, these voices arrive – mingling with the resonant footsteps of passers-by on the concrete pavements – and, depending on the day, sink me more groggily into sleep, or pierce me like arrows of light, flooding me with such intense clarity that I cannot go back to sleep.

When Madame Fossé talks about the coming day's weather, before opening my eyes I know the colour of the sky, I know that morning has come, and I find that moment conjured up by Madame Fossé's voice strictly irreplaceable. Madame Fossé calls things as she sees them, she says them succinctly, and her voice, more strident, more prophetic than the crowing of the cock, announces the advent of the day. The cock crows every morning, indiscriminately, metaphysically. Madame Fossé, though, stirs me to my soul, because she announces humanly, and by virtue of maturely digested human experience, the destiny of a day in the life of men, which will be what it will be, but the broad outlines of which she cannot change.

Last year, at the bottom of her hotel garden, Mademoiselle Ginsbourg raised a rooster, and I heard it many a time. That was how I came to compare the reverberation of its message with that of Madame Fossé. The sweeper sometimes gives his opinion on the coming day's weather, but he offers it in an offhand way, without the solemnity of the concierge. Despite his youth, this sweeper has turned this idea of the day's weather into an inescapable misfortune. Good weather or bad, his schedule never changes: he sweeps the rue Saint-Benoît, the entire length of the rue Jacob and, I believe, the rue Bonaparte. It's different for Madame Fossé, especially in the summer.

When it's fine, she parks herself in a chair in front of her door and for two whole hours, after lunch, she unravels old sweaters, which she then patiently reknits, stopping anyone she knows who lives on the street for a chat. We have had conversations about the sweeper. For a while, I was impressed by his confident stride, his handsome, intelligent expression and something noble in his bearing. We exchanged greetings every day. Planted in the middle of the road, his cap tipped over his left ear, {the Communist daily} *L'Humanité* sticking prominently from his pocket, he did his work with both sovereign efficiency and supreme casualness, using broad, even movements of his large broom, never stepping aside even for the passage of large lorries, which were obliged to drive around him. One day I asked Madame Fossé if the sweeper belonged to the Communist Party. She told me she didn't know, but that one might think so from the way he talked. I don't remember on what occasion I approached this sweeper and deftly asked my question. He told me that he was a Communist in his feelings but that he hadn't joined the party, because politics disgusted him and he would never join any party, he was much too independent for that. He told me all this with some embarrassment, and I was so surprised that I didn't know what to say. I walked away disappointed. Since then, we shake hands but never address the question of whether he has changed his mind. He retains his nobility in my eyes, but I believe less in his freewheeling ways now that I know they reflect not the clear-sighted, principled consciousness of a self-aware worker but the unselfconsciousness of a naïve and disillusioned man who fancies himself an individualist, who rejects all constraint save that of his work, work he endures without enjoyment, which embitters him more with each passing day, without allowing him to raise this {dissatisfaction} to the level of a revolutionary stance and find his salvation. I tried to explain this to Madame Fossé, telling her that a man like the sweeper, in the prime of his life, should either become a militant Communist, if he remained a sweeper, or try to change jobs, to do something else. Madame Fossé told me that this was indeed too bad, without any further explanation, but she spoke sincerely; she felt that it was too bad that he didn't belong to the Communist Party, but she did not seem truly convinced of it to me.

And, well, she and the sweeper are friends, and while I was speaking to her, she was wondering, I could tell, if my words did not reflect a certain disparagement of him. It's also true that she knows nothing about the Communist Party, and that she must have gathered that I had reservations about the Communist sympathies of her friend. He chops her wood, and when she's ill, he drags out her dustbin, in return for which she occasionally gives him a pack of cigarettes. Even if he did nothing for her, as long as he listens to her when she complains about the tenants, she considers him a true and understanding friend. I told her one day that complaining like that to the sweeper, and Mademoiselle Ginsbourg, and me, would get her nowhere, and that she needed to join the Union of the Concierges of the Sixth Arrondissement, that only there would she find recognition of her grievances, and that afterwards, if many others did as she had, the union would certainly find a way to deal with the tenants. She took her time about it but she did join, and ever since has been one of the Union's most faithful members. Her morale has improved now that she is sharing her concerns with other concierges and they are pooling their anger and indignation.

This morning, I heard neither Mademoiselle Ginsbourg nor the sweeper, only the noise of the dustbin on the flagstones and the pavement. For it's still winter, and Madame Fossé has no-one to talk to. I imagined her standing for a moment on her step, watching the rain fall, hoping the sweeper would arrive. Then she must have gone back inside. I could not fall asleep again. After I'd listened to the garbage bin, I did try to go back to sleep, but my eyelids were opening by themselves. The light was growing more distinct through the scaffolding around the medical school and the church of Saint-Germain-des-Prés and of … I heard the bells for the first Mass. I thought about what I would do that day, aside from the ordinary obligations of my work and household chores. I'd have to make up my mind about putting curtains on the sitting-room windows and moving the round table from Robert's room, replacing it with the bridge table from the dining room. I wanted Robert to have a quiet room, so nicely set up that he could work there comfortably. I was thinking that I would have liked to see R. happy and D. as well, those two in particular. And then for everybody to be happy. It seemed to me that if Robert had that square table in his room, he would be comfortable working there, and that, having worked well all day long, he would be happy in the evening. I felt kind and prepared to put myself out for the happiness of others, especially for Robert and Dionys. People were still going by in the street.

One evening, not too long ago, a man and a woman passed by beneath my windows. It was the middle of the night. They were singing a particular song, I don't know which one, but I felt that I'd heard it before, once, only once in my life, perhaps in a moment of happiness. It was a tune with a strong beat, with the tone and tempo of an old ditty. So it was the middle of the night and at that hour, meant for sleep, two people were singing that song. Alone in the world, they were singing, in quiet, careful voices; they weren't braying like drunks, they were listening to themselves sing. Only two people in love, who were still in the rush of a nascent love affair, could sing like that, in the middle of the night, alone; at that hour when the human race, weighed down by oblivion, feeds on sleep, they had spare time to devote to singing. In the middle of the empty night, where the two slopes of the night meet, arose that song: it was a red flower blooming suddenly from a night of stone. A song against death, to make you move mountains. All my flesh began to cry out and I wanted a man; the couple were long gone and I still couldn't sleep for wanting a man. I was alone. I imagined that a man could have come in. A stranger. Above all, a stranger, as unknown as the street. Why? Probably out of a concern for purity. To prevent sentiment from intruding upon this moment when I was fulfilled by the love of others, of those who had just passed by. The stranger would have entered me completely and stayed silent and motionless, and I, in the same way, would have remained motionless and satisfied, filled with what I was empty of – a man's sex, as full as a glass of wine – and linked to others, to the world by that penis lodged inside me, rooting me to the ground.

We are immobility and what we aspire to is that immobility.

*

Two passed by together, and they were talking as they walked quickly through the rain. I told myself that if everyone could listen to the street this way for a certain time each morning, they would find themselves changed.

Not too long ago, I took the metro at six in the morning; everyone reads *L'Humanité* in the metro. There's a coincidence there between the worker's lot in life and his adherence to the Communist Party, and if people were to observe this coincidence, becoming aware of it as if it were a fact, as real and indisputable as a purely material fact and as material as the realization of the great social laws that govern our society, many people would reflect and lose heart just enough to tire of imagining reality instead of seeing it, and would be disposed to accept this reality, naturally and without preconceived ideas. That's what I told myself, and also that I would have to say that simply and well, but it's very difficult. I was listening to the street, the footsteps, and I'd heard the sinister rumbling of the dustbin that – through the workings of class destiny – Madame Fossé found herself forced to drag out every morning (and that morning in particular, so alone in the rain), and I felt I was at the heart of a living reality that claimed all things, claimed my body as well as my thoughts, which were clear and distinct like things.

And then the child I am carrying moved inside me. He moved while those workers were passing, in the precise reality of the street. I had not forgotten my child, while he kept still, deep in my womb, for can one forget one is alive? But in the moment of his movement, he added himself harmoniously to the surrounding reality. It was when, tired of trying to fall back asleep, I had deliberately turned onto my back, with my ears well clear of my pillow, that he made his move. He began to wriggle just a bit above my pubis, and then I placed my hands flat on that part of my belly, to feel him. He lifted up my hands and rummaged around in there, so merrily and in such an early-morning way that I had to smile.

I wondered if he was sleeping, because there were moments of stillness and moments of movement, impatience, fidgeting. With my hands I tried to feel the parts of his body but could feel only its contour, especially the height, from just beneath my navel down to my pubic bone. He was deep inside me, almost against my back, and in this warm basin he frolicked comfortably, living inside me and bumping me around as he pleased, growing bigger and more robust every day, sucking a little of my blood every day, flexing muscles growing stronger every day until the day when, a fait accompli, he would solemnly become still to traverse that passage of my flesh still separating him from daylight. I have already had one child, and I know that this moment is terrifying when, head down, he will push at my uterus until it widens enough to let the whole of him out. At that point he will stop moving, and his heart will be pounding from his efforts. I know, for I've already had a child, that it's a terrible ordeal, and it awaits me in three months. This morning, when I felt him stir beneath my hands in the darkness of my womb, barely separated from me by that supple wall of my skin, I thought about the birth, that passage he would be making, that exit, and I could not imagine it: my womb was so closed, and my child was so peaceful there, so blissfully contained. It's an extraordinary thing. Of course, it has been experienced and said and described, but nonetheless, it is still extraordinary.

This morning, however, no matter how extraordinary giving birth seemed to me, it took its place in that totality of the dawn, and I found it no less extraordinary to hear the footsteps of the first workers along the pavement, the muffled noise of the dustbin, the slow and steady pouring of the rain, to know that the day was coming imperceptibly on and would tuck all that away into its diversity, among its many aspects. But for the moment, a few of its facets – the solitary morning workman walking briskly along the pavement; the horror of Madame Fossé's unchosen lot in life rearing its grumbling head; my child in my womb – were isolated, promoting so strongly in me what Paulhan calls "the illusion of the wholeness of the world" that I felt as if I were touching it, feeling an abstraction beneath my fingertips. While my hands were on my belly, the worker walked and moved along in the steady clatter of his footsteps, audible in the silence broken by the rumbling dustbin of the oppressed proletariat.

I would like to portray the joy of that hour. It isn't an exaltation or excitation of the mind. The joy came not from the day dawning on these things, but rather from these things arising in the dawn, just as if there existed a visible morning of things. While children are being formed, while the disgust of the oppressed proletariat grows stronger, men go to work in factories and prepare for liberation. It was an hour opening onto the future in every way. This morning, I saw that, and interpreted things in a certain way, and not because I am a Communist. (I don't think so, at least; how can one tell?) I feel that this morning, anyone else would have seen the rain, heard the footsteps, the rumbling of the dustbin, and felt her child move within her womb all in the same way, and would have found a fundamental bond that linked together these various expressions of the world.

But perhaps it is because I am a Communist that I believe that anyone at all would have perceived these things in the same way. Dionys would tell me that people don't say this, that it's false to say it. That one doesn't announce it. I belong to the Communist Party, which doesn't mean that I'm a Communist: that's what I would say. Between Pisa and Florence, I was sitting beside the driver of a lorry, and I announced it to him. I told him half in English, half in Italian. After arriving in Florence, I informed Dionys that I'd told him; that time, he said I was right. We went off to have a glass of Chianti in a cafeteria: Dionys, Robert, the driver, a mason and I. We'd been "recognized" in Pisa by the mason, who was also a comrade. We were waiting for the bus, and so was he (he was on a team of workmen helping to rebuild Pisa, and every Saturday they went home to Florence). When the lorry drove up, the mason went to tell the driver that we were French "comrades" and that he should give us a lift, because the Saturday-evening bus from Viareggio was always full. And so, while I was talking with the driver, Dionys and Robert were getting to know the mason, whom they told that they, too, were comrades. It was the end of August. The driver got going on the subject of Gasperi.[1] Whenever he said "Gasperi", he let go of the wheel, brandished his fists, then pounded them on the wheel while the lorry swerved wildly and the tarpaulins covering the back flapped in the wind. He was from Tuscany, the driver, twenty-five, quite handsome. He told me that he was an internationalist, and that he didn't make any distinction "between you and one of my comrades in Florence". When we went through villages, he drove very slowly to let me read the slogans chalked on the walls of houses: "Viva il Partito Comunista," "Viva la Repubblica," and the upside-down "V" in front of "Il Re". I read everything carefully, and told him that it was the same in France, that we used the same methods. He talked about Gasperi and I spoke of De Gaulle, and the way we'd got rid of him. He was happy, thrilled at each resemblance between our two countries.

The sky was red when we entered the Arno Valley, above the river; cypresses stood out against the Tuscan hills, the only hills in the world inhabited in a way that makes them unimaginable without this human presence, and here and there, among the villages, there were long, low monasteries with arched doors, flattened by their wide-angled roofs. "Are you from Florence?" I asked the driver, who replied, "Not from Florence itself, but I'm a Tuscan, from these parts." I looked around; between its dark banks, the Arno was green, moss-green. The vehicle sped along the road, still without headlights. It was cool, the heat of the day had passed; the coolness had come as we'd entered the Arno Valley, as if this coolness were rising from the river, a freshness made iridescent by forests of olive trees and the Arno's high banks of moss-covered rocks. Florence was waiting for us at the end of the road. I couldn't wait to see Florence. Every ten minutes the driver kept telling me, "Another quarter of an hour, twenty minutes – and you'll see, the hills of Fiesole, too. Right now we're just above the *Città!*"

I don't know why I'm talking about that driver, and the evening we saw Florence for the first time. Why wouldn't I talk about it? That hour, beside that Italian comrade, was as pellucid as this morning. It did not have the same meaning, of course, but I thought of it again this morning, and of our stay in Bocca di Magra. I thought of it because after listening to the rain and, hands upon my belly, feeling the unexpected movements of my child, I thought of my death, or rather, of my age. I'm thirty-two years old and this morning, since everything was so clear, the number "thirty-two" followed by the word "years" popped into my mind, and stuck to me. Lightning bolt. It was a number that concerned me. I had lived thirty-two years. I know those moments. Useless to describe them.

Whenever I hear it, I experience it as essentially quotidian. It's every day that it happens, every morning of every day, every day of the year. As for me, I hear it only rarely and when I do, I feel that I don't hear it every day but that it happens every day; I hear and understand it as such: quotidian. I would like to succeed in expressing this perfectly. In the abstract maelstrom of noise from a locomotive passing close by (the only noise that annihilates you, empties you out, you're a bug beneath that noise), all locomotives pass by and you feel that there are thousands of them in the world, locomotives that exist and that you don't hear, and you place yourself, in a blinding flash of consciousness, in the world of the locomotives of the world, in your world full of locomotives that – in every direction – shriek and race by, hauling swarms of carriages filled with your travelling contemporaries. In the same way – but in time, not space – the dustbin makes me feel the world of dustbins in my world, those bins full of peelings and empty tins from my contemporaries who eat, eat again, chew and chew again to soldier on, to keep themselves alive, who digest, absorb, digest again, keep themselves going, in an astonishing effort of perseverance, of such breadth and regularity that in itself it is more conclusive proof of man's desire to endure than the most famous cathedrals, which – although offered as examples – are mere record accumulations of perseverance that astonish with their gratuitousness, astonishing only those who do not hear the enormous din of chewing, the rumination daily repeated by man. That rumbling, that rumbling taken up and echoed by the dustbins – it's the most perfect noise possible to place you among your contemporaries, in your historicity: it's the cry of fraternity, because everyone eats and, refusing to resemble your enemies in any way whatsoever, you do as they do, you endure. Through this great [effort], from this soil, spring other [endeavours].

Soon she came back out and, in exactly the same way, stared again at the door to number 5 like an idiot. Leaning slightly from my window, I saw that Madame F.'s shutters were not yet open, and that Mademoiselle G. was looking directly at those shutters but without making the slightest gesture or move towards them. Have I mentioned that Mademoiselle G. was for me the very embodiment of stupidity? Mademoiselle G. is forty and a virgin. Anyone seeing her manage her residential hotel so carefully, so conscientiously, in the most perfect contentment and obvious satisfaction, anyone witnessing her happiness at the economy of her existence, the happiness of self-sufficiency, of providing that certainty for herself, would understand that Mademoiselle G. is a superlatively obvious target for crime, and the idea that her murderer might be punished for such a crime could lead to the direst conclusions regarding justice itself. Mademoiselle G. is a plaything in the hands of Madame F. And one can say that Madame F. is for Mademoiselle G. the only outlet in her life towards folly, passion, irrationality.

Through what admirable subterfuge has Madame F. arranged for Mademoiselle G. to practically feed her for free, and obtained an incontestable right to her share of the most delicious and exceptional dishes that Mademoiselle G. whips up for herself alone? I don't know. But it's an established fact that now Mademoiselle G. can hardly ever resist sharing her treats with Madame F. Each day at noon and at seven in the evening, Mademoiselle G.'s maid crosses the road, bearing to Madame F. – carefully wrapped in a spotless cloth – her rightful portion of Mademoiselle G.'s lunch and dinner.

"Not bad, your leg of lamb, but a touch underdone, if you ask me," says Madame F.

"Ah!" says Mademoiselle G. "You think so?"

"Well, that's what I said," replies Madame F., "and I don't usually talk to hear myself speak."

So I believe that Mademoiselle G. can no longer do without this kind of authority. Thus, having through mindless virtue escaped the supremacy of a male, Mademoiselle G. does not escape that of Madame F., in which she daily seeks brutal and arbitrary condemnation, exercised not only with regard to the dishes she sends her but apropos of her slightest initiatives and actions.

The sweeper is too gloomy. The sweeper has been brooding over something big for two days now. It's getting bigger, bigger. And (Madame F. admitted this to me the other day, in secret, but without giving me any explanations) he is drinking. When he's been drinking, she can tell from a mile off. If she's standing on our front step as he turns into the rue Saint-Benoît, she studies him immediately from 50 yards away, hands on her hips, and shakes her head. "Been drinking." She goes back into her lodge, gets her largest pot, fills it with water and places it on her table. And she gets on with her work without betraying her intentions in any way, except perhaps through her quickened pace. When the sweeper is close to the building, she opens her shutters and waits motionless by the window, holding the pot of water. The sweeper, who is accustomed to this, begins to chuckle, but softly. And to whistle. He only whistles when he's drunk. He's still lucid enough to sweep the street, and to provoke Madame F. by whistling quietly in front of number 5. He's sweeping: that is, he's sweeping the way one must sweep in a dream: dancing in the sunlight, without really sweeping anything, in a street from a dream. So he's whistling in front of number 5, laughing softly to himself, while keeping his eyes fixed on Madame F.'s barred window. Once directly before the window, he becomes motionless in turn, stops whistling and says, "Let 'er rip." Madame F. dumps the whole pot of water on his head. And then the sweeper starts laughing boisterously. "Pig," says Madame F. Her rage is at its peak. The sweeper's laughter has attracted Mademoiselle Ginsbourg and the waiter at the Restaurant Saint-Benoît, however. They laugh along with the sweeper. Madame F. comes out into the street as well. "That'll teach you," says Madame F. And then she joins in with her magnificent, throaty, velvety laughter that never comes completely out into the open, the loveliest laugh I have ever heard. "That'll teach me what?" hiccups the sweeper. "That'll teach you not to drink any more," says Madame F. "Next time I'll use my washbasin." They laugh together for a long while until Madame F. withdraws into her lodge and thinks about this sorrow dogging the sweeper.

Madame F. and the sweeper share an obvious complicity. I shouldn't like to put a name to it and I don't think I could. It's clear that if Madame F. were only twenty years younger, she would inevitably have slept with the sweeper. She knows this, and has certainly thought about it. He knows this, and has certainly thought about it. And she knows that he knows this, and he knows that she knows this. In short, they like each other perfectly, they suit each other. They "hit it off". But she's sixty and he's thirty.

*

[...] This drama that turns short, turns in circles, in defiance of
the most sacred and consecrated laws of drama, is one of the most
moving and unsettling moments imaginable. For if Madame F.
struggles against the sweeper's unfortunate inclination to drink,
she is struggling not only to save him but to save herself from
the fate that threatens her. Because if he continues to drink, she
must be convinced that it will end badly for her, and that a day
will come when he will kill her. He knows it. She knows that he
knows it. Which is why she empties her pot of water over him,
and why they laugh it off together.

The murderer takes aim at his victim, but his revolver jams,
and – would you believe it – victim and murderer burst out laughing at how seriously the murderer took aim, at how ridiculous
a murderer – no matter how accomplished – sometimes winds
up looking before even the most defenceless victim, and so they
"make up" at the expense of all mankind, which was expecting
the bang of a bullet through the heart, and not the blow-up of
this monumentally aborted tragedy. Victim and murderer "switch
places". The victim becomes the murderer of the murderer, by
challenging the latter's status as a murderer (a murderer whose
revolver jams in front of the victim is as ridiculous as a head of
state taking a pratfall before his subjects) and dominating the
murderer by laughing, literally diluting all his gravity – and what
gravity! – with laughter.

One day, my venerable mother, revered and forbidding, tumbled,
before my eyes, all the way down the stairs of a metro entrance.
And on her derrière, too, while I, seeing her venerability going
unexpectedly arse over teakettle, burst into uncontrollable laughter. And my mother yells at me, bellowing for me to help her
up. And people are outraged that a daughter is laughing at her
mother like that. And finally my mother, who shared the same gift
of laughter with me, laughs with me in turn, against the crowd.

Saint-Germain-des-Prés: the church
Rue Saint-Benoît: rue Sainte-Eulalie: rue du Père, rue du Fils
Mademoiselle G.: Mademoiselle Marie
Madame F.: Madame Dodin

1. Do not involve myself.
2. Avoid damning descriptions of Madame D.
3. It's not a simple psychological portrait but a story, a *novel*.
4. Return of the dustbin *necessary*.
5. Use short chapters?

- Main theme
- [Drinking]
- The street?
- *Royalty* of Madame D.
- Surprise and mother on her arse
- *We* instead of *I*
- Difficulty of writing about one's mother? about Madame D.?

- The theft of the butter
- The theft of the baby blanket
- Mention the fear Madame D. and the sweeper inspire in the neighbourhood, and the *respect*

- Return to the dustbin, unheard on that particular morning
- Madame D.'s funeral
- Madame D.'s son, and her daughter
- Conversation with Mademoiselle G., who informs me of the existence of 24,000 francs
- The sweeper

And ever since, he's been claiming that he would need an equivalent sum to go off to the Midi – to change his life – to enable him to abandon his shameful profession – change his life – to be happy. In short the game continues. It's an exceptional game, in which the players themselves don't know what's at stake. He knows she won't give him her savings. She knows he knows that. That she'll never give them up. Not only because they're six years' worth of savings (all her former savings were abandoned, twice, to her husbands) – for if the sweeper's health required it, she would certainly give them to him – but also to keep him from, as she puts it, "going under", drifting off toward a kind of seaside happiness, quite suspect, comprised of laziness, sunshine, refusal. For – instinctively – Madame Dodin does not like happy people. There would be a lot to say on that subject; she denounces her tenants' adulteries, and carefully takes advantage of every opportunity to stir up trouble between couples.

That's what Madame D. and the sweeper have come to. In addition to stealing, Madame D. has lately taken to writing anonymous letters. She's just getting started. She has sent anonymous threatening letters to a tenant – the very same one from whom she was stealing butter. [Since] she is more or less illiterate, it's Gaston the sweeper who writes them.

"If I write anonymous letters, it's because I like to, and who's to say anything against that?"

*

And so all the tenants find themselves challenged in their right, implicit until now, to have a dustbin and, therefore, to live.

Some of them, doubtless ill prepared for a war of contestations, thus find themselves treated with that same lack of consideration. But these tenants, naïve enough to become indignant, are the ones whom Madame D. hounds with the best results.

Because – setting aside, perhaps, the institution of the dustbin – nothing will ever assuage Madame D.'s dissatisfaction; nothing will ever temper what might be called her fundamental scepticism. The great nobility of Madame D. is just that: she is impervious to charity. When the nuns of the parish of Saint-Germain-des-Prés bring her the "roast meat for the elderly of the Sixth Arrondissement" at Christmas time, she looks at them and laughs.

"I'm still not going to Mass, I'm warning you," she tells them. "Not my style."

And when the sweeper [to whom she turns for confirmation] stands there laughing along with her, she tells him, "What business is it of theirs? I mean they should all get buns in the oven, those bitches, that'd teach them not to stick their noses so much into other people's affairs."

And in the same way, aside from her bosom buddy and sole accomplice, Gaston the sweeper, Madame D. will refuse all compromise with humanity, be it even through the medium of Mademoiselle G.'s kindness towards her. And as I was saying, Mademoiselle G. is nothing more for both her and the sweeper than the frightened witness of their complicity, a plaything and, so to speak, their victim. That's why, when Gaston shows up whistling 5o yards from the block of flats, and he's been drinking [...].

[...] and above all that even the last act, Gaston's murder of

Madame D., does not change profoundly. For although Madame D. worries about the sweeper, to keep him from ending up as her murderer, it's true that she esteems him nonetheless, and that to be worthy of his friendship, to hold up her end of their daily competition, she finally gives in to her deepest nature and to her hitherto repressed truth: what is commonly called vulgarity. On the whole, Madame D. blossoms along with the sweeper. She winds up writing anonymous letters and stealing. Stealing – the way I don't know anyone else her age can steal: purely. And so, even while she's deploring Gaston's propensity to drink, she encourages him in his gradual downfall. They compete with each other in saying the most blasphemous things, flouting the most sacred values, the most recognized authorities, in accomplishing the most audacious feats. In short, Madame D. wishes to be worthy of Gaston's crime.

The things they say make the entire neighbourhood shudder, which gives them great pleasure.

"The wars," says [Gaston].

To which Madame D. replies:

"The Germans […]"

And although Madame D.'s thefts are known only to a few [*illegible*], the two of them tend, ever so slowly, to make them public, they try to commit them more and more carelessly.

Along the entire range of private ecstasies, there is only the last act, the liquidation: the flowers in the gutter.[2] In other words, there was a time when Gaston believed that [*illegible*] his profession could satisfy his great curiosity. He no doubt believed that he could also be the sweeper of souls, of consciences; that he could gather in the inadmissible confessions one admits only to the sweeper. But alas, when he asks Mademoiselle G., "And your eye, how is it?" – she replies that it's doing really well. And he knows this is not so, that Mademoiselle G.'s eye is worsening every day but that she's hiding this from him because she fears (perhaps without fully realizing it) that one fine evening, when Gaston is drunk and when he knows her eye is bad enough not to recognize him, he might venture into her respectable residential hotel bent on a very, really very frightening purpose – because of his political convictions. So, the sweeper hears false news, even about Mademoiselle G.'s eye. As a result, naturally, he feels strongly that he belongs on the side of murderers, outlaws. He overdoes it in that department.

"Pierrot is dead," he announces, referring to Pierrot le Fou,[3] or else he must know everyone's name by heart [*illegible*].

"A fine crime: for a sweeper, that's the best thing that can happen to him. There's not a single crime they don't check with the sweepers. That's the sweeper's only entertainment."

Madame D. and Mademoiselle G. look at him, and after he's gone, Mademoiselle G. announces hypocritically, "For some time now, he's been saying things that ..."

And Madame D., who is on the sweeper's side, after all, replies, "A man like that, it's not everyone can understand him."

As soon as Gaston arrives, the conversation takes a more general, more philosophical turn. It's a question of their respective jobs and the advantages and disadvantages involved.

"That's a profession, at least, sweeper," begins Madame D.

"Shouldn't ever talk about what you don't know," says Gaston. "Otherwise you're talking without saying anything."

For Gaston, too, has a certain horror of his profession. But a philosophical attitude towards it as well.

"We both," says the sweeper, "have unappreciated professions."

"You certainly know what you're talking about," says Madame D.

At dawn, when the Club Saint-Germain closes its doors, along comes the sweeper.

"I always arrive too late," he says. "It's closed, music's over. In the pretty-girl department, seems it's full of 'em, but not for me. All I get to see is that there's some serious pissing on the club walls. You should have a look. The walls are black, it's even rather astonishing."

"'Course people got to piss," says Madame D., "seeing as they drink all night."

"The piss, that's for Gaston the sweeper. Gaston's promoted to these gentlemen's piss."

Madame D. looks at Gaston with love and pride. Gaston and she have the same way with words. Mademoiselle G. lowers her eyes. Everything Gaston says seems to her tainted with secret and unsavoury intentions.

"If you're judging by the piss," continues Gaston, "they must drink nonstop."

"They piss, therefore they drink," says Madame D.

"That reminds me of something," says Gaston the sweeper. "What you just said there. A philosopher must have said the same thing: I think therefore I am, he came up with that. Descartes."

"Been better off if he'd kept quiet," says Madame D. "Anyone could say that. Day carts of what?" she [ventures]. "Day carts of piss-all? And besides, how come you know that?"

"I like to read," says Gaston. "I have an arrangement with a guy on the garbage truck: he slips me the old books, I hand over the fag ends."

"In the meantime," says Gaston, "it doesn't get us anywhere."

"As to that," says Madame D., "I really don't know what would get us anywhere. And anyway we got a writer in the building, he's the worst of the lot."

"Don't mean a thing," says the sweeper.

"Mustn't generalize," says Mademoiselle G. timidly.

"You, with your De Gaulle," says Madame D., "you [get right up my nose]."

Although Madame D.'s colourfulness might possibly come close to ordinary picturesqueness through its regularity, its monotony, its repetitiveness – it would be a shame to assign her merely the standard picturesque quality, which is always dumb by definition.

Madame D. cannot share our enthusiasm for life. Were she to let herself accept, even once, a disgraceful compromise, she would be siding with her natural enemy: the tenant.

With great style, Madame D. refuses to knuckle under.

For Madame D. has a very distinctive idea of Providence (quotation) and a no less distinctive conception of the future of socialism (quotation). Still, Madame D. does throw into doubt, in its very principle, one of the most commonly accepted institutions, the most innocent, absurd, hidden violence in bourgeois society: the institution of the dustbin. Sending the letter,[4] giving her cause for satisfaction in her particular case, would make Madame D. (although I have my doubts) a replete, sovereign, contented concierge who would no longer send rampaging through number 5 rue Saint-Benoît one of those rages that truly ought to exist. All the tenants, whatever their merits, are lumped together and treated with equality, even perfect equality, of which I see no other instance in everyday life. And I really don't believe it's a bad thing that some of them should be challenged {politically like that}, even in what they feel is their right to fast on Fridays.

*

[...] every day her refusal is as complete as on the first day, as untouched as possible by any submission, any acceptance whatsoever. Madame D. could die for the cause: the suppression of the institution of the dustbin. Not a day goes by without her justifying her disgust in some way or another to [one of the] tenants. Her reasons are numerous, rooted in the most flagrant bad faith, and that's quite normal. Her passion blinds her, and she cannot put it into words when she is calm. The tenant {who suffers it} is usually the last one to empty a dustbin. This has become one of the particular little obligations of the building. To get scolded because of emptying a dustbin. A bin you emptied because you had one to empty, which you had because you eat, and because as long as you live you'll have one to empty. And that's how the many tenants unprepared for this kind of thing have learned that someone could contest their hitherto accepted legal right to have dustbins, and how those who are the most convinced of their [rights] have seen themselves treated with such [...]

The most unexpected consequence of her friendship with Gaston is that he has alienated her from her children, especially her youngest son. She no longer wants to see him: he bores her. She raised him very well and has made uncommon sacrifices for him. Her husband would drink her salary and she, to [raise her] children, she worked in a factory for fifteen years. After the factory, in the evenings, she took in laundry. Her daughter is a post-office employee. She lives in a distant *département* and rarely sees her mother.

"On that score, I've no worries."

But her son is a small farmer in Chatou. He comes to see her on New Year's Day, Bastille Day and Easter, when she invariably welcomes him by saying, "I did so much for them that I'm tired of them. All I want from them is just to stop bothering me."

Her son and daughter often ask her to come "live out her days" with them.

"Even if I'd be living like a queen with you, I'd rather croak in a home for the elderly."

Sometimes Madame D.'s son comes to see her. For Madame D. has two children. He comes to see her on New Year's Day, the anniversary of the Liberation and Easter. Just as she has constant grievances against her tenants, Madame D. has some against her son: just as vague, just as terrible.

"Children, they're all lousy bastards, and even the best ones," begins Madame D., "no exceptions."

The son takes a seat in her lodge.

"And she's off," says Madame D.'s son.

"If you can't bear to hear a few home truths," says Madame D., "just go right back where you came from."

"It's not that he's bad," Madame D. tells the tenants, "but it's only normal, he's waiting for me to croak. So naturally he's the one I've the least to say to."

And she invariably adds, "Don't like macaronis."

This seemingly benign, gratuitous remark is aimed at her daughter-in-law, who is Italian.

"Really like to know what it is you got against me," says the son.

Seeking lady with child-care experience and excellent references (preferably around forty years old) mornings nine to noon
for housework and four to six p.m. to take the baby out, except
Sundays.
  In return:
  furnished maid's room with electricity
  4,000 francs
  breakfast
  and midday meal.

We cannot sleep any more.

The opening of the Club Saint-Germain-des-Prés has turned the rue Saint-Benoît upside down. All night long, nothing but engines revving up, horns blowing, car doors slamming. It's practically impossible to close your eyes until three in the morning. Let's note that on the rue Saint-Benoît, almost opposite the Club Saint-Germain-des-Prés, there's a home for the elderly. Let's note, for example, that in number 5 alone there are eleven children. And we've learned that another Tabou[5] will be opening on the impasse des Deux-Anges. That will make three nightclubs on one narrow street and [*illegible*]. Couldn't the rue Saint-Benoît be made a one-way street? And the [*illegible*] be situated on the Place Saint-Germain, where parking will be available? And where the noise, given the size of the square, would be less unbearable?

The Socialist Party has come out against cantonal elections. It shuns universal suffrage, the suffrage of workers, housewives, the middle classes. It is afraid. And with reason. And wishing to hide its fear, it betrays, it sells, it plays the informer. During the parliamentary session devoted to the cantonal elections, it "gave up" the Madagascan parliamentarians.

And to fool its people, here's what it did: although the elections were the only subject under discussion, the party hijacked the question, starting off with a motion to suspend proceedings against the Madagascan parliamentarians. Two deputies – [Violette], the Democratic and Socialist Union of the Resistance, and [*illegible*], an independent – {then} rise to announce that the Parliament cannot block a judicial [*illegible*]. And as if struck by this fact, the socialists immediately withdraw their motion and abstain. And because of their disgraceful action, the motion is withdrawn.

And then the Socialist Party, believing it has honourably re-deemed itself in advance through an [*illegible*] initiative, having sold out the Madagascan parliamentarians to the reactionaries, [votes] against the cantonal elections and for a uninominal ballot – {voting for a single member only} – in two rounds in March 1949.

After that fresh disgrace, on the heels of a struggle that had al-ready gone on for too long, five socialist deputies and Paul Rivet, director of the Museum of Natural History and city councillor from our arrondissement, tendered their resignations. For which we congratulate them. We see a connection between their action, the creation last Sunday of the Unitarian Socialist Party, and the "fed-up" socialists, whose numbers increase by the day. And let us hope that the voice of the masses will be increasingly heard "from the bottom up" against their leaders.

It's uncomfortable sitting at a round table: your elbows aren't resting on anything and you can't lean on them to rest from writing, and while you're writing they're sticking out into nowhere, and if you don't notice that right away you tell yourself, "I don't know what's wrong with me, I'm tired," and it's because your elbows aren't resting on the table.

NOTES

1. The distinguished Italian statesman and politician Alcide de Gasperi, co-founder of the Italian Popular Party and prime mover of the Christian Democratic Party, was an antifascist and a staunch supporter of the idea of a European community.

2. In her novella *Madame Dodin*, Marguerite Duras writes that Gaston has become blasé because "he has lived too much [...] He has witnessed every event, public or private, that happens in the streets he sweeps." And so, his "personal philosophy, which is perhaps that of the true sweeper", is that all human events, "first Communions, marriages, deaths, invariably finish, according to him, in the same way, with flowers tossed into the gutter and guided by him downstream to their final destination, the sewer."

3. "Pierrot the Madman", alias Pierre Loutrel, was a criminal who came into his own during the Occupation, a "Gestapiste" and cold-blooded murderer. When the tide turned, he and his gang switched sides, shielding their pimping, racketeering, robberies and assassinations in the Resistance. When he died in 1946 after a botched hold-up, Pierrot le Fou was France's public enemy number one.

4. This enigmatic letter is not one of the "anonymous threatening letters" mentioned earlier in the text but – as explained in *Madame Dodin* – a letter the narrator has considered sending to the other tenants on the concierge's behalf concerning her complaints about the refuse situation. But such a letter, reflects the narrator, if successful, might do the concierge "more harm than good. If her tenants become irreproachable, won't she experience painful nostalgia for her enemies?" So the narrator decides not to send such a letter.

5. The famous 1950s nightclub Tabou, at 33 rue Dauphine, was frequented by the likes of Boris Vian, Juliette Greco, Miles Davis and Sartre.

II
OTHER TEXTS

Introduction

The four autobiographical texts devoted to childhood and family we have collected here under the title "Boundless Childhood", as well as the six stories that follow them, were written by Marguerite Duras during the same period as the *Notebooks*, and some of the pieces might even date from shortly before the outbreak of the war. They are published here for the first time, with the exception of the long story "Eda or the Leaves", which was published in the literary journal *Confluences* in October 1945.

The first four texts are the oldest ones in the Marguerite Duras Bequest at IMEC and can be dated roughly to the end of the 1930s. Written in pencil on sheets of paper folded into quarters, they were never neatly copied out and are sometimes difficult to decipher. Each one testifies to the significance of her family history at a time when she was gradually achieving financial, emotional and professional independence: she finished her studies and began working in 1937; she married Robert Antelme, whom she met that same year, in 1939. The last of these short pieces, which recounts the circumstances of her father's death in 1921, is the only known text by Marguerite Duras devoted to that event.

The six stories in the last section were doubtless written a little later. Autobiographically inspired in various ways, they are among the first literary exercises by Marguerite Duras. They are typed and their rough drafts show signs of rewriting. The second story, "Is That You, Sister Marguerite?", which is entirely handwritten and in dialogue form, is an exception: it is a variation of the text devoted to the death of her first child that appears in the *Beige Notebook* (pp. 185–7), and it was taken up again under the title "The Horror of Such Love" in the magazine *Sorcières* (1976) and later in the collection *Outside*.

The universe of these works of fiction already resembles that of Marguerite Duras' first two published novels[1] (see "The Stolen Pigeons") and presents certain themes essential to her future work (love and its extinction in "Horror" and "The Bible"; death and ennui in "Eda or the Leaves").

NOTE

1. *Les impudents* (Paris: Plon, 1943); *La vie tranquille* (Paris: Gallimard, 1944).

Boundless Childhood

I would like to see in my childhood only childhood. And yet, I cannot. I even see no sign of childhood there. In that past there is something thorough and perfectly defined – and regarding which there can be no possible mistake.

My childhood is utterly alien to me. I consider it the most barren period of my life, aside from a few years that are like a wayside altar there, from which I have drawn strength for my entire life. Nothing more clear-cut, more lived, less dreamed than the whole of my childhood. No imagination, nothing of the legends and fairy tales that grace childhood with the shimmer of dreams.

I don't want to explain anything to myself. That's how it is with me and my two brothers, who experienced those same years. Even so, that childhood plagues me, and follows my life like a shadow. It holds me not through its charm, for it has none in my eyes, but, quite on the contrary, through its strangeness. It has never moulded my life. It has been secret and solitary – fiercely locked away, buried within itself for a very long time.

I will speak of it at the pleasure of the inner wind that rises whenever I feel my childhood steal over me and haunt me like a forgotten – and unresolved – adventure.

I did not have long years of a settled everyday life, or the comfort that springs from them and from the rhythm of that sweet comfort, the slow way in which it frees itself from time, establishing its charm. No, I had nothing of all that: I had neither family home, nor familiar gardens, nor attics, nor grandparents, nor books, nor those comrades one watches grow up. Nothing of all that. You wonder, what's left? My mother is left. Why hide it from myself?

The story I wish to tell is hers, that astonishing mystery, never fathomed, the mystery that was for so very long my joy, my sorrow, where I always found myself again and whence I often fled only to return.

My mother was for us a vast plain where we walked for a long time without ever taking its measure, and there I see no sign of the halo of tenderness and vigilance that accompanies revisited memories. Besides, that plain is not a memory. It is a vast march that has never ended.

I know nothing of her life as a woman, a girl, a wife. I see her as our mother, that's all.

Here I stop, for I would like to be able to say what that motherhood has been and still is – and words seem insubstantial to me. I would like, in order to see her, to stand clear of her, to push away for a moment that absorbent reality she still is. That's it: before us, she must have been quite impure, tainted by so much unsanctified human passion. That's all I can say.

We arrived, all three of us; we were the salt of her life, the salt of that earth from then on made sumptuously fertile.

She experienced that passion for us without the slightest restraint. She lived it actively. Without that patience, that respite granted mothers like a benediction.

She bore her passion, alone, with an unquenchable violence, and her shoulders, still bowed from her burdens, have lost none of their beauty.

Quite young, we took part in her life. We were her friends, and I believe our sense of reality came to us from her. Her reality was our dream. We were nourished on her as other children are on wild and idle fancies. We shared her misfortunes and her joys in all their plenitude.

We came from far away, always from far away. Arrivals and departures followed one another in our life the way in others, years roll by slow and steady, bound tightly one to another. My father was a civil servant in the Far East. More details would be useless and even fatal to any impression given of our childhood. There is life growing everywhere, children who live and blossom and search for their true selves, and [*illegible*] – some in large and [lonely] walled gardens, others in kitchens, in spacious and austere flats, and some as well on exposed and desolate pavements where one may yet carve out some private life, perhaps even some mystery. As for us, we were the kind of people who are familiar with ports and railway carriages. [Well,] that never produced any extraordinary revelations. Children have the grace of plants and take from the earth only what can nourish them. They leave the rest. We had astonishments as pure and simple as everyone else's. We knew nothing of generalities, had no notion of the world and journeys, for we lived only on the present of every day.

I always see us in a rather curious light. Perpetually gaunt and tired, on the [*illegible*] mornings of arrivals in nameless and unfamiliar stations, all crowded together, huddled against my mother, fruits of a single cluster, tangled up with one another, sharing even the same flesh and the same fatigue. Mama protected us, brooded over us indiscriminately, with an affection as disorderly as our bodies.

We were very young for a long, long time. An unheard-of, inexhaustible time, which always feels immeasurable to me. We were three: my two brothers, Pierre and Paul, and myself the last – I do not see myself as having any name; yes, we were very young children for a long time. Then one day, and all of a sudden, one of us, the eldest, Pierre, became a stranger to us. He abruptly overtopped the edge, emerging from the great depths of our earliest youth towards much more enlightened and definite horizons. That was, beyond question, a cruel blow for me, because I sensed that my other brother would inevitably be struck in the same manner, leaving me bewildered, all weighed down with shadows, in my first orchard.

Then other circumstances, later on, cut me off from that passionately envied world [to which I aspired]. The commingling of our [lives] that had always reigned soon vanished, giving way to an appalling separatism that seeped even into our least little games. In spite of sublime efforts on my part to [*illegible*] my state, I was excluded and alone with my childhood.

That was something I [realized] on certain memorable days.

We were very free, let loose in a big garden in Phnom Penh. Our father was the principal of a large secondary school, and its life gave rhythm to our own.

The big bustling school paid no attention to us and lived all around without disturbing us. We were still at the sublime age of perfect ignorance, and studious zeal, albeit so intoxicating, did not affect us. But we knew that this school emptied out towards the lunch hour and suddenly became accessible, and ours.

Siesta time, conspiring, was our accomplice, [*illegible*] a calm so penetrating, so eternal, that it [bathed] us in space and freedom. Nothing in the world could trouble the torpor of those hours, and that was something we felt perfectly. We gorged ourselves on that freedom with a giddiness already pent up in our long mornings of waiting.

My brother was handsome, with a beauty completely unrelated to grace and perfectly present even in his earliest childhood.

Not that simple promise of beauty but already a kind of perfection, harmonious in all its terms. Thus it is with that young Saint John by Donatello, so noble of bearing that one cannot take him for a mere child. He is too cruel, one thinks, too crazed in his triumph not to be a child, yet kisses and caresses were not enough for him.

[This was] my brother, so handsome that I think I have never seen such beauty more [...] green eyes, tawny and indescribable, lost, making features of such delicacy and distinction that no expression could distort their lines.

He was handsome for a long while and doubtless still is. But a veil came to lay down its sadness, behind which his first countenance still lives [with] a more secret life.

To be alone, she sent us to stay with some of her relatives and left to spend two weeks in Platoriet.[1] There, I believe, she found two servants who expected and received her; placing the keys in her hand, they placed the premises and themselves in her charge. Only they had intimate knowledge of my father's last days; they spoke of him with complete respect and devotion.

They were thus able with rare tact to retrace perfectly for her the last months of his life. Those months had been quite peaceful and astonishingly mild. Although I was not there, I know their light and mellowness, touching the park in autumn when the last mists well up from the valley of the Dropt River, when all the humming, sun-nourished life deserts the grounds and leaves them silent and calm like the chancel of a church when the last service is done.

My father was weak, very weak, and he died of that weakness. His illness, although not serious in itself, gradually wore him out. When life takes its leave that way, so gently, without any shock, like an idling stream, death comes like a drowsiness and puts life to sleep with the ease of a good healthy fatigue. That is how it was for my father.

My father died in his sleep, on a fine afternoon in early winter. The spacious grounds were sleeping as well and their silence entered the bedroom like an enchantment. This silence was doubtless enough to put my father, barely alive, completely to sleep.

It must have been quite calm throughout the vast empty house, the room now scarcely alive in the infinity of those last moments.

The casement window was open to the lime trees, and the large red drapes entombed whatever remained of wakefulness in things.

A scant few birdcalls from eternity served as my father's last appeals from life. As he was late in ringing, his servant came on his own initiative. He knocked, several times, and understood that what they had been waiting since the beginning had arrived.

They knew what they had to do in that case. They did it most meticulously and with noble dignity.

With my father dead, they were masters of the premises and even so used that freedom only with absolute discretion. They did not leave the property, because they knew their role was to receive my mother when she arrived.

My father had only them. They were all alone at his death. They dressed him in his formal black suit. He was so thin and so light that he seemed like a child. Henri laid him out on the big bed and went to inform the villagers that his master was dead. Jeanne remained by the bed until the evening, and throughout the night as well. She kept vigil over the dead man in a state of servitude from which nothing could release her.

So everything was done that ought to be done.

They buried my father the next day, in the cemetery of the little village to which Platoriet belonged.

Many good people who did not know him followed his coffin, for they knew he was alone and far from friends and family.

He is there to this day. My mother had always wanted to move his body to our grounds. The site was chosen, beneath a patch of snapdragons, but time dragged and Platoriet no longer belongs to us.

I went back there when we sold the property. I walked up that long road all bathed in sunshine. It was a most beautiful April day, astonishingly lovely, so lovely that all the first roses had bloomed and were already drooping with bees. I picked a big bouquet of roses whose ashes would be there still if some vigilant caretaker had not removed them.

And then, since then, perhaps some soul has brought a few other flowers. The days, the nights pass over his body, and the shadows of the yews, so marvellously precise in the full sun, sweep his stone with lacy threads of gold. And so everything is very calm, and so slow that time itself has forgotten its work. I grew up, but his death still has for me the gentle sweetness of an afternoon nap.

NOTE

1. The author's father, Henri Donnadieu, died at Le Platier, a property he had purchased in his native region, Pardaillan par Duras in the *département* of Lot-et-Garonne. Marguerite Duras felt a strong attachment to the area and took its name for her nom de plume.

Stories

Cambodian Dancers

It was in that part of Upper Cambodia caught between mountain and sea, near the Siamese border. There is only one road left out there, which grows worse and worse and stops, defeated, at the sea. The Elephant Mountains run along its entire length and plunge into the placid Gulf of Ream, where they still surface in a few islets that grow ever more rare. Some small poor villages are scattered along the roadside, tucked away in the forest. Towards evening they light up: great fires of green wood and thick streams of resinous smoke perfume the countryside.

This *lokhon*, this dancer, went from village to village. I happened to be in Bantai when she arrived. The monotonous beat of a little tam-tam had been announcing her since that morning; unceasingly it called, it implored people to come to see her. At nightfall the paths were thronged with the curious, men and women who had come from other villages.

By the time I got there, the straw hut was dark and crowded. In the centre, on an empty platform, the *lokhon* was already dancing. Smoky lamps seemed to isolate her from the rest of the world and the night. An old Cambodian woman crouching in a corner of the hut was chanting a monotonous song with a staccato beat. Her voice was thin and hoarse. Her voice was ugly, but she knew how to express the passion of an implacable rhythm; sometimes, to follow it, she shouted, no longer able to sing, and her cry seemed one of despair.

278 WARTIME NOTEBOOKS AND OTHER TEXTS

This memory has always remained a vision for me.

The girl dances; she is still young, and yet her beauty is ripe and already prepared for the sacrifice of decline.

Dressed in tarnished fake gold, she is badly made up, plastered in white. Her arms and shoulders are bare. She must have walked long hours in the sun because her throat and chest are burned. The skin of her arms is white and cool and the heavy bracelets seem to bite into it.

She does not know how to dance: she is a pagan, a false *lokhon*. She gives her dance to everyone, she gives her youth, she does not know how to hold anything back, and after the dance she gives her body for the rest of the night. No-one would want her for a servant; she dances only at night, and during the day she sleeps in some ditch or walks along the roads with her old singer, who has nothing left except her.

Thanks to her performance I understood Khmer dancing, which for centuries has nourished a people with its magic, and brings a great ceremony even into that dark and [*illegible*] straw hut.

She and the old woman begin together. The first notes sung are deep and sombre, but one senses immediately that they are calling other, more distant notes.

The dance starts soberly, as if through the extreme attention it brings to being born at a precise moment. It begins with the slap of a heel, then climbs, sinuous and slow, up to the hips. It opens out and lives intensely in the torso which at once becomes something closed, infinitely precious, from which the dance tries in vain to escape.

The hips stop moving; the legs move apart, and the feet skilfully take their places. Then the arms and bust are abruptly touched by grace and caught up in the necessity of the dance. The supple arms seem overcome by the weight of the fragrance they receive. Sometimes they live in opposition: the one in back repelling and defending, the other held out in front, the palm swollen, imploring. The hand, the divine hand, is broken as if by too great a weight. The hand is stiff with endless pain.

Once launched, she is clearly improvising. One thinks of the supreme concentration of the court dancer imprisoned in her dance, that second life that has chosen and possesses her. This dancer, she is free and she weaves her dance in perfect solitude with herself.

She seems to stretch out of her body, suddenly weary of [embracing] so little space, of being unable to go further outside herself.

Then all of a sudden the dance stops.

The dancer returned to her cramped and tired little body. Panting and glistening from the heat, she rested. Everyone stayed there looking at her with a base and cruel curiosity. Now unclothed, her theatrical nakedness was exposed, and all at once the men desired her because of the fatigue handing her over to them.

She was obliged to dance all night. For a long time the little tam-tam sent out its tenuous call. It ceased only when cool dawn entered the hut, exhausted.

She set out again with the day, for she was one of those who cannot alight anywhere.

The mannered and sophisticated court dancer would laugh at her dance and her fate, without understanding that she, too, was chosen to bear off into the distant countryside the message of her untutored art.

"Is that you, Sister Marguerite?"

"It's me."

"Where is my child?"

"In a little place near the delivery room. A small morgue, really. He's there."

"What is he like?"

"He's a beautiful little boy. We wrapped him in cotton. You're lucky, I had enough time to baptize him. So he's an angel and he'll go straight to heaven and be your guardian angel."

"Why did you wrap him in cotton if he's dead?"

"It's what we do. It looks better for the parents who come in. It's two o'clock in the morning, you should sleep."

"You have something to do?"

"No. I'd like nothing better than to stay with you, but you must sleep. Everyone is asleep."

"Everyone is asleep?"

"Yes. I'm going to bring you a [sleeping pill]."

"You're nicer than your mother superior. You'll get me my child. You'll leave him with me for a moment."

"You're not serious, are you?"

"Yes, I am. I'd like to have him with me for an hour. He's mine."

"That's impossible. He's dead. I can't give you your dead child. What would you do with him?"

"I'd like to see him and touch him. Ten minutes, if it's alright with you."

"There's nothing I can do. I won't go."

"What are you afraid of?"

"That it would make you cry. You'd upset yourself. It's better not to see them in these cases. I'm accustomed to it."

"It's your mother superior you're afraid of. You're not accustomed to anything."

"Sleep. Your little angel will watch over you."

"Do lots of them die?"

"Two weeks ago. One of them died. Well ..."

"Well?"

"Well, the thing is, it was a dwarf, actually, a little monster, so ..."

"So?"

"So we didn't revive him. But he came back to life all by himself. *He wanted to live, the poor little dear*."

"So?"

"So we shoved a towel into his mouth. *But he wanted to live, that poor little dear*. It was difficult."

"And the mother all this time?"

"We told her we were reviving him, doing what we could."

"Who did that?"

"I did."

"You baptized him first?"

"Of course. I always baptize them. That way we're more certain."

"You baptized him and you killed him?"

"I baptized him and I sent him to heaven, straight there. It was better."

"Why are you smiling?"

"Because you seem astonished."

"I think you were right to do that. But what astonishes me is that you seem so certain about it."

"When one carries God in one's heart, one is always certain. You should pray with me and you will fall asleep."

"Get it through your head that I don't give a damn about your prayers. If you've killed a child, you could certainly bring me mine, in my bed, for a moment."

"I don't even know if he's there any more."

"What are you saying?"

"We don't keep them very long."

"What do you do with them?"

"I'm not permitted to tell you. Go to sleep."

"Say it."

"You really want me to? Here, we BURN them. Now you know. Go to sleep."

"You're not asleep yet?"

"No. He's not there any more?"

"I don't know. I didn't go to check. But after two days that would surprise me ..."

"So you burn them?"

"We burn them. It's over very quickly. In an electric oven."

"Why did you tell me that?"

"You asked me to."

"You could have lied. It's because I told you I didn't give a damn about your prayers. You should never have told me."

"I feel very sorry for you, not believing in the Good Lord and his works."

"His works?"

"If your child is dead, that means that the Good Lord has called him home. And that's good."

"I would like you to leave this room."

*

"I'm the mother superior. Wake up."

"What?"

"The priest is here. You want to see him?"

"No."

"You don't want to take Communion?"

"No. Let me sleep, as I'm sleeping for once."

"Call me Sister, please. You are in a convent here. So not even the priest, even without taking Communion?"

"Nothing. If you'd just close the curtains. I'm exhausted. I want to sleep."

"What are all these flowers people are bringing you?"

"Why are you shouting like that?"

"You don't need all these flowers. You will *at least* give them to the Holy Virgin."

"Why don't I need these flowers?"

"Since your baby is dead, what are you doing with them? You aren't even permitted to have any visits, understand? I'm going to send them to the altar in our chapel."

"I don't want that."

"You really don't? Don't want Communion, or the priest, or even a bouquet for our Holy Virgin?"

"There's no point in shouting. I don't want that."

"And you dare to complain? *She* doesn't even want to give a bouquet to our most Holy Virgin and *she's* complaining? And *she's* complaining that her child is dead?"

"I am not complaining. Get out."

"I am the mother superior. I will get out when I feel like it. You aren't complaining? Then why do you cry all day long?"

"I feel like it."

"And what did I just see on your table? An orange? Who gave you that orange?"

"It's my dessert. It was Sister Marguerite."

"And do you think that we have oranges to waste like that? In times like these?"

"Get out."

"Here oranges are something we give to mamas. To mamas who have their babies. And who are nursing them. Here we don't give oranges to just anyone, not us, let me tell you."

Horror

"Well I'll be! It's you, it's really you?" He was still on the opposite pavement. Despite the darkness of the night, she immediately recognized his step, the set of his shoulders. She felt no surprise at all as he crossed the road without hurrying, trying to behave casually.

"Always late: not very nice, from an old hand …"

He liked to joke around that way, just a bit.

When he got close to her, large as life, she was amazed not to feel that same jolt of weakness as in the past. She suggested going somewhere for a drink. Champagne. Of course: she'd been waiting six months for him to come back from Algiers, that was certainly occasion enough.

Back. He was here. But too bad – she could scream it to herself all she wanted: no effect at all.

From that moment there arose between them an overwhelming, divisive anguish. They were as far from each other as the two banks of a river, and just as close.

Suddenly she gave it a try: he touched her hand. Nothing. Or rather, she felt like pulling hers away. Strangers now, their hands no longer sought each other. In the past their desires had surged and spoken through those hands clinging greedily to one another beneath tables. Bloodless from now on, those hands, and numb.

With little sips, she swallowed the bitter champagne. She was smiling. As much as one can smile with a brightly painted face. Him, he kept his face averted. Why was she laughing for no reason?

But he didn't greet life in the same way she did, this woman who burdened herself with useless emotions. He was a man, he was, and tough. He had to be, to foil her plans ... Imperturbably, ceremoniously, he told her of his delight. Seeing her again, oh – it was wonderful. Really something, right? There'd been a lot of problems; among others, his mother was also awaiting his return. Yes ...

Deep down, he wondered if he'd made a mistake in coming back to Paris. Bold tactics: "I hadn't heard from you, I was worried. You might have been ill. I came to find out what was going on, that's all ..."

He swallowed his champagne without tasting it, lapping it daintily like a cat. Glass in hand, he studied the clear liquid against the light with a deeply stupid eye. As in the past. But back then, she'd thought it was desire that made him seem so dazed.

She did not reply; she let him talk and whinge.

Something had deserted this man. Something was leaving him behind and bereft, something very like his reason for being. How awful it was not to believe in it all any more. Without meaning to, little by little, she was abandoning him to his destruction. This man's simple presence, a few months ago, had been everything to her. Now the futility of that presence just confounded her. She continued to encourage his wretched confession, however, with a shimmering smile that periodically lit up her face, as a lighthouse illuminates the briny grimace of the ocean.

Then, abruptly, she stopped him: "Come."

He chose his tone unerringly: false, hoarse and vulgar, enough to make anyone else weep. "You're the best, you know." How horrible for her. Horror was eating into her soul. Oh, what if her strength failed her ... No, really, after all. Well, then – was she crazy?

With a triumphant gesture, she drained her glass as if saluting her own daring, but there was nothing cynical about it.

He began to wax sentimental. He felt obliged to, he had his principles. Sentiment, a trick he used but rarely. At which point he became irresistible. Women let themselves be caught like flies in the honey of his voice. This evening, he ran true to form.

"Do you remember our engagement?"

An old joke.

That's what he called the beginning of their love affair: a modest debut, hey? Ah, he'd never expected it ever to acquire that scale, that "maturity", as he put it so subtly, so intelligently.

She insisted that they move on to the old address. But ... He had earned good money as a foreman in Algiers. And in the newspaper he'd just leafed through, certain addresses – with every modern convenience – had caught his eye. Oh come, come now, she ought to let him decide. She refused point blank, and sharply. Huh! The tart, he thought, the bitch! Whatever's got into her?

She wasn't saying anything in the taxi. He felt uncomfortable. He was having to search for words, which wasn't like him. Despite his density, his grimy coating of vanity, of insensitivity, the thing was getting to him, seeping in silently, little doses but from all sides, the way water attacks a foundering ship. In the back of the car, she snuggled up to him, stiffly, perhaps so he would come to her rescue. Ha! Suddenly the voice broke, like a piece of porcelain. He was annoyed, really aggravated – his only way of feeling things. He still relied on his principles, however, and tried to show her his gratitude. Taking her awkwardly by the shoulder, he kissed her behind the ear. With the best will in the world. Because he was really worried.

He started to sing. A tune from several years ago, one built into the framework of their affair: part of the act they used to play with one another in the comedy of love. Oh my God! It made her ache all over. The nerve. What a pity! What a life. She wasn't angry with him any more. Besides, she could hardly leave him singing by himself. She hummed along. His voice, cracked until now, firmed up to recover its former strength. Without realizing it, she really was a good kid, pure and kind like a woman who gives unstintingly of herself.

Impasse de la Bastille. Once it was their neighbourhood.

He wanted to stay a little longer in the taxi. Wouldn't she think he was doing this only for one thing? He tried to kiss her tenderly. She struggled. Whenever he touched her, she could feel herself turn nasty. Crestfallen, he said nothing more. In fact, he was falling prey to a kind of paralyzing distress.

No point in putting himself out, that was clear. Such a big strong guy – and he didn't have it in him to leave, even though he didn't want anything any more. But he didn't dare; she'd got to him. Like her, he was waiting for her to make up her mind to do it.

He went first. The dark and sordid dead-end street. In the past they'd savoured the joys of wickedness there. Then, the wind would whistle through, moaning; she would already be melting at the prospect of pleasure and her willpower would vanish with the wind's first slap in her face.

He filled the room with his great height, and his movements as he undressed were so many grand gestures within which she performed, efficiently, her own. He was taking his time, stealing glances at her. He was unsure of himself.

She took off her coat, literally tore off her clothes and turned down the bed at full speed, as if her life were at stake.

"But what is it, what's wrong with her?" he wondered.

"Come on, let's get on with it!"

In a real whore's fit of temper, she spat out her uncontrollable irritation.

He stood there in front of her, helpless, stock still, wide-eyed.

"Let's talk for a moment," he pleaded.

Bluntly, she took matters in hand.

She teased him, behaved childishly. Caresses, laughter – she undressed him with elaborate ceremony, the way a page undresses a
lord. He, slowly, froze. She was making a fool of him. In any case,
this whole business seemed peculiar to him. That's right, peculiar. He felt a growing temptation to beat her. At the same time,
everything was breaking up, collapsing, disappearing all around
them. Like the end of the world. As if one by one, all the good
and beautiful things of this world were vanishing. As if the dawn
had found them out in the streets ... What was it, what was it, this
horror? They had stopped saying anything, thinking anything,
were simply shot through by random reflections as sharp and cold
as knives.

She continued to wear a stunned smile, a ghastly smile. She was
utterly still. He tried to smile as well. He was pale. He thought,
"Now, I'll have to take her." It seemed to him like the crowning
torment of his ordeal.

"You're not talking to me?"

Ordinarily, the wildest words sprang to her lips – always the same
ones, moreover. That evening, she racked her brains to find them
again. Words: once they had tasted salty-sweet and escaped from
her quivering lips like bees. Now they, too, had been murdered.
Their life poured from their open entrails. Hideous characters
parading in perfect marching order, unleashing the horror.

"Just say something to me for God's sake!"

Soon there was nothing left in the woman's mouth but the
corpses of words.

He was panting and hurting her with the weight of his whole
body. They resembled lost people looking for the way out, the
light across the sea, who row like mad for shore.

At the climax of the violence, pleasure surged up. It turned her legs limp, made her belly a basin of heat and rushed through her half-open lips, which murmured it in a moan.

"This pleasure, this pleasure you give me ..."

She said the word. First as an insult, afterward with great gentleness.

Then, they dared look at each other.

For a few seconds, they experienced the ineffable identity of love. Of no matter what love. And that was enough. The agonizing obligation to pretend now melted away. Carefully, she opened her eyes. Her face was sad, released. Her violent hurry now seemed pointless to her.

In the next room, people were talking: two voices coupling like doves; silence enclosing them in a black circle.

Sitting up in bed, head tipped back, he was smoking for the first time that evening. He was smoking the cigarette of the conqueror. He'd certainly earned it. He took deep breaths now and again to get his wind back. His hands, still shaking, were open. With those hands, he had stroked, kneaded her. The beast that hadn't wanted any of it – he'd cut its throat with those hands. At least he thought so, and was quite pleased. As if after a job well done.

He looked down and smiled at her.

Ordinarily, he didn't take long to fall asleep. That evening, he began to talk about himself, almost musingly, in a tone he felt was deftly sentimental. He spoke of his troubles, his tough life, the problems of his profession. But soon – surely she'd guessed? – she would be leaving her job, fetching the little daughter she was raising secretly out in the countryside and coming back with him. Ah, she needed to have the right idea about what a bluff good fellow he was: hard but kind and understanding. Alas, she felt him calculating his effects, weighing his words.

"Turn around," he told her roughly. "You're not going to sleep yet – we haven't seen each other in six months!"

What a bully! He took up his story in his monotonous voice.

The evening wore on. The hotel was going full tilt as on every Saturday night. Beds were endlessly made and remade. From time to time, people went discreetly past their room. Late into the night, he talked.

In the morning, he was still lying next to her. Stretched out side by side, they avoided each other even in sleep. As on the previous day, she opened her eyes slowly. An acid early-morning light filtered through the curtains and onto the bedspread. Wherever was she? Oh, yes, him!

Last evening, they hadn't had an easy job of it. She heard him grumble something: "It's noisy around here, they don't let you sleep." His face began to yawn; his mouth said, "Morning, dear."

She pretended to be sleeping. He soon dropped off again.

"It's Sunday, let's take advantage of it." That was all he thought.

She looked around the room. Her face, which she stroked gently with her warm palms, must still have had some make-up on it from the day before. Her skin was a little greasy.

Daybreak. The metro was rumbling like subterranean torrents. Cheery car horns enlivened the dawn now and then, along with streaks of colour. She thought about that first, slanting light, which must be waking Paris up already. For the first time, she thought of her little girl without sadness.

She stretched silently, rose easily from the bed. From among the clothes lying on the floor, she selected her own, and dressed calmly; he wouldn't be awakening any time soon. His deep, regular breathing meant that he'd be sleeping for a good while yet.

For six months she'd been awaiting his return. In her solitude, she had endlessly woven and rewoven the texture of this return, minute by minute, point by point.

And now it had arrived, that longed-for day ...

Before leaving, very quietly, on tiptoe, she ran to the window. To see the street, take the measure of its exquisite morning freshness. But the room looked out onto a narrow courtyard, black with soot, where open windows were already vomiting bedding {hung out to air}. Down below, in the centre of the black well, rose a tropical plant, some kind of palm. The only air it breathed came from these rooms stinking of love. Its fronds rustled softly.

She looked at it for a long moment, shut the window and left.

The Bible

He was twenty years old. She, eighteen. He'd come up to her one evening in the Café du Relais Saint-Michel. He told her he'd just come from a sociology class. As for her, she waited a few days before telling him she was a salesgirl in a shoe shop. They had started meeting in the back room of the Relais, usually at around ten past six, after she'd left the shop. She liked seeing him there, he was company for her, quiet and polite. She liked seeing someone she could be with before going home to her room at dinnertime. She didn't talk to him; he was the one who told her things, talking to her about Islam and the Bible. That didn't surprise her too much, although he did keep harping on this subject. It didn't surprise her – nothing surprised her: she was the sort who is never really surprised by anything.

That first evening, he had talked to her about Islam. The following day he slept with her and he talked to her about the Bible, asking her if she'd read it; she said she hadn't. The day after that he had brought along a Bible and read Ecclesiastes to her in the back room of the Relais. With his hands over his ears, he had read it aloud in an impassioned voice and chanting like a priest, which had embarrassed her and she'd wondered if he might not be a bit mad. Then he asked her what she thought of it. Being so embarrassed by his reading, she hadn't listened too closely; she said that it seemed reasonable to her, that it was fine. He smiled at her answer. He told her it was an essential text that everyone should know.

He had seen the fragments called the Nash Papyrus in the British Museum, he told her about that: he had stayed for several hours in front of the vitrine, had returned the next day, and the following days, and he would never forget those moments. The only thing left on the Nash Papyrus was a few lines about the Exodus. He talked to her about Exodus. "'And the children of Israel were fruitful, and increased abundantly, and multiplied, and waxed exceeding mighty; and the land was filled with them … And they were grieved because of the children of Israel.'" He spoke to her about all the Bibles: the Vulgate, the Septuagint, and also the Vatican, the Sinaiticus, the Hebrew, Aramaic, Greek and Latin Bibles.

He never talked with her about herself and never asked her if she was happy working in that shoe shop, or how she had come to Paris, or what she liked. They made love. As for her, she liked making love. It was one of the things she liked. While they were making love, they didn't speak. Afterwards he would start talking again about the life of Saint Jerome, who had spent his life translating the Bible.

He was thin, slightly round-shouldered, with dark wavy hair, pale skin, a very expressive mouth, pale lips that slid over his prominent teeth, a button nose, high cheekbones and quite lovely blue eyes with thick black lashes. He was not particularly clean. His shirt collars left much to be desired, as did his pink, rounded nails, too big for his slender hands, so that his fingertips were shaped like spatulas. His chest was sunken, he had a stoop. He had spent his youth reading the sacred texts of Islam and Christianity. He had learned Hebrew, English, German, Arabic, and was still studying the latter at the École des Langues Orientales; although only in his second year, he already knew Arabic, in fact, and was reading the Koran in the original by the time she met him.

Sometimes he invited her to dinner, but it was always in cheap restaurants. One evening he confessed that he was buying a sixteenth-century Hebrew Bible in instalments. His father was rich but gave him only a little money, yet he hadn't been able to resist buying that Bible; he'd already retired a third of the debt, which he'd pay off completely the following month. He was dreaming of the moment when he would hold that Bible in his hands.

In the three weeks they had known each other they'd never talked about anything except the Bible and Islam ... He talked constantly to her about God and the eternal attraction the idea of God had always had for mankind. Personally she didn't believe in God, she didn't feel the slightest need to believe in God. She knew that there were people who believed in a God, who felt a need for that. She believed that she would not spend her whole life in the shoe shop, that she would get married and have children. She believed her opportunity was here on earth: that was her only way of believing in God.

As for him, he didn't believe in God either, but he still hadn't got over that. He didn't care about his father's fortune. It was quite a large one, acquired by exploiting a patent for the vulcanization of automobile tyres. He sometimes spoke about his house in Neuilly and the family property in Hossegor when she asked about them. She knew the two of them would never be married. He hadn't even considered the possibility.

She had never known a man like him. He talked to her about Mohammed as if he were talking about a brother: he told her of his life, his marriages to the merchant's widow, then to Mary the Copt – he knew the individual stories of the twenty-four wives of Mohammed, Mohammed who had set out to make Islam mono-theistic. It had been a noble idea and he had defended it weapon in hand with celestial courage. It seemed like a strange endeavour to her, but she didn't mention this to him, or tell him that some-times she got tired of trying shoes on people all day long, either; no, she kept those things to herself, and besides, she thought that was normal, she didn't think such things could interest anyone at all. In the end, she had got accustomed to his ways and when he recited entire suras from the Koran in Arabic, she let him recite away, she thought he was a nice boy. He bored her.

He was kind after his fashion, he'd bought her a pair of stockings. But ever since they'd started sleeping together she had felt no joy. One evening, she thought she had the answer: "I'm not right for him ..." Around him, all her energy, her youthful joie de vivre, would shut down. She was at her wit's end about it. Yet she felt flattered: in a sense it was an opportunity, she told herself that she was learning things with him. But those things gave her no pleasure. And she had so little need to learn them that she felt she already knew them. Nevertheless she tried to please him; in the evening she read the Gospels, just as he had asked. Christ's words to his mother made her feel like crying. That he was crucified so young before his mother's eyes was even more revolting. But through no fault of her own, she couldn't get beyond a certain emotional response. She did not think he was God, that man; she thought he was a man who'd had some very noble plans, and his death made him human again, so that she could not read his story without thinking of her father's end: he had died the previous year, crushed by a tip cart, a year before his retirement. He'd been the victim of an injustice that had begun a long, long time ago. That injustice had never ceased upon the earth: it carried on throughout the generations of man.

The Stolen Pigeons

Old lady Bousque always turned up in such a rush that she seemed to be running out of time.

From Les Bugues, we'd see her pop into sight, off beyond a hedge of medlars that separated our land from her children's property. A narrow path led through the hedge, and at this gap was a hillock she climbed over as briskly as a young woman. Next, head bowed, she passed along a row of artichokes, still at the same precipitous pace. It was as if she couldn't have slowed down without toppling over.

Her body was bent sharply at the waist from all those long winter afternoons spent stooping over her fire, and her thin arms pumped back and forth like rocking levers – they looked too long, now, even though they'd shrivelled up just like the rest of her. Poor old lady Bousque. She had shrunk so much, at the end of her life, that she barely overtopped the artichokes.

"Look," we'd say every time. "It's old lady Bousque."

And we were surprised every time, as if the very regularity of the thing were astonishing.

Well before arriving, she called out a friendly word with what little voice she had left, which was scratchy and off-key. And we'd yell back at her, as if she'd been deaf.

No-one set work aside to talk or listen to her; she'd come to us and begin quite naturally to help out while telling us something, always some story.

Once in a while, however, she would take me aside and murmur what she didn't dare ask out loud.

"So, tell me, when do you think you'll be leaving?"

She truly dreaded that we might move house again before she died, for she was very fond of us. We had come from far away, so far away that she didn't know where that might be, exactly, but through the pines of Les Bugues there blew a warm wind that comforted her old carcass and gave her, at over seventy-five, not just her fill of novelty and intrigue but her only opportunity to leave her village. Now more or less invalids, the friends of her youth gladly dispensed with her company. It must also be noted that old lady Bousque, elderly though she was, had not turned pious with age, an uncommon thing out in the countryside. She only darted in and out of midnight Mass on Christmas Eve because she loved night-time and holidays, too, so although people liked her a lot, they did criticize her a little. She'd been the first in the whole region to venture out our way, making friends with the family going to live on the long-abandoned property of Les Bugues.

Despite her incredible ignorance, her mind was still agile, possessed of a quite pure curiosity. Everyone feared her a little, the way you fear those who see clearly and remember everything, the way you worry about life, too, in its inspirations, its unfathomable poetry. That's why people preferred to call her a meddling gossip, when she was only fond of fancies, but my mother thought more highly of her than of anyone else around.

For us children, she would arrive with the twilight that brought us back home, yet she was also that old woman on whom we shut our door, to protect ourselves from a darkness she seemed to bewitch. Only her eyes were still intensely alive, in a face slashed by wrinkles lined with black, like deep furrows. This face, the most extraordinary thing imaginable, was all that was old about her, however, and we felt she would never die, so well was she coping with the passing years. But a terrible thing did happen to her, which she would surely have relished in the telling, if it hadn't put her in her place for ever.

This was the wellspring that fed the violent emotions of her daughter-in-law, Jeanne Bousque.

Jeanne had never known what might be called a real childhood. Hers had passed in the feverish anticipation of command, yet her marriage had restored to her neither joy nor her wasted years. Still, she ruled this roost, and, long eager to exercise an authority denied her in her own family, she wielded it excessively in her husband's. There were only four of them: the old lady, her son Louis, Jeanne and their son, Jean, and to tell the truth, this {household} did not quite compute. But what of it! As long as Jeanne now passed for the mistress of the house in the eyes of the village.

She was something to see, making sport of old lady Bousque as if she were a child! But the old woman was much too cagey ever to lose her temper over this, for her son would never have dared take his old mother's side against his wife, nor would her grandson, of course, who was only fourteen and had other fish to fry. She resigned herself cheerfully to this tutelage, but it was precisely her good humour, proof against all assault, that stung her daughter-in-law's vanity, as if, all by herself, the old lady could make Jeanne wonder who was really in charge.

Jeanne Bousque treated the old lady more brusquely with each passing year. Whenever she looked at her, her eyes turned haggard, her face ravaged by some mysterious despair.

And just look at that little old woman, so agreeable, so easy to get on with – imagine hating her like that!

Asked for news of her, Jeanne would sigh and say hypocritically, "Of course, she is getting on – you haven't noticed? – and becoming a bit dirty, when she was always so neat, I'm told ..." Or this: "When Jean grows up, we'll give him the upstairs bedroom."

She would point to it, old lady Bousque's room, which she never entered.

But whatever Jeanne did, to other people old lady Bousque always remained the mistress of the house, even though she had already handed all her property over to her children and was very glad indeed to be fed and lodged in her little room.

One March day, her housework done, Jeanne Bousque set out promptly for the high plateau where the Pelgrin family lived.

Ordinarily, she took this shortcut only on Sunday, to go to Mass, so people were surprised to see her taking it on a weekday, especially since she was striding along and barely greeting anyone, for fear someone might stop and delay her. She headed straight through the alfalfa and took the road through the village, then began the climb up to the plateau on the path that snaked among our vines.

At around eleven o'clock, she reached the great tableland that dominated the landscape. Her face was red from the wind and she was panting a little, from hurrying up the difficult ascent.

"Well! What good wind brings you here, Madame Bousque?"

Whereas everyone called her mother-in-law old lady Bousque, they called that woman Madame, because they respected her in those parts, but also because she came from another village.

She did not immediately say why she had come. Words and phrases had been swirling through her mind when she'd set out, but they'd fallen nicely into place along the way. And now, she had it, her story, and in fine shape, after working on it all the way there. What a stroke of luck!

Where had she gone? To carry her seed as far as possible, to sow it in the best place, on the high plateau with the Pelgrin family, whose spiteful gossip, like the winds of the tableland, would scatter this seed at the very least across the three villages below. Ah! She was launching a fine attack, the Bousque woman – she knew her neighbours!

"You're acquainted with my cousins from Algiers ..."

Winded by her haste as well as her fatigue, she had to begin again.

"You're acquainted with my cousins from Algiers, the ones expected to arrive this evening. Well, imagine: last night, before going upstairs, I had prepared a couple of my nicest pigeons for them, plump ones, let me tell you! So I cook them, I put them away in the pantry, and I go up to bed. In the middle of the night, if I don't hear a noise downstairs! I nudge Louis with my elbow and we both go down – I'd even told him to grab the gun, you see you never know, not with those railway men passing through at night ..."

The two Pelgrins were all ears, and their pupils gleamed like embers.

"What do I see?" continued the Bousque woman. "I thought I was dreaming! Louis and I – we couldn't get a sound out, stunned. The old lady! She was terrifying, sitting on her stool, gobbling my pigeons with both hands, like this ... She was so changed, I could hardly recognize her. It was a good long moment before she turned around, and when she saw us she froze – I thought she'd had a seizure, but she recovered, then took off at a run, a run! You know she's spry, the old lady: she went up those stairs four at a time and shut herself up in her room."

"Oh! Well, I never!" exclaimed the Pelgrin woman. "But she did have all her wits about her, though, until now ... Who would have imagined such a thing!"

But big Pelgrin, him, he said it solemnly, as was proper.

"Then she's finished, old lady Bousque: it must have come over her all of a sudden."

"It's not that I was stinting her," said their wily visitor, "but one day or another, age will addle your brains. There are old folk who talk the entire day, others who turn nasty. The old lady, her madness will be to steal and wolf down food without real hunger. Still, we were lucky – it could have been worse."

*

For several days, old lady Bousque stayed in her room. To those surprised not to see her, Jeanne Bousque said softly with a laugh, "Oh! She certainly ate enough for two days, the old lady, with that pair of pigeons ... Mind you, it's not that I begrudge her them."

And she would say this loudly enough for the little old lady in the attic to hear.

Old lady Bousque was ashamed.

What had got into her? Old age had indeed addled her brains, as her daughter-in-law said. The outlandish craving for pigeon that had suddenly come over her, and that way of devouring them, too, like an animal – she was surely accursed, and everyone knew it: the people over at Les Bugues, the village, the whole world ...

Oh, to die would have been such a delightful thing for the little old lady: to die, and not think any more – what a relief.

But, unfortunately ...

For two days and two nights, she stared stupidly at the sky, at the clouds parading past her nose, running along the way the village children, no doubt about it, would now run after her. And she stared, without seeing it, at the enormous mid-March moon.

Sitting in the centre of the room, more bent over than ever, she no longer dared even to move her head, afraid of feeding the laughter that greeted each of her movements and bedevilled her ears ...

According to her daughter-in-law, she tried to steal yet again, but that night everything was locked up, as you can well imagine! Then, frustrated, the next day she resigned herself to coming downstairs, taking advantage of a moment when the house was empty, in the lull of the afternoon, like an animal flushed from its hole by hunger.

She returned humbly to her spot by the fire, and never left it again. Since she did not speak from that day forward, no-one spoke to her, either. Her son no longer even bothered to bid her good evening when he came in from the fields, and soon her grandson stopped kissing her when he arrived home after school, because she had become quite dirty.

With delicate tact, my mother let her die without seeing her again, but she was the only one, because nobody in the village passed up the pleasure of coming for at least one more look at her. Fortunately, by then all she could see was her fire ...

She had become so grey, really grey like her old companion: she was covered in ashes – in the folds of her dress, in her hair, in every wrinkle of her hide.

When anyone came to the Bousque house and entered the large, bright kitchen, her daughter-in-law never failed to apologize for the old woman's corner, which she just couldn't manage to clean.

"And if you saw her room," she would sigh. "A real dunghill."

Even so, she had to wait until autumn to clean the place, for that old lady Bousque, she took eight long months to die, eight months of lovely spring- and summertime – really, you'd have thought she was doing it on purpose. But in the end, the wait only heightened the pleasure Jeanne Bousque took in gathering all the old woman's tatters into a huge pile in the centre of the courtyard for a bonfire that spewed smoke through the whole village, a hearty blaze she stirred up every now and again with a long poker.

Eda or the Leaves

When Jean went to his window he saw what he usually saw beyond the red roof of the public school: the platform of the dredge. It was about a hundred yards off, on the other side of the pond. Its regular backfires carried a long way. Ten or so sharp explosions followed by a muffled one, and so on nonstop.

The man on the platform was wearing a dark green singlet that clung to his stocky torso. A small brown cap protected the crown of his head from the sun; lower down, his neck was bright red. He would occasionally shout something to the dozen workmen filling tip carts with sand and pushing them off to dump it out over behind the trees, where huge Latil lorries could be seen driving away every fifteen minutes.

Jean knew the man in the green singlet. It was Lucien. He didn't see the others clearly but from their positions could tell exactly what they were doing. The previous year he had operated the dredge for three months.

It was ten to six; Jean reflected that it was getting late. In ten minutes the noise from the dredge would stop. If it was still light, that was because spring had really arrived, this time. It was April. It had been cold until recently. They'd been waiting for nice weather for six months now, it was about time. Jean had often been cold that winter. Hungry too sometimes. With Eda, of course. But whenever he remembered that, he didn't feel bitter.

There were also the usual pigeons walking slowly along the

ridge of the school roof. With each step their throats would swell, then deflate with a curious clicking sound. They would fly off. Return. Birds were constantly coming and going on the school roof. But they were always the same ones. There was nothing to be gained from this sight. He knew it well. It was of no interest. It would even, if he kept watching, end up bothering him, as always. The pigeons moved around too much and for nothing. He gave up watching them at it – as usual.

Now the sky was uniformly grey.

Jean gave a great yawn. The sky was dark grey on all sides. Evening was coming.

Jean let his gaze drift around the empty schoolyard.

In the yard were the chestnut trees.

That's when he noticed how they had changed.

A moment before, he was still seeing the schoolyard as it had been all winter. Now they were there, thrusting up from the ground. There were eight of them.

From that moment they claimed his full attention.

They already had all their leaves. All of them, born the same day, perhaps the same instant. Maybe a week ago. Maybe less. He hadn't noticed a thing. He couldn't have said when. He told himself what they *were*: they were new and innocent, innocent and new.

They were pale, tender, these new and innocent leaves.

They would keep growing, all together, until the summer. There were some all along each branch and at the tip of each branch. Everywhere and yet every one at just the right place for it to be. Still too young to spread wide open, they were resting, limp, a bit furled. Every day they would be less young. Every day the trees would push them outside a bit more, after having contained their substance so patiently, so jealously, throughout the entire winter. Still, the trees were abandoning them with a kind of love, with care. Every day the leaves were more distinct, more themselves, more alone. Soon they would be open, Jean thought, spread flat and straight at the ends of their stems. Perhaps in a month or two weeks. He didn't know exactly. One doesn't notice things like that, the time they take. For the moment, still clinging closely to the trees, they swayed gently, now and then, but hardly sticking out at all. They made you think of things, painful things. Their flesh was so alive. More alive, more innocent, more unnoticed than the flesh of children. Through their veins, in their transparent layers, a sap that must have begun to warm up in the sun was busy circulating, collecting in small velvety cracks. And the leaves were growing, unfurling in movements so slow, so long, that they lasted for days and nights.

Jean felt unhappy. "What? What's wrong with me?"

He looked at them but so badly, so badly. He thought about them but so badly: "Those leaves there, so ... so strong. No, so young, there. At this moment ..." But still so badly. He tried to pay attention. But to what? Nothing was happening. Pay attention to what? Yet there was something to be done, that was certain. But what? And this head that was hampering him, bothering him, restless, good for nothing, cranking out words, images: "A woman is being crushed beneath you, filling your field of vision, enlarged, bloodied, better. Fists pound, at the door. Door of what? It's the Closed Door, everyone knows it well. Goddammit, goddammit. Pound, pound. The blows wear out the fists. Which hurt. But outside shutters clatter, clatter in the wind. And it's the Summons. You go towards what is open. Outside. Walls enclose gardens lush with warm, ripe tomatoes you can easily bloody with your teeth." No.

Jean sensed a kind of disaster growing inside him. He forced himself to think about sensible things, but they degenerated straightaway into fear.

"Soon, oh, soon, it will be too late, too late ..."

How could you live and lose *that* time?

But Jean didn't know what to do with that time, or why it suddenly seemed so precious.

From his room on the seventh floor, he could not see the chestnut leaves clearly. And as he tried to think about them, he began wanting to see them up close, which made his eyes and mouth water. To see them up very, very close. Perhaps to grab them as well. With his hands. That wasn't impossible: *all he had to do was go down and get himself into the schoolyard*. No, it wasn't impossible. Then, perhaps, tear {them} off. Who knows? Touch. Feel carefully. Crumple, crumple until… smell, that's it, smell. The sharp odour, male and female. The smell of everything at once in a single odour. Smell it all fit to bursting, bursting open one's chest, because of the mouth, the nose, too strong.

Really, that sight, those leaves, new and innocent – they made Jean want to plunge with all his strength into a contentment with life so new that he could not tell if it existed or where it might lead him.

From the moment he'd realized that he had to go down into the schoolyard, his unhappiness had vanished. The prospect of what he might do there to experience for an instant the dreamy taste of new and innocent leaves numbed his mind and body with a little of that dream: he felt relieved of words and images, beyond their reach. He was fine, finally free. Free to go down, or not, into the schoolyard.

A few yards away, a bit furled up, the young leaves were resting, still motionless. All unknowing of what was going to happen. Of what Jean was going to do.

But what was he going to do? Go down into the schoolyard. After that, something. He certainly wouldn't go down for nothing.

He felt they were at his mercy. Unknowing. Back again, this word was admirable, swollen with a meaning that encompassed the entire moment: Jean's desire, and the new and innocent leaves – and Jean's past. This word saved everything. Jean's hesitations melted away as he muttered it to himself. Even though it gave him no hint of what actions he would take, Jean paid no heed. He had forgotten that he was simply looking at leaves. His emotion was intense. He felt slightly giddy.

He closed his eyes. Perhaps fifteen seconds. Enormous. He opened his eyes. They were there. Still there. That's when he felt released, almost to the point of shouting about it, from whatever hardness and clarity he'd had inside his head since childhood that had always kept him from doing crazy things. A single thought stood firm while he was changing like that. A silly thought; it was that he'd be ashamed of all this if he'd had to admit it to anyone, even Eda. Fortunately, what had just happened as well as what was going to happen was nobody's business but his own. He was going to go down.

He would take his time. To begin with, he'd pick one of them. Next, yes, that was indeed what he should do, he would expose it to the sun. There was no sun, but there would be. The leaf would stay where he'd placed it. It would comply. After that, he'd see; that was foreseeable, so to speak.

Some time passed.

The precise moment of going down was biding its time. The command. And yet the leaves vanished and reappeared in a peculiar fashion, from Jean's eyes to the schoolyard. They would come closer, closer to his eyes, growing larger – not growing larger but without changing size becoming ever more precise, drawing nearer, and they would drown themselves there, in his eyes, and he couldn't get them out. And when he managed that, they would immediately be far, far away, and he couldn't make them come back in without tremendous effort. And so, there existed differences between Jean's eyes and the new and innocent leaves that were such a nuisance that he suddenly wondered whether he should bother going down.

To reach the schoolyard, he had to go by way of the stairs and the road, a path that did not ordinarily lead there.

And he remembered that he might well find himself facing leaves that, as new and innocent as they might be, would be as idiotic as always and absolutely indifferent, without interest.

It was over.

As if he'd suffered a great calamity, he told himself, "I'm going to become ill." But he began to move around and breathe deeply and he grew calm without noticing it, thinking about something else.

He began to think of Eda.

Eda was in bed in the next room, so ill, and for so long.

He should have gone to buy that medicine they'd been told about. She must already be waiting. But he hadn't much cash. And he thought there was no point in going down to the pharmacy: Eda would not get well. Although he had bought all the medicines recommended to them until now, that was only to please Eda, and anyway, for a long time now neither he nor Eda had had any illusions about their effectiveness. But when Jean brought them to Eda she smiled at him and he was happy: she understood that he'd tried to be nice. This evening, however – was it from having looked too much at the new and innocent leaves? – Jean distinctly didn't mind making Eda wait. Being less than nice to her. Her in particular. And he reflected that the money he had left could go to something besides the purchase of an unnecessary drug. For example, to have a drink at the Café de la Meuse. Lucien would surely be there. Jean liked Lucien. They could even have a walk together. Jean considered it, this idea he'd had, and felt no remorse.

It was natural that he should think of Eda this evening with a certain rancour. If she hadn't been so ill she would have been able to help him completely shake off that uneasiness provoked by the sight of the new and innocent leaves. But she was so poorly. So poorly that she no longer changed her sheets, barely had the heart to wash herself. The thought of going in to see her couldn't even really cross Jean's mind.

The leaves, they were pure. They were perfect, the leaves. New, innocent. They had never been used by anyone, for anything. For anything at all, actually, really anything, by anyone, absolutely anyone.

He would definitely go to the Café de la Meuse. Lucien would be there. He had slept. Well, it was as if he had slept. A little groggy.

It was true that the leaves had never been used by anyone or for anything. They remained completely new and innocent. In other words, if someone were too feckless even to venture down into a schoolyard, they would in fact not be used by anyone or for anything.

Jean felt a little ashamed, uneasy, and ashamed of that uneasiness.

Jean resigned himself. He told himself that if he'd kept working on the dredge, he would not have embarked upon daydreams as idiotic as this one. He spent part of each day on his balcony. Perhaps it was looking for too long at the same things that drove people insane, to the point of dreaming about tree leaves as one would about a woman and perhaps even with something more than when dreaming about a woman.

Idleness played tricks like that. Always that bitching idleness. Yet Jean did not believe that idleness alone was making him unhappy. The proof was that when he'd been operating the dredge he had been just as unhappy as when he was idle – and even more so, for thus denied the leisure to think freely about the reason for his sadness, he was deprived of his only true occupation, after all – of his sole earthly happiness, as they say.

For Eda, the question did not arise, since nothing made her sad, not her. Since not even finding herself dying affected her spirits.

To manage taking care of her Jean had gradually sold everything he owned, and quite uselessly, too, since she worsened every day. They really didn't have much of a future now and Jean was not eating well. Of course, when they'd been working, last year for example, he'd eaten better. But now Eda was ill, eating hardly anything any more: what use would the money have been?

Ordinarily the shame of working could still be justified, but with Eda ill now, no, nothing should make this ordeal worse, especially not work.

Obviously – but that wasn't the case – if Jean had been working, if Eda had been a fresh and lovely young woman, if they'd had some money, if etc., well, he wouldn't have felt so upset this evening, felt that imbecilic impulse regarding the new and innocent leaves. He would have gone in to see Eda, would have had no problem with that, no remorse. But that wasn't the case, and Jean wasn't sincere: he knew that when he was working he became so gloomy that nothing managed to distract him, neither Eda, nor eating well every day, nor being able to drink in the evening at the Café de la Meuse if he felt like it. It's just that he liked to persuade himself that he was even more unhappy than he was, and to think that he was really fed up with this rotten life – which was equally false: he was less and less fed up with doing nothing since he was looking less and less often for a job. Eda herself had always assumed that he didn't want to stick with any regular work. The nasty remarks on that subject from family and neighbours did not faze her and she must have known how things stood. Besides, Eda did not see anyone much and went to visit her mother only to fetch provisions, so what people said about {the two of} them didn't really bother her.

The last time Jean had worked had been on the dredge. For three months he had conscientiously and punctually pushed the tip carts around. At the beginning, he might almost have thought that this job suited him. First off, the effort warmed him up in the cold weather. Also, he had experienced real satisfaction, because every day he could feel the increasing suppleness and ease with which he pushed and emptied the tip carts. Unfortunately, after a month he was working so skilfully that he performed those same actions without noticing them. He was bored and wanted to do something else. He had left the dredge just when he'd become a good worker. He'd been missed. Naturally Eda had encouraged him, even decisively, in this, telling him that he would certainly soon discover a job to his liking, or words to that effect. But it was always the same story with Eda: Jean seriously suspected, even while she was talking about it, that there was no such thing as a job to his liking. But she was so clever, Eda, so persuasive, that he couldn't be completely sure she hadn't said that simply to please him. It was this sliver of doubt that until now had allowed Jean not to become completely disgusted, and to have some good times with Eda.

Eda always thought that Jean was right to do whatever he did. Others weren't wrong either to work for a great deal of their lives. But he, Jean, was right to want not to do anything. Although they never spoke of this, Jean suspected her of knowing very well that it was useless to pressure yourself to work, of knowing this much better than he ever would himself. (Unless you enjoy it, which was perhaps the case with others, basically.)

He, Jean, felt that he was understood. No point in agonizing: whenever he wavered over quitting a job, she would tell him, "Why should you stay on? Hey, you don't have to." It was so obvious that Jean was dazzled, and he would happily give notice. During the next few days they would both be perfectly content. They would wander around the city and sometimes got gently drunk together as well.

Only a few weeks later would Jean wonder why Eda was encouraging his laziness that way. Those moments of reflection were the most moving of his life. They usually occurred on the day after or the very evening of Eda's visits to her mother. With Eda gone, Jean spent his day dreaming, waiting for her. It was generally winter. Eda would get home at dinner time laden with the week's supplies. Jean would open the door for her, a bit uncomfortable on account of the provisions. But Eda? "Hello there, Jean dear!" She'd embrace him, caress him, hold her cool mouth up to him. She had the mouth of a fiancée, and told plenty of stories about her day. At once Jean would feel at ease again.

Which did not prevent Jean from sometimes wondering at night after such days who that woman he was lying next to was.

Eda's beauty – each time he felt it anew – made Jean want to die. Among all the things that could inspire thoughts of dying, that one was the champion. Until the arrival of those others, now, tonight.

Those new and innocent leaves. And yet, it wasn't the same thing. Lying next to Eda, he would have liked to be able to run away from her. How could he bear it, in fact! Then he would remember all the grievances he had against this woman, and all his reasons for loving her. Nothing saddened Eda, nothing inconvenienced her, nothing disturbed her or surprised her. She never passed judgement on anyone, not even Jean, not even murderers in the newspapers. Yet she was neither a Christian nor even charitable – and how could she have been, she who was more free than the wind and lived only through pleasure? She, she, more lovely, more natural, more new than a new and innocent leaf.

The memory of Eda who was sleeping there glittered in the darkness of the bedroom and bathed Jean's heart in a terrible clarity. More terrible than moonlight upon the sea. More terrible than every other brightness upon the sea of things. What to do with this woman? How to express to her what he felt for her, for this woman who was the chance of his lifetime, the chance – to die, to accept – of his life? To die for her – but how could one die for Eda, how, without hurting her? She who was convinced, oh, and how much, that it was useless to die for anything at all, just as it was useless to keep from dying when you had to.

You had to see her sleeping, that witch of a woman: peacefully, a pigeon. That's how she slept after every day of her life and each of those days was a feat of grace, and she was unaware of this and her grace was this unawareness. So how could one escape? You had to see her walking in the road, had to have felt her arms wrap around your neck, seen the precise colour of her black hair, to understand what Jean could bear with this woman. "Shit," said

Jean. And he would feel such love for her that he could neither kiss nor even touch her.

Jean remembered those moments while looking at the new and innocent leaves.

Once again he had forgotten Eda's serious illness. He had constantly to remind himself of it because his thoughts turned naturally towards a former Eda he would never see again. She was beautiful, then, always new, always innocent. Unknowing, unaware of herself. Unknowing in her always new and always innocent way. Her clear and naked secret remained as impenetrable as in the past, as the dark secret of the leaves. But in the past Jean could enter Eda's belly. In there, it was wonderful, my God it was wonderful. Ah! Eda was truly Jean's woman and at the same time all women, all of them, even the ones with whom he'd betrayed her. And besides, she was cheerful, Eda, and when she was in the mood, no-one was funnier. When she was in the mood she was always what you'd never have dared hope for. Now she was really very weak.

She was rarely entertaining. Very rarely. Jean felt tired and left the balcony.

The noise of the dredge had stopped. From the pond came a stale smell of water.

Eda was going to die. That was certain.

Jean went to lie down on his bed. He looked at the alarm clock. Six o'clock plus ten minutes. Six ten. The big hand had broken the line made with the other one and was falling slowly to the right. In a short while, instead of six-o'clockish it would be seven-minus-something and that would be completely different. Jean remembered: when he had gone out on the balcony it was ten to six. The clock now said six ten. It was stupid, an alarm clock. Nevertheless, it *was*. Jean had bought the alarm clock a long time ago. It hadn't cost much and worked perfectly, stoutly and precisely. If you listened to it closely, even, it was wearing itself out, killing itself keeping time. Jean was grateful to it. This evening he

wanted to be grateful to something that had served him so faithfully, that served and had served and would serve so faithfully
only him.

Eda was going to die.

For only he used this alarm clock. Eda couldn't have cared less
about the time. If the clock worked it was thanks to Jean who,
just yesterday, had rewound it. He rewound it every evening. How
long had he been doing that? And if he no longer rewound it, it
would stop, stupid, at a fixed, fixed, fixed time, would cry, "Help,
Jean!" – the time fixed, FIXED, nailed, glued there. Pfft! So much
for its purpose. Never the moment to do something. Never the
moment for anything. Still, it was useful, an alarm clock; it was
indispensable. For reasons Jean didn't want to bother understanding. Anyway, he'd never been able to bring himself to sell it.
That was proof.

Eda was going to die.

Not to sell it, to part with it, to put it in Eda's room to know
when to give medicine, no, Jean hadn't done that. That alarm
clock definitely belonged to him and only him. He would very
much have liked to stroke it, to warm its icy, unappreciated life
against his heart. Naturally he didn't, because he knew it was impossible. And he felt like smiling to himself at all the endeavours,
all the defeats that peopled his solitude, his inaction. But he had
become quite lazy, and didn't take the trouble to smile.

He ran his hands slowly through his hair, and placed them one
upon the other beneath his head.

Eda was going to die. It was hard.

The sky was now dark blue. A breeze was coming up, blowing
past the wall outside the room without coming inside, because
nothing was making it pause. Because for a long time everything
had been happening outside this room, even the wind. Everything
was stirred up elsewhere. Against here. Even that, that death,
Eda's death, death.

They, the leaves, shivered in the wind, with a violent and

childish fear. Still new and innocent leaves, they wanted to live, those leaves.

Perhaps he'd also have to think soon about eating.

So let the wind pass, and pass again. Let the spring pass too if it feels like it. We know how that works. That's none of our business any more. That can no longer do us the slightest harm. Here, away from the wind and the spring, we're doing something else – something that cannot start itself afresh. But just leave us alone, why don't you …

Eda was going to die. Yes, that's what I said, all right? – die.

In life, obviously, many things happen. Of different kinds. Example: before meeting Eda Jean had loved Lucie for six months. Eda could not prevent him from having loved Lucie in his life.

Incidentally, at that moment, Lucien was probably waiting for him in the bar in the Café de la Meuse. Lucien as well had a soft spot for Jean. He was a committed anarchist. He was always talking about blowing up the dredge one day when the boss was there, and he had asked Jean to help. "Sure," Jean had replied. On account of the model houses the boss rented to his workers after four years on the dredge. That ploy had netted him a goodly number of guys who now dreamt only of proving worthy of a house. This bomb would blow the hell out of everything for a few weeks, at least. That would shove their houses right where it hurts. Lucien had told Jean that the boss would be coming soon and that this time would be the right one. Maybe they'd get a chance to blow him up along with the dredge and maybe Jean too risked blowing up with the boss and the dredge. Ah! Now that was better. He imagined himself exploded into hamburger. This vision provoked some agitation in his body. It's true. His ever-present body, silent, powerful, always ready – for nothing – for months. He hadn't slept with a woman for months, since Eda had become ill. Through the cloth of his trousers Jean felt the pent-up strength of his body. In a friendly way he felt sorry for it, found it lonesome. Abandoned. But beautiful. Quite loyal, suddenly hard and just at the level of Eda's belly. Wanting some.

Of Eda who was going to die.

As new and innocent as forever.

Eda who was going to die new new completely new die.

He was worn out from thinking of Eda. He couldn't manage it any more. What did that mean now to still think about Eda?

He would go to the Café de la Meuse tonight. He'd go down. Eda was going to die perhaps. Surely.

The sky was dark. It was darkening with great inky streaks. And soon it was done. In the place on earth where Jean was it was night.

Jean got up, went to the window. In front of him not the least trace of sunlight left. He felt normal, relaxed. A familiar tender feeling filled his insides and made all his thoughts grow misty.

EDA, EDA, even if she was going to die ...

It was late, but he'd have dinner anyway. At the bedside of Eda, his little Eda, his dear wife. Maybe afterwards he'd drop by the Meuse, that wasn't impossible. Eda was sleeping deeply. Jean coughed to awaken her. She was his love; she would ask him, "Are you there, Jean? Tell me – is it late?" He longed to hear her voice, hers. But she didn't ask any questions and he went abruptly to her room. Eda was indeed there, but she must have been dead. Jean drew closer. She was smiling. "So, Eda, you're awake?" But Eda was dead. Jean understood it completely, even to the core of his power to understand something. He didn't reach out a finger to touch her. He felt that it was not possible to touch that and not worth the trouble. He hesitated, however. Near Eda's bed there was an empty space on the floor where he could have collapsed. But he chose to go downstairs to the road.

Going downstairs he still believed it wasn't definite, his going to the Café de la Meuse. But it was inevitable.

The *Wartime Notebooks* and the Published Works of Marguerite Duras

The first section of the notebook is devoted to a long autobiographical narrative retracing the childhood and youth of Marguerite Duras in Indochina. Although none of this narrative as it stands was reused by the author in any work she later published, the period and events described here provide the material and storylines for several works of fiction published by Marguerite Duras. The *Pink Marbled Notebook* and certain of these narratives thus share several characteristics.

Echoing this initial narrative, *The Sea Wall* (Pellegrini & Cudahy, 1952) recounts the life of a French family in colonial Indochina, once again through the characters of the mother, her daughter Suzanne and a son, Joseph. Much of the novel deals with the story of Suzanne and her first suitor, Monsieur Jo, which is also the plot of *The Eden Cinema*, a play based on *The Sea Wall*.

The Boa, a novella published in the collection *Whole Days in the Trees* (Calder, 1984), expands the episode involving the exhibitionism of Mademoiselle C. ("Mademoiselle Barbet" in the published version), who ran the boarding house where young Marguerite lived in Saigon. This memory and the subsequent visit to the botanic garden, which take up a single page in the *Pink Marbled Notebook*, become a narrative of some ten pages in the novella.

The family's life in Indochina is also evoked in the novella *Whole Days in the Trees* (in the collection of the same name), which Marguerite Duras adapted for the theatre in 1968.

Finally, the story is at the heart of *The Lover* (Pantheon, 1985), which won the Prix Goncourt in 1984. The narrative voice moves back and forth between the first and third person as the novel focuses this time on the young girl's adventure with her first lover, leaving the family story more in the background. The novel *The North China Lover* (The New Press, 1992), reworks this narrative structure one last time.

The remainder of the *Pink Marbled Notebook* consists of sketches, first drafts. Moving chronologically through the notebook, considering those fragments that will reappear in *The Sea Wall*, we see the autobiographical aspect of the texts giving way to a novelistic approach: the first-person subject becomes the third person as "I" becomes "the girl", then "Suzanne"; the brother is first called Paul, like one of Marguerite Duras' brothers, then Joseph; "my mother" is replaced by "the mother". In addition to these changes and the many stylistic variations, we should note the considerable amplification of the material in the published novel: fragments that occupy all told about twenty pages of this notebook become long chapters in the finished book.

Lastly, almost a quarter of the *Pink Marbled Notebook* is devoted to first drafts of two novellas published in the collection *The War* (Pantheon, 1986) as "Ter of the Militia" and "Albert of the Capitals". The published version of "Ter of the Militia", which is longer than the first draft, develops the portrait of the title character rather than the tableau of Paris at the Liberation; the two versions of "Albert of the Capitals" are more alike, and the rewriting there was less extensive. In both texts, the names are changed, and the central character of Théodora becomes "Thérèse".

THE *20TH CENTURY PRESS NOTEBOOK* AND
THE *HUNDRED-PAGE NOTEBOOK*

The *20th Century Press Notebook* contains two separate stories. The first pages are devoted to "Théodora", a "novel" that was never finished or published. The remaining two-thirds of the notebook reappeared, sometimes followed quite closely, in *The War*, making up more or less the first third of the book.

The entire contents of the *Hundred-Page Notebook* make up approximately the second third of *The War*. On the whole, the book published by Marguerite Duras in 1986 is reasonably close to these first versions. There are some stylistic modifications, which transform neither the tone nor the rhythm of the text. Only a quarter of *The War* was entirely original in composition, namely those passages recounting the return of Robert Antelme from Dachau to Paris, then his arrival home at the rue Saint-Benoît, and the concluding pages of the book, which describe the couple's life during the first months following Antelme's return and which were also composed shortly before publication. Finally, the author deleted a few pages that appear in the *Wartime Notebooks*, pages that were particularly "contextual" – that is, related to her commitment to Communism at the time, pages referring for example to the policies of General de Gaulle and the role of the Catholic Church during the Liberation.

THE *BEIGE NOTEBOOK*

A small section of the *Beige Notebook* (the pages describing Robert Antelme's return to life after he came home from the camps) was also closely followed by the text of that same episode in *The War*.

This notebook contains, as fragments of fewer than ten pages, sketches for the novel *The Sailor from Gibraltar* (Calder, 1966). The style is similar to that of the published novel, and the chief characters are already present.

About ten pages of this notebook reappear in *The Sea Wall*, much expanded and yet quite recognizable, even to their style and passages of dialogue.

Two rather brief segments were rewritten and published in the feminist magazine *Sorcières* in 1976, without being made part of a longer story: the text "The children of the plain" (see the detailed table of contents) becomes "The Thin Yellow Children", and "The Horror of Such Love" retains its original title and much of the original text (*Outside: Selected Writings*, Beacon, 1986).

Lastly, the long autobiographical narrative comprising the major text of the *Beige Notebook* is reprised in part in the novella *Madame Dodin*, first published in the collection *Whole Days in the Trees*. While a few pages appear almost without change in the published work, others are cut or extensively modified. The autobiographical dimension, in particular, is reduced, and the story is now centred around the character of the concierge, Madame Dodin (Madame Fossé in the *Beige Notebook*), and her friend, Gaston the sweeper. The published novella remains written in the first person, but all the clearly personal allusions (especially the references to the author's pregnancy at the time when she was writing the text) have been removed.

Index of People and Characters

CANDIDA: character in *The Sailor from Gibraltar*: 216–17.

CARMEN: character in *The Sea Wall*: 180–3.

MADAME CATS: friend and neighbour of Marguerite Duras in the rough drafts of *The War*. She is waiting for her deported daughter, who will not return. Her name becomes "Kats" in the published work, and her daughter's name is "Jeanine". The daughter will become "Théodora Kats" in *Yann Andréa Steiner*: 133, 161–4, 167.

COLETTE: boader at the home of Mademoselle C. in Saigon: 7–8, 14.

COLETTE: young woman mentioned in the drafts of "Albert of the Capitals". Her name does not appear in the published version: 83.

DIONYS (D.): Dionys Mascolo (1916–1997), who became Marguerite Duras' companion in 1942. Father of her son Jean, born 30 June, 1947: 122–4, 128, 130–3, 135, 139–40, 147, 149, 152, 154–9, 161–2, 164, 189, 230.

MADAME DODIN (MADAME D.): eponymous character of the novella Marguerite Duras wrote about the concierge of her block of flats at 5 rue Saint-Benoît: 241–9.

ELIO: Elio Vittorini (1908–1966), Italian intellectual and friend of Marguerite Duras and Dionys Mascolo. A militant Communist after the war, author of – among other works – *Conversations in Sicily* (1941): 193–7, 199.

EOLO: character in *The Sailor from Gibraltar*: 215, 217.

MADAME FOSSÉ (MADAME F.): concierge of the block of flats in which Marguerite Duras lived on the rue Saint-Benoît, who will become "Madame Dodin" in the novella of the same name: 136, 222, 224, 226–30, 232–3, 237–41, 248.

FRANÇOIS: François Mitterrand (1916–1996), leader of the MNPGD (National Movement of Prisoners of War and Deportees), a Resistance movement which Marguerite Duras joined in 1943. He was a member of the rue Saint-Benoît group and helped Robert Antelme return home from the camp at Dachau. He is called François Morland in *The War*, after his nom de guerre: 159.

GASTON: character in *Madame Dodin*. Sweeper and friend of the

Detailed Table of Contents

The titles in Roman were provided by the editors.